BEER,

FOOD, AND FLAVOR

BEER,
FOOD, AND FLAVOR

*A Guide to Tasting, Pairing, and the
Culture of Craft Beer*

SCHUYLER SCHULTZ

Foreword by Peter Zien, Brewmaster/Owner,
AleSmith Brewing Co.

Skyhorse Publishing

10 9 8 7 6 5 4 3 2

Library of Congress Cataloging-in-Publication Data

Schultz, Schuyler.
  Beer, food, and flavor : a guide to tasting, pairing, and the culture of craft beer / by Schuyler Schultz ; foreword by Peter Zien.
    p. cm.
  ISBN 978-1-61608-679-4 (hardcover : alk. paper)
1. Beer. 2. Food and beer pairing. I. Title.
  TP577.S385 2012
  641.2'3—dc23
                                        2012018215

Printed in China

To my wife, Amy.
Sharing the pleasures of life together is my greatest source of inspiration.
To my dad—your support and encouragement made writing this book possible.
And to my mom—thank you for teaching me to cook.

CONTENTS

CHAPTER SIX: THE GREATER CRAFT BEER COMMUNITY

FOREWORD

There's a lot of pressure put upon the young to choose their path and identify an occupation well before they're ready to make a good choice. And sometimes the chosen occupation can feel more like a prison sentence than a way to showcase one's talents or skill sets. I didn't find my way as a professional brewer until later in life, and I was fortunate to have understanding parents who allowed me the time to find out what suited me best. Completing my major in political science and deciding to enter law school seemed like a logical choice, though I had no idea where destiny would take me. But throughout it all my life-long interests in travel, food, and beer continued to give me the greatest feelings of happiness that I could attain. On the day that the Gulf War broke out in January of 1991, I made the decision to follow my dream of doing a job that I could actually love and gave up on any plan of becoming a practicing attorney. I went to work with my father as the president of a successful home repair finance company and took up homebrewing for the first time. I quickly realized that this hobby had the potential to change my life. Six years later, in 2002, I seized on the opportunity to purchase a commercial brewery with a respected name: the AleSmith Brewing Company in San Diego, California.

What attracted me to craft beer was the unflinching commitment to high quality that this community embodies. At a time when we, as a country, are reassessing the quality of our food and where it comes from, the craft beer segment is driving a similar renaissance of quality, growth, and acceptance among brewers and consumers. It's been ten years since I bought AleSmith, and craft beer continues to post double-digit annual growth numbers, eating away at the dominance of macrobrewers. And our choices have only increased.

A wonderful part of this awakening to quality and flavor is the ability to pair the exceptional food being prepared today with the diversity of craft beer now available. Once reserved only for wine drinkers, the simple pleasure of pairing well-made dishes with craft beer is beginning to make inroads into the larger culinary scene. It is quickly becoming evident that pairing food and beer is natural and fun, and that anyone can participate in and enjoy this enhanced dining experience. "Roasted" and "caramelized" aromas and flavors found in many dishes can also be found in many beer styles, thus creating a natural bridge between food and drink. But it doesn't stop there. For every unique cuisine there's a beer style that will accentuate its most positive aspects.

It was only after meeting Schuyler Schultz that I truly realized just how fantastic a beer and food pairing event could be. AleSmith and Schuyler have teamed up to do a number of beer and food dinners since our meeting, not to mention the wonderful beer and food pairings that he has prepared for me at his home in San Diego. It is evident in the food he prepares that Schuyler shares with AleSmith a total commitment to quality. His deep understanding of craft beer and AleSmith's lineup has aided Schuyler in coming up with some of the most delicious and imaginative pairings that can be experienced.

It has been a pleasure and an honor to work with Schuyler on this book. The knowledge and breadth of experience that is contained within will give you much more than the basics of food and beer pairing; it expresses the creativity and passion necessary to create and enjoy truly memorable experiences with food and beer. Eat well, drink craft beer, and enjoy!

—Peter Zien
Brewmaster and Owner
AleSmith Brewing Co.

BEER,
FOOD, AND FLAVOR

Introduction

THE CRAFT BEER AND FINE FOOD MOVEMENT IN AMERICA

The pleasures of food and drink are supported by long traditions of skill and knowledge, but something new is happening. The new food movement in America, with its emphasis upon local and sustainable production and consumption, has many of us making more informed choices about our food and drink based on where it comes from, how far it has traveled, how it was raised or produced, and what's actually in it. At the same time, we are increasingly curious about new ingredients, combinations, and preparations. The new food movement is in part a fine food movement, creating a sophisticated, venturesome, and highly varied cuisine. Within this context, the craft beer movement is a national phenomenon rising up from and touching down in hundreds if not thousands of localities. The craft beer segment of the beverage market is growing faster than any other. In recession-plagued 2011, when overall beer sales fell approximately 1 percent, domestic craft beer sales rose by 15 percent. With 1,938 craft breweries operating in 2011—the highest total since the 1880s—craft beer's volume share of the market exceeded 5 percent for the first time ever with 5.7 percent. National and regional craft beer festivals are growing in number and attendance because craft breweries around the country are creating vibrant local scenes with distinct regional tastes. It is becoming easier than ever—and more popular—to drink local and drink well.

To choose to drink craft beer is to participate in a growing community dedicated to creativity, sustainability, and a richer quality of life through a deeper appreciation of basic, daily pleasures. Craft beers celebrate flavor. Creative brewers are using roasted malts, aromatic hops, and distinctive yeasts to produce increasingly delicious drinking experiences. Old styles are being revived and new, modern adaptations of classic styles are being created, as well.

The food and beverage movement in America has reached the level of *artistry*, and is at the same time rediscovering the fundamentals. The finest craft beers reflect the passion of brewers employing a variety of modern and traditional methods to create masterfully complex, balanced, and nuanced beverages that can alter our perceptions of what beer *is*. Combine the brewer's passion with the talents of a chef employing the same ideals and the result can be an innovative meal of a quality not likely to be found in very many restaurants. Yet.

The impact of the craft beer movement on the restaurant experience is beginning to be felt, but slowly. Modern diners at a good restaurant can now expect cocktails made with fine spirits and fresh seasonal ingredients, as well as a carefully selected wine list assembled by a person hired by the restaurant for just that purpose. It is, however, still a surprise to find a thoughtful selection of fine beers alongside the wine list and cocktail menu. And, in truth, most of us do not yet expect to find such careful attention paid to this area of the beverage selection. Some might even view a list of high quality craft beers as a novelty at best, and at worst, a pretension. Beer has long been viewed as a beverage to be drunk quickly, ice-cold, and in large quantities. The goal of the most prevalent style available in America, in fact, is to avoid strong, distinctive flavors. Recent innovations in the field of mass-produced beer—lined cans, vortex-necked bottles, or labels that change colors when the beer is chilled—have had little to do with the substance in the bottle. But this is changing. The diversity of choices is widening and the quality of those choices is growing. It is now natural and reasonable for a beer lover to ask: "What new flavor experience can I have today?"

A confluence of talent, innovation, and popular interest now exists that soon will transform the landscape of restaurant dining. But the principles of beer tasting and food pairing that will inform this change are available right now to individuals wishing to select just the right beer for a dinner party or for a particular course within a meal. And very often these selections can be made using local beers that reflect the personality of one's home region—and at much less cost than most wines.

The purpose of this book is to guide and inspire. Simple techniques of mindful tasting can enhance our experience of a flavorful beer, and command of a vocabulary adequate to the complexities of fine beer can help us to discern and enjoy its varied characteristics. When we have learned to taste our food and beer with heightened awareness we have acquired the information needed to pair it skillfully with a variety of foods.

A celebration is afoot—of fine quality, artistry, and community. Bringing together on our dinner tables the good things newly available to us represents a resounding victory for good taste and creative expression. More than ever, the daily necessity of eating and drinking is an opportunity for daily pleasure, for a rich experience of the goodness of life.

PAIRING FINE BEER AND FINE FOOD

There will always be a place for a huge cup of lager alongside a hot dog at the ballpark, a frosted mug with a slice of pizza, or simply a bottle of whatever's in the cooler at the neighborhood barbecue. These too are pairings—situational pairings that are so commonplace and rooted in social tradition that they are never questioned. This is some of what beer does best. The style of beer in these situations matters very little—nearly any type of beer tastes great at the game or beside the grill. The point here is the *quality* of the beer. Replace the generic macrobrew with a craft beer and the enjoyment is only heightened. A better beer with a hot dog will make the hot dog taste better. Simply choose whatever style strikes you and get the best example of it. If a local craft beer is available, even better.

Around the world, long-standing culinary traditions have developed around combining local specialties. Local sausages and beers have been produced and consumed side by side in many countries for centuries. Regional styles of both beers and wines are nearly always the best choice for serving alongside the traditional foods of the region. A brief study of traditional, regional foods and beverages will reveal excellent, straightforward pairings. These are the easy ones. But let's focus on the new, emerging food tradition here in the United States, which is still forming and organizing itself. And let's focus even more specifically on fine meals, either prepared at home or by a chef in a restaurant. These are the pairing situations that offer us a bit more challenge—and an opportunity—to discover something new and original.

It is now conventional wisdom that red wine complements beef and whites go with shellfish. We can break that down further by saying that crisp sauvignon blancs from France's Loire Valley superbly complement oysters, and a rich, spicy, Chateauneuf-du-Pape is the perfect accompaniment to steak au poivre. However, the notion that a dark, strong, Russian imperial stout goes with New York–style cheesecake, or that a witbier is the perfect foil for steamed mussels, is much less accepted, and such pairings may even sound mysterious to many diners. Beer offers an enormous variety of flavors that can complement nearly all foods—and many of the beers being made today offer quality and craftsmanship equivalent to some of the world's finest wines.

Much has been said and written about food and beverage pairings, and many rules have been suggested to ensure success. The topic has been the domain of sommeliers and beverage gurus to the extent that it might appear that they claim exclusive access to this information. Yes, devotion to the intricacies of food and drink can yield exceptional results. This is the field to which these professionals have devoted their lives, and it is terrific if we can use that expertise to our advantage. But the professional's deep knowledge is not necessary, and the breadth of the field need not be intimidating, but exciting instead. And so the goals of this book will be to demystify the subject, to boost confidence, and to increase enjoyment and appreciation—without condescension or oversimplification.

STARTING POINTS

The first step in heightening one's tasting skill is to understand the framework upon which beer flavor profiles are constructed. This will require tasting lots of beer, using an orderly process to analyze the experience. Research is good.

Second, we can borrow some of the well-established terms of wine tasting and apply them to beer (where this works), adding in some new beer-appropriate concepts, to create a method of systematically evaluating the wide variety of craft beers.

And finally, we will use these experiences to successfully integrate beers into fine meals to achieve the same flavor enhancements touted by wine aficionados. As more people gain an awareness of these culinary possibilities and learn to appreciate and celebrate them, more retailers and restaurants will carry the special beers that enable these outstanding dining experiences.

However, there's one more essential point to be made: It is important to *drink what you like*. Personal preference always trumps "expert opinion." That being said, the goal here is to broaden personal preference across a wide variety of beer styles. Developing an appreciation for light and dark, hoppy and malty, and crisp and rich styles of beer opens possibilities for discovering new beers and new pairings. You never know if the next new food or beer you try will become a favorite, or possibly even open the door to an entire new array of experiences not considered before. Yes, great food and beer can change your life.

One such life-changing event occurred for me some years ago upon first tasting a craft beer brewed by the AleSmith Brewing Company of San Diego, California. It was a beer of such singular quality and complexity that it inspired me to pursue a relationship with the people that make up this small company. I went on to have the opportunity to work with them on specialty beer pairing dinners, and, years later, to assist as their culinary director in helping other local chefs conduct their own craft beer dinners with AleSmith. This relationship has given me valuable insight into the workings of a craft brewery operating in the midst of the growing artisanal food movement in America. As a result, AleSmith and its beers appear frequently throughout this book, including a detailed profile in chapter four. But this could have been the case for many of the excellent craft breweries which are practicing their art within diverse local communities across the country. But my particular journey has led me here, and I would like to note that this is not a book sponsored by or written for AleSmith, but is, in part, a response to the respect and admiration I hold for these craftsmen who have become my friends. I encourage everyone to foster relationships with local producers in your community and immerse yourself in the pleasures of fine food and beer.

The benefits to participating in the food movement are immense. It is part educational movement that serves to make us more aware of how our food decisions affect our health, the health of the community, the larger economy, and the environment. It is part aesthetic movement, asking us to slow down and take greater pleasure in the simple ritual of dining together and to realize how vital these experiences are to our culture. Whether these events with friends and family take place at home around the table utilizing locally produced farmers' market ingredients or at an independent farm-to-table restaurant, they contribute richness to our lives in the form of higher quality food that is more flavorful and more nutritious, and which helps to create a more sustainable culture.

Craft beer is a vital part of this movement. To foster an appreciation for craft beer is to take greater control over your daily choices and turn them into daily pleasures. Food and drink are biological requirements, like breathing and exercise. But meals offer us an opportunity to fuel our bodies while nurturing our minds as well. Meals are an opportunity for spending time together, celebrating, or simply taking stock of the sheer magnitude of choices we have in this country. Craft beer is an affordable luxury that can enhance all of these experiences. It is a simple and fascinating way to participate in your local food community, learn about a millennia-old craft, and bring great satisfaction and pleasure to everyday meals. Taking an active role in learning about and enjoying good food and good beer together is an attainable and rewarding way of celebrating life.

1 Tasting Beer

BEER STYLES

Wine appellations are very strictly regulated because the name of a wine or the region it is from has very specific connotations. If a wine comes from the Chablis region of France, for instance, one can assume a fair amount about what that wine will be like; it will be white, made from chardonnay grapes, with good acidity, chalky mineral flavors, and a fairly light body. It is a classic wine. However, the above description is not listed on the label. One must be familiar with the wines of Chablis to know this. And Chablis is just one of hundreds of appellations in France alone. Labeling wines by grape variety has made things easier for consumers in some respects, but it has come at the expense of regional specificity.

Beer is different. The homework to be done before heading out to the bottle shop is more straightforward: learn the basics about beer styles and you'll have a very good idea of what that beer will be like. Know twelve or so different styles and you'll be well equipped; study two dozen beer styles inside and out and you're an expert. Knowing a style's characteristics makes it easier to select new beers from unfamiliar breweries with a high likelihood of successful food pairings.

A beer's style is almost always listed on the label. Often the beer's style is the name of the beer. Brewers, like wine makers, want their beers to be true to the traditions they're based upon. However, styles are guidelines, and brewers may interpret them to create original beers unique to their brewery. This has long been practiced throughout the brewing world, but contemporary American craft brewers have been the most productive innovators. Beer styles serve as the starting point, not an ending point, for how beers should taste.

There are several organizations devoted to defining traditional beer styles and educating people about them. They have created rich resources for researching each style as deeply as you want. The Beer Judge Certification Program (BJCP) is an American organization that trains beer judges and organizes brewing competitions. It has produced very detailed style guidelines to help its judges determine which of the entries is the highest quality interpretation of a traditional style.

The Great American Beer Festival (GABF), organized by the Brewers Association, is the largest beer competition in the world, with sometimes hundreds of entries in a single style category. Eighty-three different styles were recognized in the 2011 competition. The panels of judges change each year, and the winners in each category change as well.

Though organizations strive to define styles and keep them consistent, there is no one "definitive" beer recognized for each style—many beers can share the honor, each expressing a different, valid interpretation. Brewers root their beers in tradition and use their inspiration to interpret the style. This is the essence of the American craft beer movement.

Familiarizing yourself with the major beer styles is simple. After that there are a few styles whose characteristics vary depending on where the beers are made. American interpretations of classic styles generally offer a bit more intensity than their historical versions—using American hop varieties in greater amounts in pale ales and India pale ales (IPAs), more roasted malt in stouts and porters, and so on. It is these American-made styles that are going to be of most significance to us. And the most useful styles to begin with are American pilsner lager (the only lager of the group), Bavarian-style hefeweizen (wheat beer), American pale ale, American amber ale, American brown ale, American stout (nearly analogous to a porter for our purposes), American IPA, double IPA (2IPA), Russian imperial stout (RIS), American barleywine, and American wild ale (sour ale).

Imported beer also represents a significant portion of the craft beer available to us. Many fine examples are sold throughout the country, and these often can provide us with the precise taste we're seeking. Though drinking local is a great mantra, sometimes there's no substitute for the classics when we wish to create certain food pairings. It's important to acknowledge the global diversity of beers and the role certain brewing traditions have played in shaping our own beer culture. Being familiar with historical beers is very important in understanding how styles have evolved in America. Special attention also needs to be given to the beers of Belgium, which represent a unique brewing tradition that stands alone in the world of craft beer, and which are often uncannily versatile for pairing with food.

GENERAL STYLE DESCRIPTIONS:

AMERICAN PILSNER: Light gold color. Light body with a crisp, dry maltiness and light spicy hop flavors.

BAVARIAN-STYLE HEFEWEIZEN: Cloudy pale yellow color. Light body with a slight sweetness and sometimes a faint lemony tartness. Little or no hop bitterness, with distinctive yeast flavors resembling banana and clove.

AMERICAN PALE ALE: Orange-gold in color. Medium-light body with a dry toasted maltiness, significant citrus and pine hop aromas, and moderate hop bitterness.

AMERICAN AMBER ALE: Dark red-amber color. Medium body. Very much like an American pale ale but with more caramel malt sweetness.

AMERICAN BROWN ALE: Chestnut brown color. Medium to medium-full body with significant maltiness, caramel sweetness, and roastiness as well. Moderate hop aroma with medium hop bitterness.

AMERICAN STOUT/PORTER: Opaque brown-black. Medium to full body. Significant roasted malt flavors of coffee and/or chocolate with mild to moderate malt sweetness. Moderate hop aromas and bitterness.

AMERICAN IPA: Copper-gold in color. Medium-light to medium body with strong hop aromas and bitterness supported by a dry malt body that may contain some caramel malt characteristics.

DOUBLE IPA: Like an IPA, but with more of everything. Medium to full body with very high hop aromatics and bitterness with a greater malt presence and significant alcohol.

RUSSIAN IMPERIAL STOUT: Opaque black. Very full body with good viscosity. Very complex, strong roasted malt flavors with pronounced coffee, chocolate, and toffee characteristics. High hop bitterness and alcohol.

AMERICAN BARLEYWINE: Deep golden amber to mahogany in color. Very full body with good viscosity. Pronounced malt sweetness with distinct toffee and caramel flavors. High hop bitterness and alcohol in balance with the malt.

AMERICAN WILD/SOUR ALE: Highly variable experimental style. Most often possesses distinctive sour fermentation characteristics from oak barrel aging with multiple yeast and bacteria strains.

COMMON AMERICAN CRAFT BEER STYLE CHARACTERISTICS

STYLE:	PILSNER	WHEAT	PALE	AMBER	BROWN	STOUT/PORTER	IPA	2IPA	RIS	BARLEYWINE	SOUR
Malt:	1	1	2	3	3	4	2	3	5	5	1–2
Hops:	2	1	3	3	2	3	4	5	5	5	1
Fermentation:	1	4	1	1	1	1	1	1	1	1	5
Mouthfeel:	2	1	2	3	3	4	2	4	5	5	2
Alcohol:	Low	Low	Med	Med	Low	Low–Med	Med	High	High	High	Low–Med

COMMON BELGIAN BEER STYLE CHARACTERISTICS

STYLE:	WITBIER	SAISON/BIÈRE DU GARDE	GUEUZE	TRIPEL	DUBBEL	ABT/QUAD	FLANDERS RED/OUD BRUIN
Malt:	1	2	1	3	4	5	3
Hops:	1	2	1	1	1	1	1
Fermentation:	2	3	5	3	4	4	5
Mouthfeel:	1	2	2	3	4	5	3
Alcohol:	Low	Med	Low	High	Med	High	Med

FLAVOR INTENSITY/MOUTHFEEL WEIGHT KEY: 1: Light, 2: Light–Med, 3: Med, 4: Med–High, 5: High
APPROXIMATE ALCOHOL STRENGTH RANGE KEY: Low: up to 5.5%, Med: 5.6%–7.9%, High: 8% and up

DISCOVERING SOUR BEERS

I had tried a few lambics, some experimental American wild ales, and a couple of tart fruit beers. They always struck me as an assault on the palate. They bit into my salivary glands, stung my mouth a bit, and hardly resembled anything I'd had before called "beer." I tried hard to get into them. I just wasn't able to think of the situation in which I'd be able to enjoy them. As I researched more beers I came across a collaboration ale called Isabelle Proximus made by the brewers at The Lost Abbey, Russian River, Avery, Allagash, and Dogfish Head, which was inspired by their experiences together during a trip to Belgium. This team alone piqued my interest. Brewed only once, this was a tough one to find and, when I did, it was very expensive as well—all for a beer in a style that I didn't think I liked. But, in spite of these hurdles, trying this beer changed my life. Here are the tasting notes I made:

> *Clear, light gold with a very thin, fine white head and a steady stream of Champagne-like bubbles flowing through it. Deep, pure, sour brett aroma with intense light fruitiness: light berries—fresh and bright—yellow fruits, tempered by acetic/lacto fermentation characteristics. There are some secondary cheesy aged hops and soft oak-aged characteristics here as well rounding out the complex, heady aroma. The flavor is full of completely clean, vibrant sourness that splashes across the palate and washes away clean in the finish with a brief hint of spicy hop bitterness. The body is dominated by a super acidic, mouth-watering, taste bud-cramping tartness that actually leaves a little rawness in the mouth—a very physical beer—and finishes with a fresh, lemony, puckering quality. Really fantastic, complex, pure, game-changing American sour beer. This redefines the possibilities of the style for me.*

There it was. The door had been opened. Now I understood; my whole perspective was recalibrated. I went back and tried the sour beers I had been cool to before (and many more new ones as well) with a new sense of discovery. I loved these beers now. It just took the right one to bring it all together for me. The real payoff: sour beers are among the most versatile beers to pair with food. Their acidity, not found in other styles, sets off flavor elements like few other beers. They are an invaluable asset in making inspired food pairings.

The Best-of-the-Best American Sour/Wild Beers to Search Out:

RUSSIAN RIVER: Consecration, Supplication, Temptation, Beatification

THE LOST ABBEY: Red Poppy, Framboise de Amorosa, Duck Duck Gooze

CAPTAIN LAWRENCE: Cuvee de Castleton, Rosso e Marrone

CASCADE: Kriek

THE SENSORY COMPONENTS OF BEER

Breaking a beer down into its fundamental sensory elements helps distinguish not only what makes each different from one another, but also enables us to assess the particular distinctiveness and quality of each example. When tasting a beer, consider its **appearance, aroma, flavor,** and **mouthfeel** in an orderly sequence. This analysis will help us to understand why we like what we like and can help us in seeking out more examples of beers that we'll enjoy. It also helps to isolate individual characteristics that we may want to highlight and enhance alongside a particular dish.

It's a good idea to assess a beer's characteristics in the order in which we would naturally perceive them as we drink it. By considering them in this way we can garner a better understanding of how each characteristic leads into and contributes to the next, and how the next builds upon the previous. Think of a beer's appearance in comparison to how a dish is presented in a restaurant: it immediately sets the stage for what's to follow. If the beer is dark and opaque we might expect a rich, malty beer. If it is cloudy with a big head perhaps there are some interesting fermentation aromas and flavors.

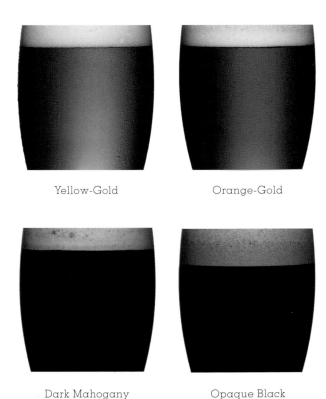

Yellow-Gold

Orange-Gold

Dark Mahogany

Opaque Black

SAMPLE COLOR DESCRIPTORS:
Light, medium, dark; yellow, gold, orange, amber, copper, red, mahogany, tan, brown, black; clear, opaque, hazy, cloudy.

SAMPLE HEAD DESCRIPTORS:
small, medium, large; dense, loose, rocky, fine; long-lasting, quickly dissipating.

SAMPLE HOP AROMA DESCRIPTORS:

Fruity: citrus, apple, stonefruit, pear, tropical fruit; Piney: resin, needles, wood; Floral; Herbal; Eucalyptus; Earthy: loam, dry leaves, bark; Spicy (not cloves or coriander); Cheesy

---

SAMPLE MALT AROMA DESCRIPTORS:

Cereal/Nutty; Lightly Roasted Malt: toast, biscuits, grain; Medium Roast: caramel, toffee, brown sugar, molasses; Dark Roast: coffee, dark chocolate, soy sauce, treacle, dried fruits (currants, raisins, prunes, figs); Smoky.

Next, we savor the aroma in anticipation of the flavor. Is it clean and straightforward, or dark and complex? We may expect bitterness from a large hop presence in the aroma, or some sweetness if caramel malt notes are present. Then we taste. Is it what we were expecting from the style of the beer? If not, how does that dissonance make us feel? Is it a delightful surprise or is something missing? This pattern of satisfied expectation or surprise is an essential part of experiencing the beer.

Finally, how are all of the beer's elements—appearance, aroma, and flavor—supported by the physical sensation of the beer in the mouth? Is it watery or does it have a medium or heavy viscosity? How much warmth or even heat of alcohol is present? Is there a pleasant astringency provided by the presence of malt tannins? What is the beer's carbonation level and how does that feel? And when we register the combination of mouth sensations produced by viscosity, alcohol warmth, astringency, and carbonation level, we can begin to speak of a beer's "body," which may strike us as being weak or strong, light or heavy, thin or full.

Among a beer's traits, its body is one of the most ephemeral and difficult to describe. The traditional use of the word in wine tasting does not translate well to beer-tasting. Because wine is made by fermenting one ingredient—grapes—we can speak of a light- or full-bodied wine in terms of its density of the flavors extracted from the grapes and its alcohol level. But given the multiple ingredients of beer—hops, malt, water, and yeast—and the multitude of ways they are employed by brewers, the situation is more complex. The sensation of body in a beer has much to do with the structure of its different flavor components and the balance (or lack of balance) among them.

We can consider a beer's appearance, aroma, taste, and body separately, but of course they interact in the overall experience. And in the best beers these dimensions form a distinct framework in which they complement one another. In a well-balanced beer each sensation and flavor holds the others in clear relation so each can be experienced more individually and fully. When we experience this we will say that the beer has good structure. For instance, a watery mouthfeel may leave a beer's hoppy bitterness lying flat on the tongue, but the presence of some pleasant malt astringency can provide a crispness that will complement and support the hop bitterness.

Savoring a beer's aroma is essential to fully enjoying it. Great pains are taken by careful brewers to produce precisely crafted aroma profiles in their beers that can easily be overlooked if the beer is drunk too cold or from the bottle. The aroma can set up what's to come in the flavor or prove to be in surprising contrast once the beer is tasted. Some beers have such complex aromas that you can enjoy them for minutes on end without taking a single sip.

SAMPLE FERMENTATION DESCRIPTORS:

Clean (no overt aromas); Estery; Phenolic; Musty; Spicy; Fruity; English: apples, pear, autumn spice; German Wheat: banana, clove, bread; Belgian: honey, candied fruit, sour fruit, "animal," barnyard, cheesy.

SAMPLE FLAVOR DESCRIPTORS:

See above aroma descriptors, but which are also/instead present in the flavor. The aroma and flavor profiles of beer are closely linked and are often very similar, but this is not necessarily true in every case. The overall flavor profile can be described as: straightforward, dense, one-/multidimensional. Alcohol, however, has its own flavors that are only detected by tasting.

Recognizing specific characteristics of appearance, aroma, taste, and body comes with practice in tasting and comparing different types of beer. And having a rich vocabulary of qualities with which to name the specific ways that beers look, smell, taste, and feel can actually help us to distinguish those qualities more clearly and enjoy them more fully. Here, in summary, are several terms you will find useful as you become increasingly mindful in your beer-tasting:

APPEARANCE—How the beer *looks*: color; clarity; size, color, and shape of the head; any other physical characteristics that present themselves.

AROMA—How it *smells*. This includes general aromatics from the ingredients: hops, malt, and yeast. What do the hops smell like? How is the malt contributing to the aroma? Yeast can also contribute specific aromas (and flavors) to a beer, ranging from subtle nuances to tart or vinegar-like elements, buttery diacetyl, or particular esters and phenols (fruity, spicy, or even solvent-like characteristics formed by specialized yeasts or flaws in the brewing process). Certain fermentation characteristics are closely linked to particular styles.

FLAVOR—How it *tastes*. Again, follow the same steps as in evaluating the aroma. Many aspects may be very similar. If you smell orange

SAMPLE ALCOHOL FLAVOR DESCRIPTORS:

Mild, medium, strong; Sweet; Harsh; Honey; Sherry; Solvent; Cidery; "Boozy"; Oxidized.

SAMPLE MOUTHFEEL DESCRIPTORS:

Viscosity: thick/viscous, thin/watery, light, heavy, coating; Alcohol: weak, warm, hot, burning; Bitterness: soft/light, sharp/harsh, nimble, heavy, straightforward, dense, clean/clear, sticky; Carbonation: soft/fine, sharp/prickly; General: light, medium, full, vibrant/lively, flat/dead, lifting, weighty.

peel or caramel are those same elements present in the flavor as well? Is the beer sweet, dry, or in between? As you learn about different beer styles you will construct a set of expectations for how each is likely to taste.

MOUTHFEEL AND BODY—How is the beer perceived in the mouth? Does it feel light, heavy, thick, thin, or watery? Does it seem "dead" on the palate—coating it with one sensation—or is it "lively," offering up varied sensations? The main elements to consider here are: What is the viscosity of the beer? Can the alcohol be felt? How is the bitterness perceived? What is the carbonation level? And how do these elements interact together? Does the beer give an overall impression of lightness or richness? How does drinking it make your mouth actually feel?

These are the general categories that the sensory elements of beer fall into and many of the specific qualities within each category. Distinguishing these qualities and noting how each contributes to the overall experience of drinking the beer is the key to imagining how it might pair with specific foods. Will the heaviness of a beer, despite a complementary flavor profile, overwhelm the dish? Does the bitter grapefruit flavor of the beer complement or compound the presence of citrus zest in the food preparation? These are questions to which the answers will come quite easily and naturally as one learns to perceive beers both in terms of individual traits and as the sum of all their intricacies.

EVALUATING CRAFT BEER —A TASTING VOCABULARY

Having broken down the experience of registering a beer's appearance, aroma, taste, and body into an orderly sequence, we can delve deeper into how we register a beer's flavors. Here, too, an orderly process will help us have a fuller experience and inform our food pairings. Breaking down the *act* of tasting helps us to deliberately look at the entire perception of the tasting *experience*.

Accurate naming clarifies experience. And so we need a rich and nuanced tasting vocabulary, not only to articulate our beer tasting but also to enable perception and discrimination. Here are some terms, including both established wine-tasting vocabulary and concepts newly adapted for evaluating craft beer. These will provide us with the language needed to fully capture the complex and nuanced experiences offered by the brewmaster's art.

INITIAL TASTING TERMS

ATTACK: The very first sensations when the beer enters the mouth constitutes its "attack." Describing a beer's attack, we might say, for instance, that it "immediately coats the mouth with roasted malt bitterness," or that "intense sourness leads into vibrant tart fruit flavors."

PRIMARY/SECONDARY/TERTIARY FLAVOR CHARACTERISTICS: Primary flavors are those that are experienced first and most prominently, which then give rise to secondary flavors that are experienced more subtly, then tertiary flavors and so on. I find tertiary flavors to be quite rare and very noteworthy when experienced clearly—a mark of a highly complex and sophisticated beer.

FRONT/MID/BACK PALATE: Different flavors are experienced on different areas of the tongue. The physical location of taste buds correlates only loosely with the notion of where flavors are experienced on the palate. Flavorful hop bitterness experienced on the tongue, for

PROPER GLASSWARE AND SERVICE

As with wine, having the proper glass is very important to bringing out a beer's full potential. Also, proper pouring allows carbonation to be released, forming the head. Too little head and the beer can't express its full aroma; too much can make the beer flat. And a head that's too big can concentrate hop oils in the foam and give it a metallic taste on the attack. The beer's temperature also plays a huge role here. Too cold and the aromas can't properly volatilize, or escape into the air and provide a bountiful aroma. The same goes for the flavors: too warm and the body of the beer can be put out of balance—the alcohol can volatilize too much, the hops can become sticky rather than crisp, and the malt can be perceived as cloying instead of pleasantly sweet.

TEMPERATURE—Most beers in America are served too cold. Straight from the fridge is usually too cold. From an ice bath is definitely too cold. In general, aim for a temperature somewhat warmer than refrigerator but cooler than the room. Ideal temperature varies by style, but 45–55 degrees Fahrenheit suits most beers. Experiment with different types of beers to determine what you prefer. This often happens naturally over the course of a pint. Take note of how the flavors and aromas change as the beer warms in the glass.

THE GLASS—A glass is assumed here. Drinking beer from the bottle eliminates the ability to experience the aroma, thereby significantly reducing the beer's impact. Insist on a glass, please. A simple, clean pint glass (without any detergent residue) will suffice in the majority of cases. Wetting the glass offers extra protection from any residue, and also minimizes the nucleation points that, too numerous, can produce overly vigorous foaming. A tulip glass can enhance the experience of any beer because its wide bowl helps to collect the aroma. This is especially important when drinking a complex beer. A red wine glass can also be used, and really shows a fine beer a lot of respect. Many beer styles are associated with traditional glassware. Building a collection can be a lot of fun. One can taste well, however, with just a few heavy pints, some tulips (or wine glasses), and perhaps a few tall, narrow glasses if you are going to be drinking a lot of wheat beers. Some very fine glasses are now being made specifically for beer. I have found that the Spiegelau crystal tulip-shaped "Stemmed Pilsner" glass from their "Beer Classics" line is the ideal glass for virtually any beer.

THE POUR—Hold the glass at an angle and gently pour the beer down the side. Turn it upright about two-thirds full and continue to pour straight down the middle. Leave room for about an inch of head to form (again, depending on style and preference). Styles with lower carbonation require more delicate treatment. Some, such as hefeweizens and many Belgian beers, should be poured with a larger head. Guinness and other beers carbonated with nitrogen have their own pouring techniques to allow them to cascade down the insides of the glass and form a signature head. Pour smaller amounts of special beers into tulip glasses so they'll have the chance to develop more quickly and so there will be enough room in the bowl to collect the complex aromas. Swirl these beers like wine to release their aromas and to form a small head.

instance, delivers a sensation different from bitterness that stimulates the back of the throat. Alcohol characteristics are also experienced differently in different areas. Some may be more "up-front" offering sweet, fruity flavors while others may give warm sensation in the throat or on the back of the tongue. Front is usually associated with the attack, back with the finish, and mid for what's experienced in between.

FINISH: The beer's "finish" is made up of the flavors and sensations that remain in the mouth/throat after the beer has been swallowed. This term should not be used interchangeably with "aftertaste," which, strictly speaking, describes a taste that remains on the tongue, not the entire finish experience, which includes both flavors in the mouth and aromas lingering in the soft palate. Aftertaste can also describe negative flavor characteristics that are present during or after the finish.

BALANCE: If a beer is balanced, its aromas, flavors, and body characteristics complement one another in a harmonious combination. In an unbalanced beer one aspect negatively overpowers the drinking experience. This does not preclude balanced beers from being very hoppy or very malty, for instance. In the case of those beers with extreme flavors, balance is achieved by the hops, malt, or other characteristics being supported and enhanced by other aspects of the beer, such as the alcohol presence and a vibrant mouthfeel. This is a different kind of balance—like a soloist playing above the rest of the orchestra. In a truly unbalanced beer, however, one might only taste and feel a high level of alcohol with little malt flavor, hop bitterness, or a substantial mouthfeel to support it.

DIMENSION: Having a complex set of well-balanced aromas, flavors, and body characteristics gives a beer dimension. A beer with only one aroma, one flavor, and a nondescript body could be considered one-dimensional. A beer with a high level of complexity that offers an evolving experience with each sip and keeps us going back to examine its characteristics from different angles could be considered to be multidimensional. Multidimensional beers can offer more opportunities for food pairings because of their complexity—giving us more points to highlight through a variety of different approaches or preparations. One-dimensional beers aren't necessarily bad; they offer simplicity and straightforwardness. They may lend themselves only to a few, very specific food pairings.

SAMPLE BEER ANALYSES

1. TASTING AN ALESMITH X PALE ALE

APPEARANCE: Medium orange-gold in color with a medium-finely textured, medium-thick, off-white colored head.

AROMA: Lots of bright, vibrant American hops consisting of citrus (orange peel) and pine needles followed by a soft earthiness with mild malt sweetness.

FLAVOR: The first impression (attack) is of a marked transition from the powerful hop aroma to a well-balanced flavor profile that includes crisp maltiness along with a subtle alcohol presence. The hops present themselves with mild but assertive bitterness along with some fresh orange and pine-needle flavor. Dry maltiness with a hint of alcohol sweetness.

BODY: The mouthfeel is neither watery nor heavy, but is crisp with straightforward maltiness, alcohol, and bitterness lending the beer a light body that conveys these aspects in an easygoing, lively fashion, yet still provides good presence into the finish.

COMMENTS: A classic, if somewhat forward, American pale ale. The hops profile is the focus here, but in a way that expresses an emphasis on American hop aromas, and is characteristic of San Diego ales. The bitterness is quite mild in relation to the amount of hops in the aroma, which is key to the successfulness of this pale ale—it is not an IPA. There are noticeable malt and alcohol flavors as well, yet the beer is dry and mild. There is no sacrifice of flavor or aroma. This beer highlights a hop-driven drinkability in appropriate balance with the American pale ale style's characteristic light, refreshing body.

WITH FOOD: Think of this beer when you want an assertive aroma to complement a distinct yet mild flavor in a dish. For instance, think of the citrusy notes of this pale ale as complement to the briny flavor of Pacific oysters and the sourdough flavor of a crusty bread with butter. Or pair with artisanal salami (with a distinct old-world cure flavor) and Italian green olives. The focus of these pairings should be on the distinctive characteristics of the fine foods that will be in turn supplemented by a fresh, cleansing citrus hop aroma, and a light, refreshing flavor profile that leaves the palate ready for the next bite.

VINTAGE BEERS

Though no longer brewed, bottles of this exceptional English barleywine can still be found and are well worth seeking out for a taste of brewing history.

While most beers are best enjoyed fresh, especially lighter-bodied hoppy ales such as pale ales, IPAs, and fruity wheat beers, there are some that can age quite well and develop unique flavors while doing so. Often beers that are intended for aging will be labeled with a vintage date. Otherwise, a beer's style characteristics, such as a high alcohol content or level of maltiness, can suggest its aging potential—sturdy, malty, high alcohol beers will stand up better over time. A beer's unique characteristics—being barrel-aged, bottle conditioned, or fermented with wild yeasts—can also indicate how well a beer will age. Beer that has already seen time in barrels, aging in bourbon barrels or re-fermenting in oak, has already been subjected to quite a bit of oxidation. As a result, these beers tend to be quite sturdy and are among the types most worthy of aging. Also, bottle conditioned beers still have live yeast in the bottle that will continue to work and protect the integrity of the beer over time.

Beer styles that can generally stand up to one to five years of aging include barleywines and old ales; Russian imperial stouts and robust porters; Belgian strong ales and Trappist ales; and sour ales such as lambics and gueuzes. However, this is highly dependent on the original quality of the individual beer; to be able to develop over time a beer must have good character from the beginning.

Ideally, all aging beer should be kept at a constant cellar temperature of 55–65 degrees

Fahrenheit, though less fluctuation is more important than a cooler temperature. Store beers straight up, though cork-finished bottled may be stored on their sides for extended aging. Typical aged-beer characteristics include:

- the development of oxidative characteristics including sherry-like flavors
- faded hop aromas and flavors
- a softened malt body and a thinner mouthfeel
- a mellowed alcohol profile, which can become more exposed
- sourness can sharpen and intensify

Though some of these traits may sound like they have diminished the beer, this isn't necessarily the case. A softer alcohol profile can bring a beer into balance. Malt sweetness or sour fermentation profiles can develop additional complexities. Unanticipated unique flavors can also develop to produce one-of-a-kind drinking experiences.

Here are some classic vintage beers:

- J.W. Lee's Harvest Ale (English Barleywine)
- Fuller's Vintage Ale
- Greene King Olde Suffolk
- Sierra Nevada Bigfoot Barleywine
- North Coast Old Stock Ale
- Many Belgian sour ales are routinely vintage dated, including Vintage Rodenbach and many editions from Cantillon, Hanssens, and Drie Fontienen

Finally, be on the lookout for Thomas Hardy's Ale, a classic English vintage barleywine. Sadly, Edridge Pope, the original maker, sold the beer's rights to O'Hanlon's Brewing Co. in 2003, and five years later O'Hanlon's let it go out of production. Bottles of this world-class beer can age for a decade or more, so keep a look out for these gold foil-topped bottles hung with a golden medallion. In the meantime, we wait in the hope that another brewery will revive this excellent beer.

2. TASTING A DOGFISH HEAD PALO SANTO MARRON

Appearance: Opaque, very dark mahogany brown color with a thin, finely-textured dark caramel-colored head.

Aroma: The powerful, malt-driven aroma is redolent of dark toffee and caramel along with significant alcohol sweetness and a slightly smoky, almost oily, edge. This is combined with highly intriguing spicy sandalwood-like notes—certainly from the influence of the unique Palo Santo wood vessels used to age this beer.

Flavor: The prominent alcohol flavors flow out from around the edges of Palo Santo Marron's enormous malt profile which is spiked with notes of pleasant roasted bitterness and a complex dark fruitiness. Nearly all aspects of the aroma show up in the flavor as well. Spicy hop characteristics also assert themselves but are restrained for a beer of this heft. Despite its heaviness, the flavor delivery is smooth and deliberate.

Body: The thick, chewy mouthfeel delivers the robust flavor profile squarely on the tongue, coating it with its dense block of flavors. It may be somewhat heavy and blunt, but it is nonetheless nuanced. The malt certainly plays the dominant role, but is supported by bitter and spicy flavor peaks.

Comments: Dogfish Head's characteristic brashness and ingenuity is on full display here in Palo Santo Marron. None of the unconventional flavors seem out of place, however. In fact, each manages to meld seamlessly with the beer's more traditional palette of rich, roasted malt elements. This is truly an enormous beer to be sipped and savored; yet it is certainly not so ponderous as to prevent casual drinking, for which it is equally well-suited.

With Food: In this case the conventional wisdom holds true: the significant malt and alcohol characteristics, combined with the smoky influence of the wood, dictates that this beer be served alongside grilled meats—namely, a thick rib eye with chimichurri sauce. The Paraguayan origins of the wooden casks reinforce this notion. Carne asada tacos with handmade corn tortillas, or bison chili with fire-roasted green chilies would also pair excellently. Feel free to push the limits for cheese pairings here; a beer this solid can certainly stand up to assertively flavored cheeses. Spanish San Simón reinforces Palo Santo Marron's smoky aspects while a creamy, mushroomy blue such as the novel Cambazola, a proprietary fusion of Camembert and Gorgonzola-styled cheeses, counters the beer's alcohol sweetness. English Cotswold—studded with chives and spring onions—matches the straightforward strength of this beer with prominent flavors of its own.

3. TASTING AN ALESMITH SPEEDWAY STOUT RUSSIAN IMPERIAL STOUT

APPEARANCE: Opaque black in color with a medium-thin, very finely textured, creamy, mocha-colored head.

AROMA: Full, slightly sweet aroma with lots of coffee and roasted malt characteristics including bittersweet chocolate, toffee, and a hint of creaminess.

FLAVOR: Rich expressions of the aroma characteristics appear in the flavor as well. The well-balanced alcohol sweetness appears first, and combines with the dark malt profile giving an impression of espresso and dark chocolate liqueur balanced by a steady bitterness from American hops and roasted grain.

BODY: Extraordinarily smooth and balanced in the mouth with a thick, but not at all heavy or syrupy, viscosity. The fine, creamy carbonation delivers the intense flavor profile so delicately on the palate that you scarcely know it hides an alcohol content of 12%. Only a whisper of warmth in the finish, combined with complex roasted bitterness, gives any indication of this beer's strength.

COMMENTS: The most remarkable thing about this beer is its balance. It contains 12% alcohol, a huge, darkly roasted grain bill, and more hops than a double IPA, yet each component interacts in such unison that no one characteristic takes over. A huge coffee flavor, from the addition of actual coffee beans, is tempered by dark caramel and chocolate malts. The thick mouthfeel that smoothly delivers these strong flavors is accented by precise, creamy carbonation and a backbone of aromatic hop bitterness. The alcohol adds dimension on the palate as well and is in turn tempered by the rich flavors. This graceful dance paradoxically conveys a notion of lightness to the huge, rich, and intense beer.

WITH FOOD: Normally, a beer with this much horsepower could be paired only with a handful of rich, strongly flavored, meaty foods—or creamy or chocolate desserts. Speedway, too, would be outstanding with such foods, but because of its exceptional balance, we can utilize its intense roasted flavor profile alongside foods that would otherwise be overpowered by a beer of this magnitude. Classic choices like grilled steaks, chicken molé, smoked pork shoulder, or lamb cacciatore would be excellent. But so would focaccia with grilled stone fruit and blue cheese, or sourdough bread pudding with brandied cherries and dark caramel sauce. All sorts of robust cheeses would pair splendidly too. Stilton, extra-aged gouda, and Taleggio spring to mind.

2 Pairing Craft Beer with Fine Cuisine

ar mission at The Vine Cottage is to serve delicious food made
h seasonal, all-natural, organic, locally-sourced, and sustainably-
oduced ingredients whenever possible.

We believe this approach provides the most healthful and flavorful
cuisine while promoting an awareness of the role independent and
forward-thinking companies play in supporting our local communities.

etizers
ad Black Mussels 13
with Yukon gold fries
nire – white wine, butter, shallots, fines herbes
gar – wit beer, cream, roasted garlic, goat cheese
r –sausage, leeks, tomato, Spanish smoked paprika

ine Cottage Bruschetta8
...t Crust White Bean – roast peppers, herbs, extra virgin oil
Olive Tapenade – capers, rosemary, lemon, goat cheese
..Mushroom Duet – portobello, shiitake, cream, Cognac, herbs
...– tomato, basil, fresh mozzarella, aged balsamic

...a Taps 13

...Ranch Pork Belly w/ Bacon Broth Stew10

Entrées
Grilled 'Niman Ranch' Pork Rib Chop 22
Fig glaze, sautéed broccolini, fingerling potatoes
Cioppino – San Francisco-Style Seafood Stew 19
Lingcod, Carlsbad mussels, shrimp, crab claws, robust tomato broth
Pan-Seared Salmon w/ Herbs19
Leeks, shiitake mushrooms, fingerling potatoes, pinot noir reduction
Grilled, Marinated 'Jidori' Chicken 18
Mediterranean tarts, grilled radicchio, goat cheese, aged balsamic
Braised Beef Short Ribs22
...san wine reduction, coconut, dried plums, fingerling potatoes
Cornerstone Farms Sliced Angus Flank Steak25
Caramelized... spelone, red wine, Romesco, dairy arugula
The Vine Cottage Grass-Fed Beef Burger12
...Cheese Co.King "Island" Merlount, onion, Guardian Gold ...
...Goat Farm Chevre, roasted onion and prosciutto, fresh sage, hot'em

WHAT MAKES A GOOD PAIRING?

The nature of beer is adaptable enough so that you're likely to come across only a few truly disastrous pairings. Most often a pairing of random food A and random beer B will yield an adequate, enjoyable experience. So, even a light application of conventional wisdom can immediately improve the quality of beer and food pairings. And beyond that, putting in some deep consideration and satisfying research can achieve remarkable gustatory pleasures.

The goal here is to create an experience in which the combination of the beer and food in a meal together add additional interest and character to the experience in a way that wouldn't be possible if each were enjoyed separately. Each component contributes its own element to the meal, as does the combination of the two. A pairing will not cover up a flaw in either the food preparation or the beer, but it can bring better balance to each.

Experimentation is key, guided by some basic principles (we'll avoid "rules"). But even then, given the diversity of beer and food, great pairings can be discovered out of seemingly incompatible matchups.

A hearty autumn meal paired with craft beers can showcase a variety of different beer and food pairing techniques.

COMPLEMENTARY AND CONTRASTING PAIRINGS

Complementary pairings focus on matching like flavors in the food and beer. The fact that similar flavors are still perceived quite differently across beers and foods keeps this approach from producing mere redundancy; instead, the experience can be very thought provoking while adding another dimension to the meal. Avoid thinking too literally about "like" flavors. Do not limit your pairing inspirations to searching out uncanny flavor similarities. This will only limit the beers you'll be able to work with. Think of like flavors in more general terms such as "fruity," "bright," "toasted," "floral," and so on. A huge Russian imperial stout might pair very well with a spice-rubbed prime rib-eye steak charred on the grill over searing hot coals. The "grilled" flavors do match, but so do the respective weights of the food and beer. This is a rich piece of meat and needs a beer with a big body

Grilled Colorado Lamb Chops with Charred Brussels Sprouts and Herb-Horseradish Fingerling Potatoes. The rich flavors of grilled lamb complement dark, strong, malty beers very well while the mild mustardy bitterness of Brussels sprouts complements their hops characteristics.

and a lot of flavor. The high alcohol content of the beer definitely cuts through the fat, and the dark malt flavors interplay with the gamey and spice notes of the seasoned beef. Russian imperial stouts are extreme beers and can be limited in their pairing ability. The same holds true for robust, fatty pieces of meat. So like flavors in this case can mean bold flavors that can stand up to one another.

A salad made with arugula will showcase its bold, spicy, slightly bitter flavor. Think IPA right away. Serve it with a dressing whose acid component is tart citrus juice, or citrus vinegar, and you have another matchup with any citrus-like American hop flavors. The

CLASSIC, TIME-HONORED BEER AND FOOD PAIRINGS

Oysters on the half-shell	Dry stout
Stilton cheese	Barleywine (more on beer and cheese later)
Bratwurst	Märzen/Oktoberfest lager
Steamed mussels	Witbier
Dark chocolate	Russian imperial stout

Try out this interesting, classic pairing yourself. The brininess of the oysters contrasts with the stout's roasted flavors while the creamy mouthfeel of each complement one another. Pictured here are Carlsbad Lunas with North Coast Old No. 38.

Uni with Roasted Golden Beets, Scallion, and Usukuchi Soy. The creamy brininess of fresh sea urchin and the roasted beets' earthy sweetness contrasts with the dry crispness and hoppy bitterness of American pale ales.

type of acidity found in dressings can prove problematic for many pairings by interfering with the flavor and body of the beer, but not for an IPA. Its bitterness, instead of compounding the arugula, is of a different sort, and complements it while also not bowing to the intensity of an acidic dressing.

Contrasting pairings pit different flavors in the food and beer opposite one another to create a contrast that clarifies the perception of each. The flavor variation between each sip of beer and bite of food highlights the distinctiveness of each. Going to extremes is not the idea here. A very delicate white fish preparation would be obliterated by a barleywine with a huge malt profile. However, if the fish is prepared with a brown butter sauce, garlic, parsley, and lemon, then perhaps the Belgian strong golden ale Duvel will work very nicely. At 8.5% alcohol it's as strong as many barleywines. Nonetheless, its surprisingly light body combined with a soft sweetness and crisp, subtle hops and fermentation aspects makes it a very good foil for the delicate fish with its richer, aromatic sauce.

Save the barleywine for a rich, baked macaroni and cheese made with aged sharp white cheddar—with a nice crispy golden crust on top. The strength of the barleywine with its assertive alcohol and hops profiles will cut right through the mouth-coating richness of the cheese sauce. The sweet caramel malt elements will provide

Roasted Pumpkin Stuffed with Bacon, Gruyere, and Sourdough Bread. Sweet-fleshed winter squashes, like pumpkin or kabocha, develop deep flavors when roasted. Combine this with a creamy, hearty filling and you have an ideal match for strong, malt-driven beers with some sweetness of their own.

Crème Caramel, a classic dessert, employs complimentary and contrasting flavors to its own success. Both elements—its bittersweet burnt sugar caramel and silken creamy custard—possess richness and sweetness in different forms. A beer pairing can highlight either aspect: a sweet, dark Belgian strong ale or a tart cherry beer each play off of different aspects of the dish in both contrasting and complementary ways to delicious effect.

an excellent contrast between bites of crispy, cheesy pasta.

Since neither food nor beer expresses just one flavor, sometimes pairings can **simultaneously complement and contrast**. These are the truly masterful pairings that can really express the synergy of food and beer. These are the ones we're shooting for. They take advantage of our precise knowledge of the specific flavor profiles of the food preparation and the particular beer.

Discovering rewarding pairings depends on working with high quality, flavorful beers and foods. These are beers that we savor for their depth and complexity and that offer an evolving experience throughout a pairing. Similarly, the types of foods we relish in these situations are deeply flavored and multidimensional ones that contain several components with interplay amongst themselves. Rodenbach Grand Cru is a sour Flanders red beer that is a blend of one-third one-year-old and two-thirds two-year-old beer that has been aged in huge traditional oak vessels known as *foeders*. Its complex sweet-sour, malty aspects combined with many different fermentation characteristics offers a rich tapestry of flavors that can play off of a wide variety of foods. Pair this with, for example, seared Colorado lamb tenderloins marinated with garlic, cumin seed, and mild chili. Plate the lamb with a fresh carrot and raisin salad with a tart ginger-yogurt dressing accented

WHAT MAKES A BEER FOOD FRIENDLY?

A beer termed "food friendly" is one that can be successfully paired with a wide variety of foods. Food-friendly beers are not necessarily those without distinctiveness or assertive flavors. In fact, the most food-friendly beers are often those with the most complexity. Complexity equals versatility. A high degree of complexity offers many flavor facets which can be highlighted by many different kinds of food.

Many "simple" beers can be enjoyed alongside food just fine, but to achieve truly exciting pairings the beers should be as serious as the food. Beers with a lot of dimension possess enough character to stand on their own as a focal point of a meal but can also work together with fine foods so that each can build on the other. A beer with a complex, well-structured body also has the ability to be flexible across diverse gourmet preparations. These characteristics offer the most opportunities for beers and foods to complement and contrast with one another in pairings.

Certain beer styles with very strong flavors, which are certainly quite complex as well, are food friendly, but only within certain categories of food. Those with very strong malt profiles are versatile for pairing with a wide variety of meats, for instance, including beef, lamb, pork, and game. Beers with intense hop flavors and bitterness can work well with rich, deeply flavored food preparations like stews, curries, braises, and a wide variety of aromatic, bitter greens and herbs. Belgian-style beers with complex fermentation profiles, which can possess some acidity, wood-aged characteristics, or utilize multiple yeast or bacteria strains, and may or may not be sour, are likely to be very friendly among foods which themselves have highly complex flavor profiles.

Some fun examples of widely available, highly food-friendly beers to try include: Orval Trappist Ale, Duvel Strong Golden Ale, Duchesse de Bourgogne Flanders Red, Lindeman's Cuvee Renee Gueuze (all from Belgium). Also, Bear Republic Racer 5 IPA and Red Rocket Ale; Deschutes Inversion IPA; Anchor Porter; Jolly Pumpkin La Roja Flanders-Style Red and Oro de Calabaza Belgian-Style Golden Ale; and Bell's Oberon Wheat and Best Brown Ale.

The vinegary tang and often spicy bite of artisanal pickles can prove difficult to pair with many wines. Beer on the other hand can handle these strong flavors quite well. A quick snack of picked, vegetables, fruits, or meats alongside a craft beer can make for a great demonstration of beer's pairing versatility.

by fresh mint. Then try to find all of the complementary and contrasting elements that jump out at you as you eat and drink. The distinct flavor of Colorado lamb in its meaty, yet lean tenderloin form complements the oak-aged beer's musky, wild fermentation flavors while the spice of the cumin seed contrasts with its sweet malt notes. Additionally, Grand Cru's sourness and the creamy tartness of the yogurt work together, even as the straightforward crisp, sweet carrot and raisin salad contrasts with the beer's deeply complex body. These are just a few of the myriad interactions that can take place in an artful and thought-provoking fine beer and fine food pairing.

PAIRING BEER TO FOOD—SELECTING BEERS USING "AREA OF FOCUS"

The sheer diversity of ingredients and preparations used in global gastronomy need not be daunting when thinking about foods that lend themselves to pairings with craft beer. Different food preparations each have an "area of focus," very much like a beer. Among beers, for example, the area of focus for an IPA is bitter hop flavor and aromatics; for a stout it's dark roasted malt; and for hefeweizens its light, fruity fermentation flavors. Particularly complex examples may have multiple areas of focus. Though the diversity of food preparations is far less regulated than the clues beer style designations offer us, generalizations can still be made from well-written menu descriptions in restaurants, or from close readings of recipes we prepare at home. One can safely assume that a barbecue preparation's area of focus will be meatiness, smokiness, and maybe a sweet, tangy sauce. An articulate recipe for steamed mussels should imply its area(s) of focus as we read it. For instance, the area of focus may be determined by the preparation (cream, tomato, herbs, or curry, for instance) combined with the mussels' ocean-like flavor. But, of course, the most certain way to accurately determine a food's or beer's area of focus is to try the food or beer, or to adapt a recipe to prepare yourself.

Determining the areas of focus for foods and beers is a starting point, and a good way to practice honing your understanding of successful complementary and/or contrasting pairings. However, when the situation allows, digging deeper into the specific particularities of familiar foods and beers, and selecting a pairing based on the interplay of the unique qualities of each, will yield the very best results and will ultimately provide the most substantive experiences. Such a detailed approach is most feasible when you are preparing the foods yourself and are able to create or select recipes specifically tailored to highlight the areas of focus you wish to present. These closely calculated pairings also may be made when you are very familiar with both the beer and the food and desire to make a pairing to showcase a particular connection between the two.

In my work to create specially paired food and beverage events I nearly always begin with the beers or wines that will be featured for the meal. This is because I cannot control what's inside the bottle, but can only select the particular flavor profiles each beverage already possesses. Since I am able to closely control the characteristics of the food being served, first selecting the beers or wines for the meal is the best method for me. However, it is likely that most people go about pairing food and beverages the opposite way, beginning with a food selection. While this approach is perfectly valid and reasonable, I must offer my ardent support of the beer-then-food approach to pairing whenever it is possible—and especially when cooking at home. Exercising our creativity to first think critically about a chosen beer, and then to create or modify a dish to accompany it, helps to develop our palates, hone our culinary "chops," and foster a deeper understanding of flavor construction. Of course, it's not always feasible to begin with the beer. Especially when dining out, we often need to pair beers to what's on the menu. Therefore, it is also important to possess the skills to successfully pair beer to food.

PAIRING EXERCISE 1: FROM FOOD TO BEER—FIVE DISHES

As an exercise in determining the area of focus of a dish and using this focus to select a beer pairing, I have chosen five dishes that cover many foundational ingredients—beef, chicken, fish, vegetables, and starches—and offer an array of beer-friendly flavors for potential pairings. They also contain a variety of flavor combinations—lemon and aromatic herbs, smoky and spicy marinade, hearty braising liquid, rich and creamy sauce, and sweetly spiced preserved fruit.

A word of qualification: it's important to remember that some of the most exciting pairings do not come out of best-case scenario situations. The challenge of utilizing local, seasonal products, or simply whatever's available on hand at a given moment, offers some of the best opportunities for creative discovery.

We can quickly analyze their general areas of focus, then use the focus to choose an accompanying beer. We'll limit the pairing pool to the beers of the Anchor Brewing Company. Anchor's lineup offers a diverse range of styles that are widely available across the country and are suitable for pairing with many types of cuisine. Any pairing situation will have limitations; I have yet to find the El Dorado of liquor stores that offers every bottled beer available. Still, successful pairings can be made from almost any well-stocked bottle shop. In any event, becoming familiar with the craft beers produced by this venerable brewer is a valuable exercise regardless of the experience.

1. BROILED WILD-CAUGHT PACIFIC SALMON WITH GARLIC, PARSLEY, AND LEMON HARICOTS VERTS AND BUTTERMILK MASHED POTATOES
   - Areas of Focus: meaty salmon; creamy, starchy potatoes.

ANCHOR STEAM
   - Area of Focus: balance of mild malt, hops, and fermentation notes.

This is Anchor's flagship beer, an American classic, and a unique style. It is made with a lager yeast but is fermented at a higher temperature normally used for ales. This adds unique fermentation characteristics to the beer. Anchor Steam is at once mild and malty, softly hoppy and distinctly aromatic, multi-faceted and yet not terribly complex. All of these characteristics give it great versatility with foods, but not deep areas of focus to draw on. Beers like these are valuable go-to options. Wild salmon, the clear choice for sustainability, has a lot of flavor that is enhanced by the bright freshness of parsley and lemon and the depth of garlic. The potatoes and green beans here round out a hearty, home-style preparation. A beer like Anchor Steam envelops these characteristics and lightens their perception without interfering with or dominating them. It is a clear, straightforward, workmanlike, and delicious pairing.

2. GRILLED JAMAICAN JERK-MARINATED PASTURE-RAISED CHICK-EN THIGHS ENDIVE AND ORANGE SALAD
    - Areas of Focus: sweet-spicy-smoky dark meat chicken; bitter greens with sweet-tart aromatic citrus.

LIBERTY ALE
- Area of Focus: clean and crisp dry malt with distinct earthy, orange Cascade hops characteristics.

Liberty is hoppy, not huge like an IPA, but crisper and more distinctive than the average pale ale. This is definitely our best option for the spicy, slightly sweet, smoky jerked chicken thighs. The thigh is the juiciest, most flavorful, and most versatile part of chicken. It is an excellent canvas for mild or strong flavors and a variety of cooking methods. In this case we're pairing to the flavor intensity of the jerk marinade. The chilies, allspice, thyme, garlic, and other robust seasonings are the focus. The juicy richness of the thighs, as opposed to the dryer white meat of the breast, also benefits from being paired with the beer's crisp hop bitterness. This is an example of complementary aromatic aspects and contrasting "textural" elements. This is also a classic example of beer's ability to tame spicy foods, both through its bitter hoppiness and its cleansing effervescence on the palate.

3. 100% GRASS-FED BEEF POT ROAST WITH BRAISED CARROTS, CIPPOLINI ONIONS, AND YELLOW POTATOES
    - Areas of Focus: rich, tender, braised beef; sweet carrots and onions.

ANCHOR PORTER
- Area of focus: dark roasted malt balanced by robust hoppiness.

Beef pot roast is a beautifully simple dish. 100% grass-fed beef is the wisest choice in terms of flavor, healthfulness, and sustainability. For pot roast a tough, flavorful cut full of connective tissue from the chuck (or clod) is braised. This combination of searing and moist heat cooking methods renders the beef very tender. The cartilage and connective tissues break down and add a delicious silken texture to the resulting sauce. This sauce is a combination of the reduced cooking liquid, which usually consists of stock and beer or wine, along with aromatic vegetables, which is fortified by the meat cooked in it. This results in accentuated meaty, roasted flavors, and sweet, tender carrots and onions. The Porter is the clear choice here. Its caramel and roasted malt flavors and its full mouthfeel complement the flavors of the meat and sauce very well. The slight malt sweetness of the beer also complements the sweetness of the vegetables. It's hop bitterness and slight grain astringency contrasts with the richness of the beef too. This pairing represents the straightforward matching of rich, roasted meat flavors with dark roasted malt flavors—a classic combination.

4.   AUTHENTIC SPAGHETTI CARBONARA MADE WITH EGG, PECORINO AND PARMIGIANO CHEESES, AND PANCETTA

- Area of Focus: rich, cheesy-eggy sauce with salty cured pork.

OLD FOGHORN BARLEYWINE

- Area of Focus: caramel malt and alcohol sweetness and robust hop bitterness.

This specific matchup is not a conventional pairing, but the principles behind it are. Carbonara is an indulgence. True carbonara sauce is made with tempered eggs mixed with Parmigiano and pecorino cheeses, and pancetta. The hot pasta is what cooks the egg, melts the cheese, and thickens the sauce. It contains no cream. This is a rich dish. In addition to eggs and cheese, it contains pancetta (or guanciale), which is Italian-style un-smoked cured pork (belly for pancetta, jowl for guanciale). All of these fatty elements combined demand both alcohol and hops to balance them out. The malt and alcohol sweetness of the Old Foghorn is not an obvious choice to pair with pasta, but I find them very appealing together in this case. The beer adds to the decadence of the meal while simultaneously balancing out its richest elements. It eases the saltiness and cuts through the creaminess.

5.   RICE PUDDING WITH SPICED FRUIT COMPOTE AND CHOPPED PISTACHIOS

- Areas of Focus: mild, creamy richness; dark, sweet, preserved fruits with "autumn spices."

Christmas Ale (AKA Our Special Ale)

- Area of Focus: caramel malt with aromatic spices and herbs.

This is not only my favorite Anchor beer, but also my favorite holiday seasonal ale. It has dark, yet not strongly roasted, malty flavors combined with complex, spicy, herbal characteristics. The secret recipe, which changes slightly each year, tastes of cola, spruce, and sassafras. This darkly aromatic flavor profile is highly complex. This beer would pair well with many hearty main course dishes, but I like it here with this dessert. Rice pudding, served cold, has a wonderfully thick texture that coats the palate with both creaminess and the soft suggestion of its rice grain texture. These qualities contrast the dense flavor profile of the beer. The addition of fruit compote made with spices such as cinnamon, clove, or cardamom, adds both sweetness and an additional level of aromatics. Chopped pistachio nuts offer a texture contrast and roasted nutty flavor. These elements complement the spice and herbaceous aspects of the beer. I also like this beer at the end of a meal, where we can contemplate its complexities after the dishes have been cleared.

Anchor's portfolio also contains other excellent seasonal and year-round offerings that are worth examining as well. Anchor's beers are classic, approachable renditions of traditional styles with an American craft beer twist. They serve as good introductions into craft beer styles and familiar and reliable go-to options.

PAIRING EXERCISE 2: FROM FOOD TO BEER —A TASTING MENU

Here is an actual tasting menu that I prepared in the restaurant that was specially created to pair with specific wines from importer Eric Solomon's European Cellars portfolio.

ERIC SOLOMON
SELECTIONS
PLACE OVER PROCESS

EUROPEAN CELLARS—ERIC SOLOMON SELECTIONS
PRESENTED BY VIN SAUVAGE LAS VEGAS, NV
JUNE 24, 2008

Amuse Bouche:
Lump Crab Salad with Yellow Pepper and Hothouse Cucumber

1st Course:
Olive Oil-Poached Tuna Fillet "Provençale" with Haricot Verts, Hard-Boiled Egg, and Aïoli
Niçoise Olives, Sungold Tomatoes, Smoked Paprika
Wine Pairing: 2001 Gramona Cava *Imperial*

2nd Course:
Duck Confit with Wilted Frisée and White Nectarines
Dijon Mustard Oil, Tarragon
Wine Pairing: 2005 Domaine Bott-Geyl *Les Pinots d'Alsace*

3rd Course:
Tyrolian Speck with Grilled Bread and Marinated Cannellini Beans
Fresh Brussels Sprout and Pecorino Toscano Cheese "Salad"
Wine Pairing: 2004 Domaine la Lorentine Lirac

4th Course:
Braised Lamb Shank in Red Wine with Piquillo Peppers and Horseradish Gremolata
Crispy Potato Discs, Herbs
Wine Pairing: 2003 Clos d'Agon Tinto

Dessert:
Ames Farm Basswood Honey Panna Cotta with Amaretti Cookies
Fresh Raspberries
Wine Pairing: 2003 Château Tirecul la Gravière Monbazillac *Cuvée du Chateau*

The dishes on this tasting menu convey a progression of flavors that can be paired with craft beers instead of wines. So, as an experiment, let's take this actual menu and do the beer pairings. Since these preparations are a bit more complex we'll examine their areas of focus in terms of primary and secondary flavor characteristics. I've chosen several craft beers for each course, rather than just those from a single brewery, to demonstrate different pairing possibilities.

AMUSE BOUCHE: Lump Crab Salad with Yellow Pepper and Hothouse Cucumber

Areas of Focus
- *Primary*—creamy, mild, sweet shellfish flavor.
- *Secondary*—light vegetal freshness.

This would be a great opportunity to feature a light, crisp, flavorful pilsner or witbier. The crab salad and cucumber provide a fairly neutral palette that could be taken in many directions, but easily overpowered. A beer with a light, crisp area of focus and a bit of its own pizzazz to contrast the neutrality of the food's flavors is necessary. Craft-brewed pilsner, witbier, or hefeweizen would all bring their own distinctiveness and serve as an excellent opening to the meal.

BEER PAIRINGS:

Victory Prima Pils, North Coast Scrimshaw Pilsner

Why it works: light, crisp malt presence accented by spicy continental hops of the beers contrasts with the sweet, creamy crab salad.

Allagash White, Jolly Pumpkin Calabaza Blanca

Why it works: refreshing, fruity fermentation profile with a light, slightly tart body combined with a touch of spice from coriander seeds and orange peel in the beer contrasts with the creaminess and compliments the mild sweetness of the crab and yellow bell pepper.

COURSE ONE: Olive Oil-Poached Tuna Fillet "Provençale" with Haricot Verts, Hard-Boiled Egg, and Aïoli
Niçoise Olives, Sungold Tomatoes, Smoked Paprika

Areas of Focus

- *Primary*—the richness of meaty oil-poached tuna, egg, and aïoli.
- *Secondary*—"Mediterranean" vegetable flavors of green beans, sweet tomato, and salty Niçoise olives.

For this course a beer needs to provide a contrast to the meaty richness of the tuna's oiliness along with the aïoli and boiled egg. The pairing should provide both substance and lightness and serve as a counterpoint to the generally subtle, yet rich qualities of the dish. Styles such as saison, bière de garde, or Belgian-style pale, with their bright carbonation, soft hops spiciness, and medium-light body would work excellently.

BEER PAIRINGS:

The Lost Abbey Red Barn or Saison Dupont

Why it works: The overall lightness of this beer offers an immediate affinity to the food. After further contemplation, the complexities—spice, earthiness, and subdued toasted maltiness—reveal themselves and contrast with the clean, straightforwardness of the dish.

Orval

Why it works: Oval is unique. Immediately recognizable as Belgian but not necessarily as Trappist since it possesses a more singular, focused, flavor profile that is refreshingly different. The flavor contains notes of spice and a light, crisp tartness akin to green apples along with an effervescent body and soft malt presence. These qualities set up a highly complex contrasting pairing with the dish.

COURSE TWO: Duck Confit with Wilted Frisée and White Nectarines
Dijon Mustard Oil, Tarragon
Areas of Focus

- *Primary*—very oily, deeply flavored duck.
- *Secondary*—fruity, slightly acidic sweetness.

Duck confit is deliciously rich with a nice robust yet understated dark meat flavor. When combined with the aromatic mustard and tarragon, the crisp bitterness of frisée, and sweet-tart nectarines, the richness of the dish is nicely balanced. This is the perfect opportunity for an amazing IPA pairing. It can handle the richness with ease while contributing an aromatic fruitiness of its own to complement the nectarine and tarragon.

BEER PAIRINGS:

AleSmith IPA, Russian River Blind Pig IPA, or **Bear Republic Racer 5 IPA**

Why it works: The ripe fruitiness of the hops perfectly complements the nectarine and tarragon while the crisp bitterness contrasts with the richness of the duck. Perfect.

Victory Hop Wallop or **Stone Ruination**

Why it works: Take these same principles a bit further with a double IPA. With more malt, alcohol, and hops the experience is amplified. Be careful to select just the right double IPAs that remain dry, crisp and not overly malty to maintain the emphasis on the hop aromatics in this pairing.

COURSE THREE: **Tyrolian Speck with Grilled Bread and Marinated Cannellini Beans**
Fresh Brussels Sprout and Pecorino Toscano Cheese "Salad"

Areas of Focus
- *Primary*—smoky, salty, and fatty cured pork.
- *Secondary*—mustardy aromatic crispness of fresh Brussels sprouts.

This was my favorite course of the evening. I thinly sliced raw Brussels sprouts and combined them with a rich, salty, crumbly pecorino Toscano cheese and a little lemon juice, olive oil, and parsley to create a crisp, slightly bitter, aromatic salad accented by the creamy, salty cheese. The speck's main characteristics are its salty smokiness, fatty richness like prosciutto, and subtle juniper berry spice. Add in the grilled sourdough bread and cannellini beans marinated with garlic, rosemary, and black pepper, and you have a lot going on here. A fitting beer here would need some complexity, but could stand to play a supporting role in terms of flavor intensity here. A well-structured brown ale with a touch of malty sweetness and nutty roasted qualities would work very nicely.

I would not choose an overly humble example of the style, which can often be the case with brown ales, but something unique with a good amount of character. This philosophy could be taken a bit further with a well-balanced porter with good substance but not too much coffee or chocolate malt characteristics.

BEER PAIRINGS:

AleSmith Nut Brown or Bell's Best Brown Ale

Why it works: The rich, maltiness of these beers serves as an excellent base for the many more assertive flavors presented in the food. These beers can hold their own and they contribute excellent contrast to the rest of the dish.

Dogfish Head Indian Brown or Surly Bender

Why it works: Both of these beers offer non-traditional takes on the style, which in this case works well to add interest to the pairing. The Indian Brown has amped-up hops and malt while the Bender includes oats for a complex mouthfeel. These represent alternative contrasting pairings.

COURSE FOUR: **Braised Lamb Shank in Red Wine with Piquillo Peppers and Horseradish Gremolata**
Crispy Potato Discs, Herbs

Areas of Focus
- *Primary*—dark, rich, gamy meat flavors.
- *Secondary*—subtle fruity spiciness of roasted peppers.

Lamb is a very flavorful meat, and the shank is an especially flavorful cut. Here is an opportunity to pair a very strong, complex beer. Braising tenderizes the meat and softens the connective tissue while infusing the meat with the flavors of the cooking liquid. This produces a robust sauce, which I based on red wine but could easily be adapted to beer. As such, even foods that are cooked with wine can be very successfully paired with craft beer. In this case a high alcohol style with a prominent malt profile is called for. Wee heavy is a roasted malt-driven Scotch style that would work very well. Taking a different direction, a big, hoppy barleywine would be excellent, or, occasionally a brewery will make an amber or red ale with a bigger malt and hops profile than most others. Sometimes referred to as "imperial red ales," these beers have significant, yet nicely balanced alcohol, malt, and hops characteristics. For any approach, the beer must be strong enough in flavor and body to stand up to the depth and heaviness of the lamb preparation. The horseradish gremolata serves to add some brisk zest to the dish and is complemented by the beers' hops as well.

BEER PAIRINGS:

Sierra Nevada Bigfoot Barleywine or **Founders Dirty Bastard Scotch Ale**

Why it works: Bigfoot's significant hop presence overlaying a sturdy dark malty profile complements the lamb's richness and can bring extra vibrancy to the braising-liquid sauce it's served with. Dirty Bastard accomplishes the same but with an emphasis on maltiness and a hint of smokiness with its hops following behind.

Bear Republic Red Rocket, Green Flash Hop Head Red, Port Shark Bite or **Port Shark Attack Red**

Why it works: These beers possess significant malt and hops. Though they have less alcohol and lighter malt profiles than the barleywine or Scotch ale, they still can stand toe-to-toe with the food while providing a contrasting lightness to the palate.

DESSERT: **Ames Farm Basswood Honey Panna Cotta with Amaretti Cookies**
Fresh Raspberries

Areas of Focus
- *Primary*—thick and creamy richness.
- *Secondary*—honey sweetness and aromatics.

Although this is a rich dessert, the light texture of the panna cotta and the aromatic, nectary sweetness of the basswood honey it is flavored with adds unexpected lightness to the creamy texture. The rich, sweet, honey-infused panna cotta needs some alcohol to contrast the sensations on the palate. Again, a barleywine would work very well, though one that this time focuses on precise malt and alcohol sweetness rather than big hops and roasted malt characteristics, preferably with an aged, oxidized aspect to it. The English-style barleywines would be excellent, and there are many special editions that are either vintage bottlings or have been aged in various types of wooden casks that formerly held spirits. A Russian imperial stout with just the right amount of dark roasted malt characteristics, and preferably with some barrel-aging traits as well, would also provide a nice contrast. The bottom line is: provide something to mediate between the sweetness and creaminess.

BEER PAIRINGS:

J.W. Lee's Harvest Ale or Anchor Old Foghorn Barleywine

Why it works: The rich, malty sweetness complements the honey flavors while the alcohol warmth contrasts with the dessert's cool, creamy richness.

Deschutes The Abyss Russian Imperial Stout

Why it works: Very similar concept with pairing 1, but with added emphasis on some darker malt flavors to contrast with the creaminess.

NAVIGATING RESTAURANT BEER LISTS

Although excellent craft beer lists are not the norm in most American restaurants, more and more fine dining establishments are creating them to offer diners this excellent option to pair with their meals. As the farm-to-table philosophy of cooking increases its presence in our dining culture, offering local craft beers is the natural next step in fulfilling its possibilities. If there isn't a craft beer list, ask the proprietor to consider adding one. The best establishments always welcome constructive feedback and are eager to learn of their customers' interest in their business.

There are many ways of organizing a beer list. The best include information about the beer's producer, style, and region. When faced with a lengthy or, sometimes, disorganized list, it can be useful to break it down mentally. Most lists can be broken down into five general categories, which may help you hone in on your cravings.

MACROS—Ignore these. They're just there to appease the non-curious and inflexible.

LOCAL CRAFT BEERS—A well-chosen list will likely have several nice examples in a variety of styles from noteworthy local breweries. These beers are also likely to be on draught, if the restaurant is so equipped. In that case, don't be shy about asking for a sample to confirm your ideas about a potential pairing. Eating and drinking locally is a fun way to experience the culinary "sense of place" of the region in which you are dining.

NATIONAL CRAFT BEERS—These are widely available, familiar craft beers that have been selected for their popularity (unless they happen to be local to your area). These can represent some great choices that you've most likely already experienced and offer the ability to create a pairing based on a crowd favorite.

IMPORTS—Read: *Belgian*. Other imported beers are usually in styles that can be found in local offerings. Most Belgian beers are available nationwide, age well, and are generally food friendly. For these reasons they are very attractive to beer list designers. Having a good working knowledge of the classic Belgians will guide you well if your meal is crying out for one of these distinct offerings.

"RESERVE" BEERS—These are the high-end "limited edition," or "brewery only" releases that give the list an opportunity to show off. Such beers don't often make it too far from the brewery where they are produced, so they're likely to be local, or maybe the proprietor has a special relationship with his or her favorite brewery. Whatever the case, these are likely to be more expensive, but still represent great values when compared to the relative quality of the least expensive bottles of wine available (and many are packaged in 22-ounce or 750-milliliter bottles). If you see something that catches your eye here, I would strongly consider ordering your food based on what would go well with this special beer. These are always some of the most exciting beer drinking opportunities for me.

Breaking a list down in this way can make it seem less daunting. Similarly, if the establishment has an extensive list, there's likely to be someone there who can help you out with it. A knowledgeable server or sommelier will be able to help guide you through the list. Be sure to ask some questions about any new, interesting beers you see. Take advantage of this opportunity to learn about the establishment's passions for craft beer and see how it relates to yours.

Read the menu closely and order with beer in mind. If you're a steak person, have a good working knowledge of the malt-driven styles available. If you're in the mood for seafood consider the lighter, aromatic offerings. And perhaps plan out a progression of several beers throughout your meal. Sharing these with your dining partner is a great way to try more things and get another perspective on the beers and the pairings you choose together. Many restaurants also offer "flights" of draught beers. These are several small portions of beers that offer the perfect opportunity to try multiple styles with multiple dishes.

PAIRING FOOD TO BEER —CREATING MENUS

Designing your own recipes to showcase specific aspects of your favorite beers can be one of the most personally satisfying ways of enjoying craft beer and food pairings. You may not be able to control what's inside the bottle, but you can choose which bottles you want, and you can control what the food will be like. This is why beginning with the beers to be paired when creating menus is the most certain way to experience the most exciting beer and food pairings.

I have been fortunate in my restaurants to be able to plan many specially paired beer and wine events. What follows are the narratives that describe the considerations that went into planning four craft beer dinners with three outstanding breweries: two with AleSmith, and one each with The Lost Abbey and Bear Republic. These events served as valuable opportunities for me to explore the possibilities of combining some of the finest American craft beers with high-end cuisine specifically designed to complement them, served in a fine-dining setting. This truly is the setting in which these beers deserve to be served. It was tremendous fun to collaborate with the brewers for these events, and they, in turn, enjoyed having their products presented in this manner.

ALESMITH BREWING COMPANY
OF SAN DIEGO, CALIFORNIA
SEPTEMBER 4, 2008

1st Course:
Grilled *Summer Ice* Oysters
Cilantro-Orange Compound Butter
Beer Pairing: Horny Devil Belgian-Style Ale

2nd Course:
Mizuna Salad
Roasted Sweet Potato, Enoki Mushrooms, Pine Nuts,
Mixed Citrus and Tamari Dressing
Beer Pairing: IPA

3rd Course:
Braised Berkshire Pork Belly with Pearl Barley
Caramelized Onion, Roasted Carrots, Micro Amaranth, Celery Greens
Beer Pairing: Anvil ESB

4th Course:
Sliced Prime Beef Bavette Steak
Grilled Japanese Eggplant, Shiitake and Hon-Shimeji Mushrooms,
Shiro Miso Jus, Chives
Beer Pairing: Wee Heavy Scotch Ale

5th Course:
Selection of Artisanal Cheeses
Rogue Creamery Crater Lake Blue, Brie de Meaux, Ossau-Iraty
Beer Pairing: 2006 Vintage Grand Cru Belgian-Style Strong Ale

Dessert:
English Toffee Pudding Cake
Made with 2003 Barrel-Aged Speedway Stout, Whipped Cream, Fresh Figs
Beer Pairing: 2007 Barrel-Aged Speedway Stout

As I planned my first craft beer dinner in Las Vegas with Ale-Smith Brewing Company, I began (as I did with each event) by selecting the beers. I wanted to be sure to feature one of their special releases that are always highly sought after and would surely draw a crowd to the event. Barrel-Aged Speedway Stout, which spends a year aging in oak barrels that formerly held Bourbon, is one of the most prized beers in the craft beer community, and I was fortunate that the brewery had it available. I had my finale beer, which would be paired with dessert. Not only that, but a few non-carbonated bottles of the 2003 edition were available to cook with as well. The challenge was offered and accepted.

AleSmith also had a 2006 vintage bottling of their Grand Cru available—a natural choice. This dark Belgian-style strong ale has lots of dark caramel notes and fruity Belgian yeast esters. Due to its bottle age, this version would have a nicely mellowed flavor profile and well-rounded body that would disguise its 10.6% alcohol.

I needed to use their IPA. It is my favorite IPA and one of my favorite beers of any style. It represents a very nuanced and complex example of a style that can often pose challenges for food pairings. It's 7.3% alcohol and immense hop bitterness and aromatics makes a big impression. But this beer's balance and tightly woven structure makes it very manageable in the right pairing scenario.

Anvil was another certainty. An ESB, it is a terrific example of a style often overlooked by American craft brewers. It resembles a maltier, less hoppy pale ale with a great body and an appealing flavor of the actual grains used in the brewing process. These characteristics would be useful in creating a dish to pair with it, and would serve as a break from the other heavier, higher alcohol beers that would be served that evening.

I had two beers left to choose for the evening. I needed something fairly big to anchor the main course, but something that would also contrast with the Grand Cru and the Barrel-Aged Speedway Stout. Wee Heavy would do nicely. This Scotch-style ale emphasizes deep maltiness with a hint of nuttiness, smoke, and low bitterness. This is a full-bodied beer that expresses very different characteristics than Speedway.

Finally, Horny Devil seemed a good choice to round things out for the evening. It is one of AleSmith's signature offerings and is another Belgian-inspired ale. Clear, bright gold in color, and quite strong, it offers nimble fruitiness and spiciness—including actual bitter oranges and coriander seeds—contained within a bright, honeyed malt body.

This is a diverse lot with enormous potential. Some ideas for the food were beginning to take shape. The stout would be last with a dessert that utilized it as an ingredient as well—something with some dark richness and caramel notes to play off of the boozy Bourbon qualities. The complexity of the vintage Grand Cru meant that it should come later in the meal, and would therefore need to be served just before the Speedway. It has a natural affinity for cheeses, which I always like to include in a multi-course tasting menu, and could be served just before dessert. The Wee Heavy would need to precede that, and would work well with some roasted meat—a fitting main course. The Horny Devil, with its fruitiness, would make a great introduction to the meal and would come first. The bitter hoppiness of the IPA is a good match for a special salad that would logically follow. All that was left was the Anvil, which would go with practically anything, and thus gave me a lot of flexibility in my food choices at this point in the meal. Now I had my beer lineup and was ready to plan my course-by-course pairings.

HORNY DEVIL, BELGIAN-STYLE STRONG GOLDEN ALE: First Course.

I wanted to begin with seafood since this would be the only opportunity to incorporate some into the meal—shellfish rather than finfish made sense to me. Citrus zest and cilantro, the plant from which coriander seeds come from, would be fun to use since they are both present in the beer. The appetizer needs to be somewhat light in advance of the following courses, but also with a little richness to play against the alcohol. A cilantro-orange compound butter (with some scallion for depth), placed on top of fresh Pacific oysters, warmed over the grill would serve very well as my first course.

AleSmith **IPA**, India pale ale: **Second Course.**
This beer, redolent of bright citrus and tropical fruits, resiny and
herbaceous, crisp and bitter—but with some malt presence as well—
would pair well with a salad at this point in the meal. Mizuna is one
of my favorite salad greens. It is exotic yet approachable, beautiful to look at with its sharply toothed leaves, and has a distinct
mild mustardy bitterness along with its lush crispness that would
do nicely alongside the IPA. The salad should have some grounding elements as well to acknowledge the malt aspects of this beer.
Cubed roasted sweet potato would contribute sweetness, earthiness,
and color in addition to a tender textural contrast. Fresh enoki
mushrooms would also provide a nice visual element—thin white
stalks resembling the white stems of the mizuna—and additional
earthiness to play off the hops' secondary flavor characteristics.
A few toasted pine nuts would mimic the resinous qualities of the
beer and provide a creamy nuttiness in accordance with the beer's
malt profile. The dressing would need to tie everything together
and give the salad some heft to stand up to the IPA. I admire the
artisanal citron vinegar from Huilerie Beaujolaise in France for its
complex citrus qualities, which I mixed with bottled yuzu juice and
fresh orange juice. These ingredients, too, play off of the citrusy
hop aromatics while adding acidity as a counter to the bitterness.
A light touch of tamari (itself a fermented product) darkens the
flavor profile, complementing the malt, mushrooms, and sweet
potato, while maintaining the Japanese theme that is emerging in
the dish. I finished the dressing with grapeseed oil, a light, fairly
neutral oil that will emulsify these flavors together (with a little
help from some Dijon mustard and chopped garlic).

Anvil **ESB**, extra special bitter: **Third Course.**
Lots of possibilities here. I needed an appetizer preparation that's
a little richer to build on the salad, and a starch that will complement the grainy malt profile that I love so much about Anvil. I
chose pork, in rich belly form, braised in an aromatic stock (with
some of the beer added) until it's tender and luscious. Barley, the
brewer's grain, in pearl form for the kitchen, simmered in the
braising liquid and fortified with butter, would be the perfect complementary pairing here. Tasting the same grain side by side in two

very different forms will provide a fun juxtaposition. I thicken the remaining mirepoix-infused braising liquid with a nutty roux and added some flat-leaf parsley to freshen the aromatic profile. Some vegetables are necessary to complete the various stew-like elements coming together in this course. Baby carrots are a mainstay, and some sweet caramelized pearl onions would provide a tie-in with the dark, toasty malt profile, along with some sharply herbaceous celery greens to round out the trio. Micro amaranth provides a flash of color with its deep burgundy leaves, and is another alternative grain-producing plant. I placed a small pile of the cooked barley in the center of a small plate with a few slices of the delicate pork belly on top of it. A spoonful of the sauce over the top and around the plate is next, followed by a few cooked carrots, caramelized onions, a sprinkling of the celery greens, and a small bouquet of micro amaranth.

WEE HEAVY, STRONG SCOTCH-STYLE ALE: **Fourth Course.** The rich maltiness and subtle smokiness along with significant alcohol cry out for a rich, almost gamey cut of aged meat. The bavette steak, short for *bavette d'aloyau*, is the French term for what butchers call, quite unromantically, "flap meat." (It also sometimes goes by the name "inside skirt.") It is my favorite cut of beef. Little-known and under-valued, it is highly flavorful and offers a pleasant meaty texture—the opposite of beef tenderloin. It is very well-suited to the grill, especially when marinated with fresh garlic, rosemary, black pepper, and olive oil. Japanese eggplant—preferred over the large Italian *globe* variety for its thin, edible skin, firm texture, and nutty flavor—is also fantastic on the grill and offers a great contrast to the beef when both are sliced thin and layered together. These elements would go well with any malty, full-bodied beer. But when paired with the additional nutty earthiness of sautéed shiitake and hon-shimeji mushrooms immersed in a shiro miso broth, the particular complexities of the AleSmith Wee Heavy will be fully highlighted. The broth is a traditional dashi made with smoked bonito flakes and kombu that is fortified with clarified beef stock into which the salty, slightly sweet white miso (also a fermented product) is whisked. This combination creates a deeply flavorful, lightly smoky jus that brings together all of the elements of the mushrooms, grilled eggplant, and beef with a dose of rich umami.

This pairing possesses both complementary and contrasting elements: nutty, earthy mushrooms in sweet miso jus interact with the beer's dark, sweet caramel malt; the smoky grilled eggplant and rich, deeply flavored bavette steak complement and contrast with the Wee Heavy's varied roasted grain and alcohol characteristics.

2006 Vintage Grand Cru, Belgian-style dark strong ale: Fifth Course.

Beer and cheese are old friends (a relationship that will be discussed more thoroughly in the following chapter). The rich, outgoing nature of the vintage Grand Cru is capable of complementing a wide variety of cheeses. Rogue *Crater Lake Blue* is an excellent West Coast artisanal nutty blue cheese made from cow's milk. Its slightly spicy characteristics contrast nicely with the malt sweetness present in the beer. Brie de Meaux is the real-deal *appellation d origine contrôlée* (AOC) cheese from the Brie region of France near the town of Meaux. It is made from cow's milk and, with its characteristic soft bloomy rind and yellow interior, is rich and unctuous and goes perfectly with the Belgian yeast flavors present in Grand Cru. Ossau-Iraty is another French AOC cheese. This one is made from sheep's milk and is from the Northern Basque Country. It is semi-firm with a creamy mouthfeel, softly sweet nutty flavors, and a slight sheepy piquancy which harmonizes with the dark fruitiness of the beer. With the addition of some Spanish Marcona almonds I had my cheese course.

Bourbon Barrel-Aged Speedway Stout, Russian imperial stout: Dessert.

This course created the most excitement for me, and as you read earlier, provided the seed around which the rest of the meal grew. This may seem unusual, in that dessert is often thought to be the most challenging course to pair with beer. But, inspired by Speedway, this was the first recipe I created for the meal—the one I was most certain of, and still like best.

I had enjoyed English toffee pudding cakes before in British pubs. With their inclusion of dried dates and burnt caramel topping, they seemed a natural pairing for certain traditional "dessert beers" like imperial stouts and barleywines. But they could never fully stand up to the strength and complexity of my favorite examples of those beers; I needed more than a simple dark cake. Among the many recipes I studied for traditional pudding cakes, I found a bare-bones recipe that expressed the basic essence of this traditional dessert. From this I created my own version with more, higher quality dates, raisins, and the addition of the powerful, viscous beer itself as the cooking liquid. Now this once humble pub dessert had gravitas. With the addition of a richer caramel sauce topping that would easily brown beneath a broiler to create a dark toffee flavor profile, and a generous garnish of vanilla whipped cream and seasonal fresh figs, our meal now had a fittingly *haute cuisine* finale.

Artisanal foods, remarkable beers, and a six course tasting menu: This was a white tablecloth meal, and the beers were served, fittingly, in crystal. Fine beer and fine food are made for each other and deserve the same presentation we extend to any haute cuisine dining experience.

ENGLISH TOFFEE PUDDING CAKE MADE WITH BEER
with Whipped Cream and Fresh Figs

Ingredients:

1 cup flour + 1 Tbs. flour

¾ cup total of raisins and/or chopped dates

4 Tbs. unsalted butter, softened + 3 Tbs. unsalted butter

¾ cup sugar

1 large egg, lightly beaten

1 tsp. baking powder

1 tsp. baking soda

1 tsp. natural vanilla extract

1¼ cups dark, sweet, full-bodied beer (preferably Bourbon barrel-aged: AleSmith Speedway Stout, Sam Adams Triple Bock, Goose Island Bourbon County)

5 Tbs. dark brown sugar, firmly packed

2 Tbs. heavy cream

Pinch kosher salt

Method:

Preheat oven to 350 degrees Fahrenheit.

Butter an 8″ round cake pan.

Sift the 1 cup flour and the baking powder together.

Toss the raisins and/or chopped dates with the remaining 1 tablespoon of flour.

Beat together in a mixer the 4 tablespoons of butter and the sugar until light and fluffy.

Beat in the egg on low speed and add roughly ¼ of the flour mixture; mix until smooth. Add the remaining flour mixture and mix until just incorporated.

Bring beer to a simmer. Then, in a small bowl, combine the raisins/dates, baking soda, vanilla, and simmering beer. Add this mixture to the batter and beat until well blended. Pour the mixture into the cake pan.

Bake for 30 minutes or until set and well browned.

Remove the cake from the oven and preheat the broiler.

In saucepan heat the remaining 3 tablespoons butter, brown sugar, cream, and salt until the mixture simmers. Simmer until thickened and bubbly (about 3 minutes). Pour this topping over the hot pudding.

Broil the pudding until the topping bubbles while watching carefully to prevent burning.

Cool the pudding briefly and serve warm.

Serve with:

Whipped cream, sweetened to taste with vanilla

Sliced fresh figs (optional)

Yields 8 servings.

The Lost Abbey

THE LOST ABBEY BREWING COMPANY
OF SAN MARCOS, CALIFORNIA
FEBRUARY 12, 2009

1st Course:

Infused Valencia Orange and Red Grapefruit Suprêmes

Rose Essence, Honey, Vanilla Bean, "Tangerine Lace" Herb

Beer Pairing: Witch's Wit Witbier

2nd Course:

Vermont Cheese & Butter Creamery *Bijou* Artisanal Goat Cheese

Spiced Roasted Golden Beets, Red Beet Gastrique, Micro Beet Greens

Beer Pairing: Avant Garde Bière de Garde

3rd Course:

**Braised Niman Ranch Duroc Pork Shoulder
and Berkridge Kurobuta Pork Belly**

Dried Plums, Saffron, Cumin

Beer Pairing: Red Poppy Flanders-Style Red with Cherries

4th Course:

Seared Dry-Aged Prime Beef Loin

Indonesian Sweet Soy, Grilled Onion Relish, Forbidden Rice, Persimmon

Beer Pairing: Judgment Day Belgian-Style Quad

5th Course:

Anise-Scented Sweet Pearl Barley

Greek Yogurt Ice Cream, Mint

Beer Pairing: Serpent's Stout Russian Imperial Stout

Dessert:

Calimyrna Fig and Pistachio Tart

Brandy Caramel Sauce, Aged Balsamic Whipped Cream

Beer Pairing: Angel's Share Brandy Barrel-Aged Barleywine

I wanted very much to do a beer dinner with The Lost Abbey's brewmaster Tomme Arthur. Tomme's work with the local chain of Pizza Port brewpubs produced many of the iconic Southern California beach-themed beers now brewed by Port Brewing, the other label he produces at The Lost Abbey brewery. The Lost Abbey label focuses on high-end Belgian-inspired specialty beers. Its portfolio includes some of the finest barrel-aged and sour beers brewed anywhere. These beer styles are highly food friendly and would provide excellent contrast to the portfolio of flavors expressed during my previous AleSmith dinner. Additionally, including some of The Lost Abbey's greatly anticipated special releases in my menu would fuel interest in the event and give me the opportunity to work with a few of these exciting beers. So, when Tomme agreed to come to town for the dinner with his head brewer, Mike Rodriguez, I knew immediately that I wanted to feature their Red Poppy and Angel's Share special editions. Luckily, they had reserved a few cases of these beers for special events like this.

Red Poppy is a Flanders-style red ale is aged in oak barrels where a secondary fermentation is encouraged to take place using wild yeasts and bacteria including brettanomyces, lactobacillus, and pediococcus. Cherries are added to the barrels during this process and are fermented as well, imparting a complex sweet-tart fruit flavor to the beer. The terrific acidity of this beer is key to its pairing ability, and I thought it would work very well with an appetizer-like dish leading up to a heavier main course.

Angel's Share is another cult barrel-aged beer. In this case the beer isn't soured in the barrels. The emptied brandy barrels (or Bourbon barrels for some editions) it is aged in are used to flavor the beer with complex caramel, vanilla, and oak notes while oxygen slowly seeps in and mellows out the alcohol component. Angel's Share would come last; it's a dessert sipper for sure, and would overwhelm anything that would follow it.

Avant Garde, a bière de garde, or "beer for keeping," is one of Lost Abbey's signature offerings and Tomme requested that I include it in the lineup. I did so with pleasure; the light, nutty, toasted grain flavors and soft European hops spice would fit very well into a cheese course near the beginning of the meal.

Judgment Day was also available for the dinner. This serious beer showcases the darker, caramel malt side of Belgian strong ales along with a huge, complex, fruity fermentation profile. These types of beers are often referred to as abts, quadrupels, or quads, and many of the most famous Belgian abbey beers fall into this category. Its varied flavor profile could be paired with a wide variety of main courses.

Described by Tomme as "kind of a sleeper" in his portfolio, Serpent's Stout, a big Russian Imperial stout packed with roasted malt flavors, would also appeal to enthusiasts and stand out among the other beers with more pronounced fermentation flavors. It would provide a nice contrast to the other beers in the lineup.

Finally, I needed something very light to balance out the heavier beers of the second half of the meal and that could serve as an opening aperitif of sorts. Witch's Wit would be perfect. It's a fun interpretation of the classic, refreshing Belgian wheat beers made with bitter orange peel, and coriander seeds. In this case grapefruit zest and grapefruit honey are used to subtly flavor the beer.

The beers were chosen and the serving order was becoming clear. The beers' body characteristics and their flavor complexities pointed to Witch's Wit as the first beer, followed by Avant Garde, and then Red Poppy. I also knew that Angel's Share needed to be last, and that Judgment Day should precede Serpent's Stout. So, my lineup was set and ideas for the food were beginning to take hold.

WITCH'S WIT, BELGIAN-STYLE WITBIER: **First Course.**
Light and aromatic, this beer is the prefect easygoing entry point into what was going to be a serious progression of intense beers. Taking a cue from the grapefruit zest and honey used in the brewing process, I designed a small appetizer of red grapefruit and Valencia orange segments marinated in the fresh juices of those fruits along with rose nectar and vanilla beans. Each bite, which included a sprig of the zesty and aromatic chrysanthemum-like "Tangerine Lace" herb, would rev up the palate and prepare it for the heavier flavors to come.

AVANT GARDE, BIÈRE DE GARDE: **Second Course.**
Cheese is often served just before dessert, which is a fine place for it, but the intricacies of artisanal cheeses would often fall upon palates fatigued by the preceding main courses. Moving it up to the beginning of the meal promotes the notion of cheese as a principal part of the meal. In this case, the refined *Bijou* goat cheese from the Vermont Butter and Cheese Creamery, modeled after the French small ripened goat cheeses Crottins de Chavignol, provides a

delicate, creamy focal point to the beginning of the meal. Roasted beets seem to have been permanently paired with goat cheese on menus across the country, but for good reason. The many varieties of goat cheese, and preparations that beets lend themselves to, justify the continued exploration of this popular combination. Here toasted caraway seeds recall the soft, nutty spiciness of Avant Garde and the sweet tanginess of the beet gastrique—a reduced sauce made with vinegar and sugar—embellished with the fresh earthiness of micro beet greens, come together in contrast with the mushroomy richness of the aged goat cheese. I think of the beer in this course as establishing the milieux in which the characteristics of the food interact with one another, and various aspects of the beer.

RED POPPY, FLANDERS-STYLE RED ALE BARREL-AGED WITH SOUR CHERRIES: Third Course.

This is one of my very favorite beers, and so I was excited to create a dish to pair with it. Though it is a low alcohol beer, its acidity cuts through fats on the palate in much the same way that alcohol does, but it does so with the addition of a contrasting flavor element. Whereas alcohol seems to physically interact with fats on the tongue, the sourness of this beer offers that same effect combined with a sweet-tart flavor that enlivens the heavier elements of a dish. Pork is a favorite meat of mine, which can be quite rich, and provides an excellent foundation to build flavor upon. When braised, both the shoulder and the belly cuts become meltingly tender and provide a hugely rich mouthfeel. I added sweet and aromatic elements in the form of dried fruits and spices to highlight various aspects of Red Poppy's complex flavor profile. Here, dried plums are reminiscent of the fermented cherry flavor in the beer, and the mélange of blood orange, fresh ginger, capers, cumin, saffron, and cinnamon provides a deep pungency that recalls the host of flavors formed during the oak barrel-aging process.

JUDGMENT DAY, BELGIAN-STYLE QUAD: Fourth Course.

The beers turn big as we roll into the main course. At 10.5% alcohol this beer needs something substantial to accompany it. My restaurant was a steakhouse, and I was proud of the dry-aged steaks we served. The flavor of dry-aged beef used to be the norm when butchers would hang primal cuts in their coolers and sell only hand-cut steaks to customers. The aging process creates extraordi-nary nutty and gamey flavors and gives the steak a more concentrated "beefiness." It also adds a lot of cost to the product. I really can't say enough positive things about dry-aged beef. Seek it out at finer steakhouses; you won't go back to enjoying so-called *wet*-aged steaks the same way. I served roughly a three ounce portion of New York strip steak pavé style, in the shape of a small cobblestone, seared on a flat grill to form a crisp crust. Judgment Day is fairly dark, with sig-nificant malt and fermentation flavors. Using Indonesian *kecap manis*, a sweet soy sauce with a molasses-like flavor, as an accent pulled at the malt angle while reconstituted dried fuyu persimmon slices highlighted the beer's fruity fermentation esters. Dried persim-mons offer a complementary fruity flavor here, less obvious than the dried plum and fig notes that usually spring to mind for this style of beer, which is remarkably close to the actual flavor of the beer itself. A relish made from chopped grilled onion slices mixed with a little Pedro-Ximenez sherry vinegar added a counterpoint of acidity to contrast with the rich meat. And finally, the deep nuttiness and dark purple-black color of forbidden rice provided both a textural and visual contrast while rounding out the substance of the dish.

SERPENT'S STOUT, RUSSIAN IMPERIAL STOUT: **Fifth Course.**
Beers like this can very easily be one-dimensional, offering only straightforward coffee and bittersweet chocolate flavors to work with in a pairing along with a heavy, alcoholic mouthfeel. While those flavors are present in Serpent's Stout, they are balanced alongside undertones of dark candied fruit and licorice with substantial tex-tural elements like roasted bitterness and a hint of astringency. This unique, subtle anise characteristic intrigued me the most. Anise is a divisive flavor: it seems that people either love it dearly or hate it pas-sionately. It would be an interesting challenge to present this flavor front-and-center to guests in a way that could be enjoyed, I hoped, by all of them. I wanted to create an unusual dish that would circum-vent potential reservations that people might bring against anise. This would be the first of two desserts, and would act as a dénoue-ment of sorts after the climactic dry-aged steak, and could be brack-eted in peoples' minds as a pre-dessert—not overly rich or elaborate, but interesting and thought provoking. I still really liked the idea of using barley as an ingredient in a beer dinner and I wanted it to be

a common theme in my menus. I infused a simple syrup, sweetened with molasses, with star anise and fennel seeds. I then used this as a cooking liquid for the pearl barley. As it simmered the liquid thickened and the barley softened. When served at room temperature the barley grains were draped in a slightly sticky, dark, sweet, anise-flavored syrup. I made ice cream from plain, tart Greek-style yogurt that I minimally sweetened. Its rich creaminess was the ideal contrast to the softly *al dente* barley. With an essential aromatic garnish of a fresh mint chiffonade, the beer played beautifully against the tart, smooth ice cream and the sweet, rustic barley. After the meal several guests told me that, prior to their having tried this dish, they thought they didn't care for anise, but had enjoyed it in this context. I was very pleased with how this experiment turned out.

ANGEL'S SHARE, BRANDY BARREL-AGED AMERICAN BARLEYWINE: Dessert.

This last course would be a much more conventional dessert offering. Angel's Share is another big, dark beer. I wanted this preparation to highlight completely different aspects of the beer then the previous course had done. A small custard tart flavored with dried golden calimyrna figs and toasted pistachio nuts would pair complementary flavors in the beer and would have the requisite richness to counter Angel's Share's strong alcohol component. Brandy barrel aging not only infuses the beer with a distinct, strong brandy flavor, but also slowly exposes the beer to air that seeps through the wood and softens those alcohol flavors through oxidation. This is a very desirable characteristic for a beer as strong and richly flavored such as this one. The oxidation process also imbues the beer with flavors of vanilla, dried fruits, and nuts. So, the choice of dried figs and pistachios is quite a straightforward pairing strategy. The beer is certainly the more complex side of the equation here. Each strong, boozy sip rewards close contemplation for many minutes. A bite of the tart would give the palate a break while reinforcing different iterations of the fruity, nutty, and richness characteristics in both the beer and the dessert. As the meal wound down at this point guests got up and milled about the dining room chatting with one another, snifters in hand. This is the great thing about complex, after dinner sipping beers such as this: they stimulate and inspire and, because they take a while to drink sip by sip, pleasantly extend the afterglow of a fine evening together.

BRAISED NIMAN RANCH PORK SHOULDER
with Dried Plums, Saffron, and Cumin

Ingredients:

¼ cup olive oil for frying

2–2¼ lb. Niman Ranch bone-less pork butt/shoulder, cut into 2″ cubes (approx.)

1 large yellow onion, ¼″ dice

1 cup light, dry white wine

6 cloves garlic, peeled

1 cinnamon stick

1 blood orange, quartered (may substitute a small navel or Valencia orange)

1 oz. fresh ginger; peeled, minced

2 bay leaves

1 tsp. saffron

2 tsp. ground cumin

1 tsp. Piment d'Espelette (may substitute ½ tsp. crushed red pepper flakes)

2 cups chicken or pork stock (plus ½ cup more if needed)

2 oz. salted capers; soaked, rinsed (may substitute brined)

8 oz. pitted prunes, halved (may be combined with dried apricots if desired)

¼ bunch flat-leaf parsley; stemmed, chopped

Drizzle of aged balsamic vinegar (optional)

Salt and pepper to taste

Method:

Pre-heat oven to 275 degrees Fahrenheit. Heat olive oil on high in a heavy-bottomed pot with a lid that is large enough to hold all the meat in a single layer (a Dutch oven works well).

Fry pork cubes until a golden crust forms (3–5 min. per side).

Remove pork, reduce heat to med., and add diced onion. Sauté onions until translucent while scraping up browned bits from the bottom of the pot with a wooden spoon (3–5 min.).

Deglaze with white wine and let reduce by half.

Add garlic, cinnamon, blood orange, ginger, bay leaves, saffron, cumin, and Piment d'Espelette to the pot; stir together with the onions and let cook for a minute.

Return pork chunks to the pot and arrange in a single layer with the cinnamon, orange, bay leaf, and garlic arranged evenly between them. Add chicken or pork stock until meat is about ⅔ submerged in liquid (2 cups).

Cover pot, bring to a simmer, and then place in the oven. Braise for 1½ hours while occasionally checking the liquid level in the pot and the tenderness of the pork.

Add dried apricots, prunes, capers, (and an additional ½ cup stock if the pot is getting dry) and braise for an additional hour.

Remove orange quarters, cinnamon stick, and bay leaves. Check the seasoning and add salt and pepper as desired.

Notes:

The idea is to have just the right amount of liquid remaining when the pork is done to form a thickened sauce with the other ingredients to serve with the meat. The meat should be moist and very tender so that it breaks apart easily with a fork. This dish tastes best when left to cool and then held in the refrigerator overnight in the Dutch oven so that all the flavors continue to infuse. When ready to serve, reheat Dutch oven on the stovetop.

Serve with:

Pasta or rice is an excellent accompaniment
Chopped Italian parsley (as garnish)
Aged Balsamic vinegar (as garnish, optional)
Yields 8 servings as a main dish.

ALESMITH BREWING COMPANY
OF SAN DIEGO, CALIFORNIA
APRIL 9, 2009

1st Course:
Marcona Almond Soup
Green Grapes, Piment d'Espelette
Beer Pairing: Nut Brown Ale

2nd Course:
Chimay *with Beer* Trappist Abbey Cheese
Mâche, Easter Egg Radish, Chive, Tenuta di Capezzana Extra Virgin Olive Oil
Beer Pairing: Lil' Devil Belgian-Style Ale

3rd Course:
Barley "Risotto" with Mushrooms and Carlsbad Black Mussels
Porcini and Oyster Mushrooms, Mushroom and Mussel Crème, Herbs
Beer Pairing: Winter YuleSmith Double Red Ale

4th Course:
Grilled Colorado Lamb Tenderloins
Montmorency Cherry Demi-Glace, Potato Discs, Thumbelina Carrots,
Micro Mustard Greens
Beer Pairing: 2008 Decadence Anniversary English-Style Barleywine

Dessert:
California Date Shake with Steamed Cacao Nib Cake
Oasis Date Gardens Medjool Dates, Vanilla Bean Syrup
Beer Pairing: 2007 Bourbon Barrel-Aged Decadence Anniversary Imperial Porter

It wasn't long after our first craft beer dinner together that Ale-Smith team and I began talking about doing a second one. Seven months later it was actualized. The synergy that we established at that first event, and fostered though the budding relationship that followed, impelled us forward to explore more deeply the possibilities that AleSmith's beers offered to the fine dining, fine food realm. As we discussed the finer points of AleSmith's philosophy of beer and the intersection of craft brewing and artisanal cooking, the shape of our next dinner took form in my mind. We would feature beers that we hadn't in the first dinner; Nut Brown and Lil' Devil were draught-only releases available only in select markets, and the remaining beers would be special seasonal and one-time-only releases. These would include YuleSmith winter edition, a robust imperial red ale—a robust amber ale with much more malt and hops than normal, and two editions of the annual AleSmith anniversary release, Decadence, which is brewed with a different recipe each year. The first of the anniversary releases would be the 2008 English-Style Barleywine. The second Decadence, the 2007 Imperial Porter, would be our final beer of the evening. Our dinner would be the first opportunity for anyone to try this barrel-aged version, a sub-edition of an already limited beer. This had been the easiest beer selection process yet.

NUT BROWN, ENGLISH-STYLE BROWN ALE: **First Course.**
At first glance this brown ale comes across as an unassuming beer. It often seems that little attention is given to this style by serious craft brewers in the United States. Brown ales are frequently plain, insipid, or not made at all, ceding the category to the ubiquitous Newcastle Brown Ale. AleSmith Nut Brown is entirely different. This beer has both dimension and flavor. The body is maltdriven but also possesses a distinctive hops profile. This flavorful, easygoing beer would be a perfect starter to the meal. Almonds are an obvious choice to pair with this nut brown ale. I served a Moroccan-style chilled soup made with Marcona almonds, my favorite variety, to open the meal, which immediately put across the fact that this menu was going to explore new territory. The soup is creamy but also light and refreshing on the palate, this dish truly is an appetizer—it whets the appetite and paves the way for the next course.

LIL' DEVIL, BELGIAN-STYLE GOLDEN ALE: **Second Course.**
Here again I decided to go with a cheese for the second course. I
was very satisfied with how a cheese here added to the progression
of the Lost Abbey Dinner and I felt that the same would work here.
Peter Zien is an avid cheesemaker and I knew that he feels a kinship
with the tradition of brewing beer and making cheese alongside one
another. The cheese here is made by the monks of the Scourmont
Abbey who also produce the world-famous Chimay Trappist ales.
The Chimay *with beer* edition is a washed-rind cheese that develops a
wonderful rich and meaty funkiness from aging. These characteristics are perfectly matched by the light crispness of Lil' Devil Ale.
Similar in flavor to Horny Devil, the lower alcohol here delivers a
brighter, crisper experience that complements the distinctive flavor
of the cheese without competing with it. This match-up is rounded
out by tender, buttery mâche greens; crisp, peppery spring radishes; and grassy, aromatic extra virgin olive oil from one of my
favorite Italian artisanal producers, Tenuta di Capezzana.

YULESMITH WINTER HOLIDAY ALE, IMPERIAL RED: **Third Course.**
Among the bounty of local specialties produced in the San Diego
area, the European-style black mussels raised by Carlsbad Aqua-
farm are one of my very favorite ingredients. Mussels and beer
share a special affinity. Served together in *moules-frites,* the de facto
national dish of Belgium, mussels steamed in beer and spiked with
cream, herbs, et cetera, are a classic example of simple beer cuisine. I would dress up this concept a bit for our event, and because
Winter YuleSmith is a considerably heftier beer than those that
would customarily be served with these shellfish. Using pearl barley
again, I turned it into a "risotto." After steaming the mussels, I
simmered the grains in the fragrant liquor they released. I then
reduced the remaining liquid into a concentrated shellfish essence
and blended it together with tangy crème fraîche. Pearl barley
does not produce the same creaminess as Arborio or Carnaroli
rice when prepared as a risotto. Folding the mussel-infused crème
fraîche along with the steamed mussel meats into the cooked barley
gives the dish its requisite richness while producing a distinctive,
lighter interpretation of this classic. The barley risotto plays very
well against the heavier malt, alcohol and prominent hop bitterness

in Winter YuleSmith. A final brightening garnish of chopped flat-leaf parsley, chive, and chervil helps to bridge the risotto's richness and the beer's aromatic bitterness.

2008 DECADENCE ANNIVERSARY ALE, ENGLISH-STYLE BARLEYWINE:
Fourth Course.
The differences between American and English-style barleywines can be quite dramatic. American versions often possess big, aggressive citrus and resinous hop characteristics, sometimes along with a darker malt profile. English versions tend to focus more on a rich, sweet malt body with strong caramel, toffee, and/or molasses elements that also often convey notes of dried fruits. Both have significant alcohol profiles. An awareness of these distinctions is essential to creating a successful, nuanced food pairing with such a substantial beer. AleSmith's regular barleywine offering—Old Numbskull, an American-style—is arguably the finest barleywine made in America, of any style. This one-off Decadence recipe gave them a chance to explore another side of barleywines, one in contrast in many ways to Old Numbskull. Here, dried fruit notes, cherry in particular, are present alongside sweet caramel malt, earthy hops, and warming alcohol.

Thinking of English barleywines conjures a specific image in my mind: sipping a snifter in a darkened corner of a quiet, cozy pub. While certainly not the only way to enjoy these beers, mentally playing out this scene rewarded me with an idea for a food pairing: shepherd's pie, an English pub staple. While not wanting to serve that dish specifically, I found the combination of lamb, potatoes, aromatic vegetables, and a rich sauce very appealing as a companion to this hearty beer.

Lamb tenderloins are not often seen in meat markets. The larger size and more delicate flavor of Colorado lamb tenderloins are something special and luxurious, especially when marinated with garlic and grilled over coals. Thumbelina carrots are small and round like radishes and very attractive when served whole on the plate. Small potato discs, roasted until crispy, provided the starch element, and micro mustard greens stood in as a fresh condiment garnish. Finally, tart Montmorency cherries added to a silken house-made demi-glace would evoke the beer's subtle fruit characteristics, enliven the dish's overall flavor profile, and unite each element with rich flavors of roasted lamb bones, mirepoix, and a slight dark sweetness.

2007 BOURBON BARREL-AGED DECADENCE ANNIVERSARY ALE, IMPERIAL PORTER: Dessert.

Few beers can successfully follow a barleywine in a tasting. This particular Decadence spent a year in a Bourbon barrel while the previous beer was being brewed. Strong boozy elements along with dark chocolate, vanilla, burnt caramel, and some softening oxidation from the aging process cap off a hugely diverse progression of flavors and textures expressed across the span of this meal. A beer as boozy and rich as this one requires an equally rich accompaniment. A duo of desserts would serve to both complement and contrast with the many facets of this beer. I served them together on either side of a long platter. On one side, a traditional Southern California date shake; on the other, a dense, gooey, individual steamed chocolate cake with bitter cocoa nibs garnished with a sticky vanilla bean-infused syrup. In many ways the beer comes across as a distillation of these two desserts. A bite of each, followed by a sip of beer offered at once holistic and deconstructed perspectives on the flavors in play here. This was the most complex, labor-intensive course I had prepared for a special event, but the effort was certainly worth it for a one-time-only beer of this magnitude.

MARCONA ALMOND SOUP
with garnishes

Ingredients:

8 oz. Marcona almonds

4 cups (more if desired) plain, unsweetened almond milk (homemade chicken stock may be substituted for a heartier soup)

½ cup extra virgin olive oil

¼ cup freshly squeezed lemon juice

5 cloves garlic; peeled, halved

1 oz. (approx.) crusty country white bread, torn into chunks (optional, for a thicker consistency)

1 tsp. piment d'espelette (½ tsp. Spanish paprika may be substituted)

1 Tbs. kosher salt

Suggested Garnishes:

Chopped herbs such as chives, parsley, and/or chervil

Green grapes, halved

Smoked paprika/chili powder

Method:

In a food processor blend almonds, garlic, and a few cups of almond milk together to produce a smooth, consistent paste. Add remaining almond milk, olive oil, and lemon juice and continue to blend. Add remaining ingredients and blend until smooth. More almond milk may be used to adjust consistency if desired.

Serve chilled in small bowls topped with a variety of garnishes.

Yields 6–8 appetizer portions.

BEAR REPUBLIC BREWING COMPANY
OF CLOVERDALE, CALIFORNIA
JULY 16, 2009

1st Course:
Butter-Poached Viking Village Sea Scallop
Tsar Nicoulai Truffled Tiger-Eye Whitefish Caviar, Tahitian Vanilla, Chervil
Beer Pairing: 7 Year-Aged Sammy's Strong Ale

2nd Course:
Grilled Treviso Salad with Heirloom Tomatoes and Sunflower Sprouts
Baby Lolla Rossa Lettuce, Mint, Huilerie Beaujolaise Citron Vinaigrette
Beer Pairing: Racer 5 India Pale Ale

3rd Course:
Artisanal Nuernberger Bratwurst
Brown Butter, Sultanas, Fried Parsley, Potato Purée
Beer Pairing: Red Rocket Ale

4th Course:
House-Smoked Niman Ranch Pork Leg with Grilled Peaches
Peach Chutney, Grilled Scallions
Beer Pairing: Big Bear Black Stout

Dessert:
House-Made Caramel Corn
Spiced Cashews, Madagascar Chocolate
Beer Pairing: 2000 Vintage Olde Scoutter's Barleywine

Bear Republic is a unique brewery that manages to make a large amount of beer and distribute it across a wide range while still maintaining the true feel of a family-run business and producing a quintessential artisanal product. I met Richard Norgrove, brewmaster and co-owner along with his wife Tami, during a visit to the brewery to discuss the possibility of doing a dinner together. That day they would be firing up their new state-of-the-art bottling line for the first time, but Richard still managed to lead me on a lengthy tour of the facilities that included detailed discussions of using hop "tea" in beer (for better freshness and hops utilization), and propagating specific generations of their own yeasts to brew with (for maximum consistency and viability). When the tour was over he insisted that we take a particular route through Sonoma's vineyards as we drove to the brewpub in nearby Healdsburg for lunch and samples of special releases. This sort of friendliness, professionalism, and attention to detail can be tasted in the exceptional craft beers produced at Bear Republic Brewing Company.

Soon after our initial meeting we had chosen a date for a craft beer dinner together in Las Vegas and were discussing what beers we would like to feature for the event. Richard offered two well-aged special bottlings from his personal cellar. These rarities would offer guests the opportunity to sample some aged beers that few consumers ever get to experience. I would use these two specialties as bookends to the meal. Sammy's Strong Ale, a Belgian-style golden strong ale, was brewed to commemorate the birth of the Norgroves' son in 2003. It had been lovingly cellared since. This would be the first beer of the night. Fresh palates would best be able to appreciate its subtle complexities. Olde Scoutter's, a classic strong, hoppy, and malty American barleywine, is often available at the brewpub in Healdsburg, CA, but never in bottles. This was a special batch that had been brewed in 2000 and cellared away. This would be the perfect conclusion to the meal.

Racer 5 is an enormously popular, award-winning American IPA that I have consistently enjoyed. Check. Red Rocket is a robust American amber, which is a style with a lot of pairing versatility. Red Rocket in particular is a great example of the bolder side of this style and its versatility. And, to round things out, Black Bear: a big American stout that's intense but not quite as strong as a Russian imperial style. Full of dark, roasted flavors, this beer continues the steady rise of intensity that I was trying to put together without overdoing it, in anticipation of the meal's final, aged beer. This lineup presented a solid showcase of sturdy American-style craft beers, each balanced and full flavored, including some, unique aged specialties. I was excited to begin planning the food.

7-YEAR-AGED SAMMY'S STRONG ALE, BELGIAN-STYLE STRONG GOLDEN ALE: First Course.

Belgian golden strong ale is a bit of a catch-all style. Beers listed as such can vary greatly. This particular brew was made with orange peel, coriander seeds, grains of paradise spice, and candi sugar for added body—and is fermented with a Belgian yeast strain. It's difficult to predict what seven years in the bottle would do to any beer—especially a style that's not normally aged for great lengths of time—so developing a food pairing could be tricky. Its 7.5% alcohol would have helped to preserve it, but the hops, fermentation, and spice notes would likely be completely different now. I had to sketch a general outline of the meal before I received the shipment of beers, so my initial thoughts for this first course were formed before I had tried this beer. I would add the accents to the dish later, once I knew the direction that this beer would lead me in.

Seafood is usually well-suited to the types of beer that work well at the beginning of a meal. Scallops were an easy choice. They are versatile, popular, and one of my personal favorites. When selecting scallops it is essential that they be packed "dry," which indicates that they have not been treated with sodium tripolyphosphate. This chemical preservative causes the scallops to absorb water—plumping them up and increasing their weight. When cooked, this water comes right back out, interfering with the cooking process (they are unable to be seared or grilled properly), and leaving an unpleasant chemical aftertaste.

Butter-poaching is a wonderful cooking method that is easy to execute and one that makes it difficult to overcook foods. Gently melt unsalted butter with a very little water or cream to form an emulsion and soon you have a pot of melted butter that hasn't separated. Slowly cooking seafood in this emulsion keeps it moist and infuses it with the rich flavor of the butter. At the same time, some juices from the scallops enter into the poaching liquid, turning it into a wonderful shellfish butter sauce to serve with the scallops. This method creates a perfect base to build other elements of the dish upon.

When I did receive the beer and sampled it for the first time I was amazed: it tasted both quite aged and strikingly vibrant at the same time. The alcohol had thinned out a bit, giving it a marked impression of lightness on the palate, while darker, earthy malt flavors mingled with spikes of soft fruit and spices. Inspired by this contrast, I made some additions to my recipe. For the dinner I added a touch of orange zest and fresh vanilla bean to the butter poaching liquid to round out and deepen the flavor and spooned a generous dollop of black truffle-infused whitefish caviar on top of the sauced scallop. This combination of light and dark, fruity and earthy flavors in a way recreated the various dimensions of the beer. The dish, like the beer, was a combination of unexpected contrasts to surprise and delight my guests. This was one of the fortunate instances where a pairing turned out even better than I had planned. It was great fun for both me and my guests.

RACER 5, AMERICAN INDIA PALE ALE: **Second Course.**
My first course turned out to be quite a bit more fancy and decadent than I had at first envisioned. It would be a great entrance into the meal, but from here on I wanted to return to an initial idea that had come to me when thinking about my impressions of Bear Republic's beer portfolio as a whole. Our dinner was in the middle of July—the heart of summer—and I was inspired to create the feel of a family barbeque in the park, but put forth in our fine dining setting, of course. A fresh, aromatic, summery salad would be perfect at this point—a notion bolstered by the success of the IPA/salad as the second course of my first AleSmith dinner. Grilled greens, such as chicories—radicchio, endive, and escarole—are amazingly flavorful and lend substance and distinctiveness to the salad. In this case I used treviso, which is essentially radicchio formed into an elongated head similar to romaine, and grills very well. I sliced the grilled treviso halves and added to them fresh, young greens along with crisp, earthy sunflower sprouts and the aromatic piquancy of fresh peppermint, additional herbs, and another dressing made with my favorite French citron vinegar. This bright and varied mixture very nicely accompanied the citrusy and herbal hops components of Racer 5 IPA.

RED ROCKET, AMERICAN AMBER: **Third Course.**

Red Rocket is a truly American beer. The amber style is interpreted in so many ways, ranging from plain amber-colored beers with very limited hops and malt flavors, to flavorful expressions of darker malt and hops that straddle the hoppiness of IPAs and the maltiness of porters. The Bear Republic interpretation hits it right in the sweet spot—significant hops and malt aspects balanced to express nuances of each without being overbearing in either category. Red Rocket, therefore, is a highly malleable food beer that can be utilized in many different ways. I love sausages, which can also be a very important part of any barbeque. Nurenburger-style bratwursts are made primarily with veal and have a smoother texture and slightly more delicate flavor than the traditional bratwursts that we're most accustomed to. The richness and spice influence of these particular sausages, which I purchased from a traditional Old World-style producer, conveyed a sophisticated, artisanal quality that really shone when doused with a simple, nutty brown butter sauce in which some golden raisins had been warmed. I made a very smooth, rich Yukon gold potato puree to accompany the sausages and garnished the dish with crispy fried parsley. The richness of the sausage, potatoes, and brown butter was matched by Red Rocket's refreshing hops while the malt and alcohol components, accented by a bite of sweet golden raisin, provided a foundation for the dish's meaty grilled flavors.

BIG BEAR BLACK STOUT, AMERICAN STOUT: **Fourth Course.**

Growing up in Iowa, pork chops were a grilling staple. Since I was serving veal sausages in the previous course, I didn't want to follow with a juicy slab of pork loin, but I did want to do something different with pork. The richness of pork is not only very suitable as a main course, but also a great companion to the richness of the Black Bear stout I would be serving with this course. The pork leg is a large cut that is excellent when slow cooked and smoked over hardwood coals. I was lucky enough to have access to a large oak-fired smoker, which I used to cook the two bone-in pork legs that I had previously brined and coated with a brown sugar and spice dry rub. After developing a dark, crispy crust in the smoker, the succulent leg was sliced and served with a sweet-tart peach chutney—a fruit wholly associated with warm weather. I now had many elements working together in this dish: the rich, smoky pork leg with its spiced crust; the sweet, vinegary peach chutney; and finally, the charred earthiness of grilled scallions to round out the collection of flavors. These three components conveyed the essential elements of a summer barbeque, and when combined with the hearty roastiness of the Black Bear Stout, coalesced tightly around the central grilled theme of the course. This was a flavorful, filling, and satisfying combination that evoked vivid memories of past summer barbeques.

2000 VINTAGE OLDE SCOUTTER's, AMERICAN BARLEYWINE: Dessert.

Barleywines' strong malt and alcohol components make them very age-worthy beers. The oxidation that normally takes place as a beer ages in the bottle can often prove ruinous to less sturdy styles. But in the case of barleywines the softening effect of this process adds nuance and complexity. At ten years old, this was an elderly brew, but certainly not out of range for a well-made example. Upon opening, many dark, sweet aromas and flavors presented themselves, including caramel, molasses, toffee, brown sugar, treacle, and candied fruits. The hops had faded, leaving only enough bitterness to balance out the malt so that it was not cloying at all.

I wanted to continue playing off these variations on the dark sugar theme, and in keeping with my notion of summer fare I thought of caramel corn. Cracker Jack is an iconic treat at summer ball games. My goal would be to call upon those memories with a fresher, more artisanal version. Caramel corn's crunchiness introduced a new texture at this point in the meal to enliven guests' palates while they compared side-by-side the flavor of actual caramel and the caramel flavors found in the beer. My mother has a fantastic old recipe for caramel corn that she prepares for special occasions when friends and family are around. We always ended up eating way too much of it, whatever the size of the container, and regardless of our appetites. I took fresh oil-popped kernels made on the stovetop and delicately folded them together with dark, bubbly caramel. I spread the mix onto buttered sheets, then baked the kernels to help distribute the caramel evenly into their contours and turn the caramel sauce into a brittle candy coating. Combined with some spiced whole cashew nuts and shards of fine dark chocolate, it became the ultimate gourmet snack, and a highly festive end to our mid-summer meal.

SALLY'S CARAMEL CORN
with Spiced Cashews and Chocolate Chunks

Ingredients:

8 quarts popped corn kernels, from approx 1 cup unpopped popcorn (Use fresh oil or air-popped popcorn kernels. Do not use bagged microwave popcorn.)

½ lb. unsalted butter

2 cups brown sugar

½ cup corn syrup

1 tsp. salt

½ tsp. baking soda

Method:

Preheat oven to 250 degrees Fahrenheit. Butter a very large mixing bowl and add popped corn.

Melt butter in a heavy-bottomed pan, and add sugar, corn syrup, and salt.

Boil for five minutes and turn off heat.

Add the soda while stirring vigorously. Take care at this point as the mixture will bubble profusely.

Pour caramel sauce over kernels and gently fold to coat them. Coating will not be entirely even, but will even out during baking.

Transfer mixture to large buttered roasting pan(s) so that it is in an even layer about three inches thick.

Bake for one hour, stirring gently every 15 minutes, so that the caramel distributes itself evenly throughout the kernels and the corners of the pan(s) do not burn.

When finished, the caramel coating should be crisp and brittle and not chewy.

Keeps well in an airtight container.

SPICED CASHEWS

Ingredients:

2 cups whole, dry-roasted cashews

2 Tbs. unsalted butter

1 tsp. paprika

1 tsp. cumin

½ tsp. smoked paprika

½ tsp. coriander

¼ tsp. cinnamon

¼ tsp. allspice

¼ tsp. white pepper

1 tsp. fine salt

You may adjust any or all of these spices to your individual tastes.

Method:

Melt butter in a sauté pan.

Add spices and stir quickly until their aromas are released (approx 30 seconds).

Add cashews and toss until evenly coated and warmed. Add salt.

Chocolate Chunks: Coarsely chop a high quality dark chocolate bar (70%+ cacao).

FARMERS' MARKET CUISINE AND CRAFT BEER

The farmers' market is the ultimate source for locally produced, seasonal, sustainable, natural, whole foods—the perfect companion to craft beers. Each season offers its own delicacies, some of which may only be found at farmers' markets. A few of my personal favorites include: pea tendrils, green garlic, and rhubarb in the spring; squash blossoms, heirloom tomatoes, purslane, Japanese eggplant, and stone fruits in summer; rainbow chard, romanesco broccoli, Brussels sprouts, winter squash, and heirloom apples in autumn; and an enormous variety of citrus fruits and root vegetables in winter.

Vegetables can be used in innumerable preparations that can be paired with virtually any beer. However, here are a few quick, basic suggestions for utilizing the season's bounty.

- Salads with a variety of mixed greens, bitter chicories, and aromatic herbs in a light vinaigrette work very well with IPAs.
- Roasted, caramelized root vegetables such as parsnips, rutabagas, turnips, and carrots, along with sweetpotatoes, winter squash, and fingerling potatoes are a natural match for porters, stouts, and brown ales.
- Braised greens like chard, collards, kale, and mustard greens can be matched with nearly anything, but pale ales and ambers work very well.
- Grilled, marinated eggplant, summer squash, onions, and heirloom cherry tomatoes contrast nicely with malty Scotch ales or strong red ales.
- Cauliflower, romanesco broccoli, and Brussels sprouts are all fantastic slightly charred in a sauté pan with brown butter. The nutty, slightly mustardy flavors pair very well with Belgian beers with complex, spicy fermentation profiles.

These are just a few ideas to help you get started brainstorming on how to utilize the boundless possibilities of ingredients and preparation combinations at the farmers' market. Because of vegetables' versatility they can be easily adapted to accompany any beer. Add in some artisanal cheese or a little pasture-raised meat for flavor and you'll have a meal that perfectly expresses the essence of the local, seasonal foods movement.

When roasted, many vegetables—such as these squash, potatoes, carrots, eggplant, peppers, onions, and corn—develop excellent sweet caramelized flavors that complement the roasted malt flavors in brown ales and porters.

3 Beer and Cheese
Long-Standing Companions

THE BEER AND CHEESE PAIRING

Cheese and beer share a lot in common. Both are produced with a limited number of ingredients using methods that are varied slightly to create an enormous diversity of styles, each with its own distinctive flavors. Both depend on the workings of tiny microorganisms to achieve the finished product. Each stylistic choice made by the brewer or cheesemaker brings its own set of variables to contend with, which can dramatically effect on the end result. Close attention to time, temperature, and sanitation are the keys to success in each pursuit. Of course these factors are important to cooking too, and especially to baking, but rarely will such a minute adjustment have such a large impact on the final product, determining, perhaps, success or failure. I've brought many a stew back from the brink with some quick thinking and a trip to the walk-in, but missteps in brewing and cheesemaking are not so easily corrected. Simply heating the mash for a few degrees out of range can drastically alter a beer's final character by extracting different fermentable compounds from the malt into the wort. Cooking the milk just a degree or two out of range can create an entirely different texture in a cheese. It is the complete understanding of the significance of each step in these delicate processes, the precise manipulation of variables throughout their production, and the proper utilization of each specific ingredient that bonds the brewer and cheesemaker together in their respective arts.

It is also uncanny how especially delicious beer and cheese become when consumed together. There are few ideas as generally true as this: beer + cheese = delicious. I have yet to find a craft beer and a quality cheese that do not taste good together. That being said, not all pairings are equal. Some are fine, but do not add to our appreciation of the beer's or the cheese's individuality. Others—the result of the simple application of a few creative considerations—are truly amazing. This is where the fun begins.

WHAT'S AT WORK IN A PAIRING?

So why exactly do beer and cheese go together so well? What is it about these two products that accent and enhance one another in such distinctive ways? When answering these questions it is useful to remember the principles that go into making a great food and beer pairing. The notions of complementary and contrasting flavors and aromas are certainly at work here with cheese pairings as well. In this discussion, however, it is first important to point out some basic similarities across all cheeses and beers.

With rare exceptions, all **cheeses have fat and salt**, and all **beers have alcohol and carbonation**. These basic sensory factors highlight what's at work in the mouth when beer and cheese are enjoyed together. The fat in cheese coats the tongue and gives us the perception of richness in the mouth, while the salt adds dimension to the perception of this fat and heightens its flavor. The alcohol in beer asserts itself in the mouth despite the cheese's richness—we have said that in this way the alcohol cuts through the fat. And the carbonation in beer is experienced on the palate in a lively or cleansing way, which contrasts with how the richness of the fat is perceived. So when eating any cheese, any beer refreshes the palate.

Beyond these basic physical interactions in the mouth, we can add the flavor and aroma elements of a specific cheese and a specific beer to create a special pairing. A case can be made for any pairing that has some thought behind it, whether it's a traditional pairing based on regional associations or a new melding of recent artisanal innovations. In Europe, some types of cheeses have been consumed with particular beers for hundreds of years. In America, some pairings of newly invented craft beers and artisanal cheeses are just as remarkable together. Moreover, in any combination our perceptions of the beer and cheese paired together are at least slightly changed as each casts new light on the other. Sip by sip and bite by bite, the variables of flavor, aroma, and texture in the beer and cheese alter the final perception of the beer and cheese together.

To make truly special pairings we must understand the origins and characteristics of the flavors and aromas of cheese as we did previously with beer. Indeed, we can discuss basic artisanal cheese styles the way we talked about craft beer styles in chapter one. The individual characteristics of each side of a pairing—the malt sweetness and hop bitterness of the beer, and the texture and milk flavors of the cheese, for instance—determine why particular beers and cheeses will or won't combine to form great pairings. As you discover how the individual characteristics of your favorite cheeses interact with the flavor and aroma components of beer you can then explore pairings in much the same way we did with food in general—determining complex complementary and contrasting elements.

CHEESE BASICS

There are three main elements to consider when looking at styles of cheeses: the type of milk used to make the cheese, the texture of the cheese, and what ripening process has been used to finish the cheese. Caring for the milk-producing animals by providing them adequate grazing areas and proper shelter gives the cheesemaker access to the essential high quality raw material. Applying meticulous cheesemaking methods determines the type of cheese that will be produced. Finally, using the appropriate ripening techniques transforms the cheese into its final, perfected form.

MILK: THE RAW MATERIAL

Milk, of course, is the basis of cheese, and each type of milk has its own flavor that you'll easily learn to recognize after trying a few different cheeses made from each one. Of almost equal significance to the type of milk used is what the animals ate to produce the milk. The quality of an animal's diet has a direct impact on the flavors found in cheeses made from their milk. Contented cows, sheep, and goats grazing in specific pastures provide milk with unique flavors that are influenced by the plants and conditions in that particular pasture. Seasonal variations in animals' diets also play a role in a finished cheese. A diet containing more pasture blossoms in summer gives the milk higher levels of carotene, which produces cheeses that are more yellow colored, for instance. During winter, when many animals are confined to the barn, the animals' diet may consist primarily of hay and grains, which also has an effect on the qualities of the milk. Many dairies also partner with local breweries and reap mutual benefits. Dairies help the breweries by hauling away the spent grain from the brewing process and using it to supplement their animals' diets. This relationship strengthens the bond between local producers and lends the cheeses made from this milk a unique origin story.

RAW MILK AND CHEESEMAKING: Any discussion of the milk used for cheese must address the topic of raw milk. It is certainly the controversial issue in the artisanal cheese world today. Many artisanal cheesemakers tout the benefits of raw milk while FDA regulation and inspection regimes threaten its use. Cheese shops give particular attention to cheeses made from raw milk, the virtues of which—including improved flavor—are touted again and again by connoisseurs. Raw milk retains all of the beneficial microorganisms naturally present in the milk, and their effects help to better produce and preserve the cheese, and create deeper, more nuanced flavors in it. Pasteurizing the milk can also change the flavor of the milk—think of the flavor of steamed milk—and diminishes the subtleties imparted to the milk by the animals and the pastures it came from. The FDA requires that all cheeses made with raw milk must be aged at specific temperature and humidity levels for at least 60 days before they can be sold or imported. It is thought that during this aging process the salt and acidity in cheese helps to reduce any harmful bacteria that may be present.

The FDA also conducts occasional random inspections of cheese samples and cheesemaking facilities. While the spirit of these practices has the best interest of consumers in mind, and often result in certain production improvements, some artisanal cheesemakers argue that this sort back-end regulation is based on industrial production methods, and not on farmstead cheese production—how the majority of raw milk cheese is produced. If the manufacturing process begins with clean, wholesome milk and proper production techniques and sanitation practices are followed throughout—of equal importance for both pasteurized and raw-milk cheeses—then clean, safe, wholesome cheeses will result. Much of the information surrounding this contentious issue remains in debate, and the bureaucracy—including its looming threat of an all-out ban on raw milk cheeses—continues on.[*]

---

[*] Though it is tempting to discuss the many unfortunate laws that surround the sale and distribution of craft beer around the country, it is beyond the scope of our present topic.

Regardless of where one stands on this issue—and the conflicting scientific claims surrounding it—producing farmstead cheese from raw milk is the most traditional approach to cheesemaking, and a vital option for producing truly authentic, artisanal products. There are very many truly excellent, classic cheeses made from pasteurized milk, and products made from it do not constitute a lesser class of artisan cheeses. However, given the degree to which we value all of the artistic touches that craft brewers apply to their beers, the production model for artisanal cheesemakers should allow them similar opportunities to safely produce whatever expressions of their art form that they choose.

COW'S MILK: Cow's milk cheese is the most common type that you're likely to encounter in the United States. Cows need large, lush pastures to graze in to produce the best milk, and also require a bit more attention to raise than goats or sheep. They also produce the largest amount of milk. Cow's milk generally has a mild, buttery flavor that is made into a multitude of cheeses. Depending on the amount of carotene-rich plants in the cows' diet, cow's milk cheeses can range in color from pure white to rich yellow-gold. Classic cow's milk cheeses include Cheddar, Parmigiano-Reggiano, Gruyere, and Stilton—to name only a few.

GOAT'S MILK: Goats also appreciate green pastures and woodlands but can easily clamber around rocky crags to seek out hard-to-reach tufts of grass and herbs. Goats are affable, lower maintenance, and are raised as successfully in France's bucolic Loire Valley as they are in dry, coastal Mediterranean climes. Goat's milk has a fresh, creamy tang that varies in strength depending on the type of cheese it's made into. Unlike cow's milk cheeses, goat's milk varieties are always white. Fresh goat's milk cheeses are mainstays in the kitchen and are delicious in many dishes from salads to desserts. Many types of classic goat cheeses often possess a characteristic smooth, clay-like paste texture. On the other end are the dry, crumbly feta-type cheeses often made from goats' milk. Firmer, creamy-smooth goat goudas are increasingly common and irresistibly delicious. But the absolute classics are the chèvre-style cheese from France.

SHEEP'S MILK: Sheep also thrive in dry or difficult foraging areas. The prevalence of sheep's milk cheeses in a particular region, such as large areas of Spain, often reflects the region's sparseness. Sheep's milk is ideally suited for cheesemaking with higher levels of fat and solids than both cow and goat milk, however, each sheep produces significantly less milk. Sheep's milk cheeses are highly prized for their richness and their distinctive nutty or grassy flavors, which are often combined with a hint of sweetness. Many possess complex, gamey flavors that can become highly developed when aged. Roquefort, Ossau-Iraty, Manchego, and Pecorino Toscano are some of the world's most revered sheep's milk cheeses.

MIXED MILKS: Many wonderful cheeses are made from a blend of two or more types of milk. These cheeses can convey the qualities of each type of milk without being dominated by any one characteristic. They can be quite complex and well-balanced. Some classic examples are Robiola due and tre latti and traditional Cabrales.

TEXTURE AND RIPENING: THE CHEESEMAKER'S HAND

TEXTURE: A cheese's texture doesn't necessarily indicate where it's from or what type of milk it was made from, but it does tell you is how it's going to interact with your palate. Learning some general cheese styles will help you form mental categories when tasting different cheeses and remember how texture relates to the tasting experience.

The main factor that affects the texture of a cheese is how much moisture remains in it, which is in turn largely determined by how the curds were handled during production. Generally speaking, the larger the curds are that go into the cheese, the softer and creamier the resulting cheese will be. The smaller the curds are cut, sometimes down to the size of rice grains, the harder the final cheese will be. Other processes also contribute to texture. The curds can be "cooked," a process during which the curds are heated to a specific temperature, which causes them to contract further and expel more water. After the curds have been molded into their final form, they can be "pressed" to dry them even more. The hardest cheeses can have as little as 30 percent water, while the moistest ones can maintain water levels as high as 80 percent.

RIPENING: Specific ripening procedures produce dramatically different cheeses. After the curds are molded into a shape resembling the finished cheese, many microorganisms go to work, slowly breaking down the milk and producing many of the complex aromas and flavors that we cherish. The first starter cultures begin to acidify and coagulate the milk and break down proteins and fats. Later, secondary cultures may be added, each of which contribute to the unique qualities of a particular type of cheese. Each different bacteria or mold contributes its own flavor and texture effects to the finished cheese; indeed, some classic cheeses are defined by the type of mold or bacteria at work in them.

Each ripening method produces a different type of rind on a cheese and imparts distinctive characteristics. Blue cheeses are inoculated with particular strains of mold that produce their distinctive blue-green veining. Washed-rind cheeses are bathed in brine or alcohol to stimulate the growth of beneficial bacteria on their surfaces, which produces a pungent, orange-colored coating. Cheeses with a "bloomy" rind have special molds in them that produce the soft, snowy, mushroom-scented coatings that we closely associate with cheeses like Brie and Camembert. Other cheeses are given a light dusting of vegetable ash, wrapped in leaves, "bandaged" with cheesecloth, coated in herbs and/or spices, or covered with wax. Each of these methods enlists different bacteria and molds, or utilizes different chemical processes within the cheese, to produce different results in the fully ripened cheese.

Sometimes the absence of any aging or ripening characteristics defines a cheese. These fresh cheeses are eaten soon after production. They can be formed into shapes but do not have rinds. Fresh goat's milk cheese (often referred to as "chèvre"), plain "farmer's cheese," and feta, which is preserved in brine, are widespread examples of fresh, rind-less cheeses.

We prize artisanal cheeses for their complex flavors and aromas that we use to form the basis of excellent pairings. The ripening process is a main source of these valued characteristics, and the method used determines how they will develop. Much like the fermentation process in beer, ripening is essential to developing a truly full-flavored and aromatic cheese.

HARD CHEESES: The curds for hard cheeses are cut very small and are often cooked. These cheeses often have a dry texture that breaks up into granules as you bite and chew the cheese. These particles melt on the tongue with a lot of combined surface area to deliver the flavor that gives them intensity on the palate. These cheeses can have an appealingly sharp, salty piquance, which is sometimes accompanied by a sweet nuttiness. Parmesan and Alpine cheeses are typical examples of hard cheeses.

SEMI-FIRM CHEESES: These cheeses may undergo one or more of the drying processes that create hard cheese, but to a lesser degree. Their curds are often cut quite small, but are not cooked, only pressed. This is a very large category, containing a wide variety of cheeses that can range from tender and moist to quite hard when aged. Farmhouse cheeses, tome-style, and most blue cheeses are all part of this varied category.

SOFT-RIPENED CHEESES: These cheeses have the highest moisture content retained from uncut or minimally cut curds. Some possess a bloomy rind consisting of a dense coating of delicate, white cottony filaments produced by the Penicillium candidum mold. French-style goat cheeses are often dusted with vegetable ash before their surface mold begins to develop. Whatever the method, the key aspect of these types of cheeses is that they ripen inward beneath a layer of surface mold. Their interiors slowly transform into a creamy, gooey, silken-textured paste that provides a rich, palate-coating mouthfeel. Their flavors can range from mild and delicate fresh milk to robust and meaty with notes of earthy mushrooms. The soft-ripened category also includes double and triple-crème cheeses, which are as decadent as they sound. Their pure expressions of butterfat are some of the most luxurious to be found in the cheese world. Brie and Camembert are quintessential examples of soft-ripened cheeses.

BLUE CHEESES: The cheeses in this huge category all share the distinctive striations caused by the Penicillium roqueforti mold. Named for the famous strain of mold discovered in the caves where Roquefort is made, it has been a part of cheesemaking since ancient times. Some examples of blue cheeses are pierced with needles to allow air into their interiors and spread the blueing more quickly, and their blueing patterns often follow the paths created by the needles. Other traditional blues are left to slowly mold from the inside, which creates intricate feathery or web-like patterns within the cheese. Whatever the method to spread the growth of this mold, the flavor impact it has on the cheese is immense. As the mold slowly breaks down the proteins and fats, pungent, complex aromas and flavors are released that range from toasted hazelnuts to damp hay to an unctuous root cellar. The most classic examples are aged in underground caves in which the ambient mold spores work their way into the cheeses as they slowly age under ideal temperature and humidity conditions. The paste of some blue cheeses remains mostly white and retains a fresh, tangy milk flavor spiked with earthy blue accents, while others become dry, turn a deep golden brown, and develop an intense, spicy nuttiness. Textures can range from dry and crumbly to very soft and spreadable. Blue cheeses are often heavily salted, and their strong flavors are ideally matched with strongly flavored beers.

WASHED-RIND CHEESES: These might be considered the "advanced" cheeses because of their very strong aromas. Like soft-ripened cheeses, washed-rind cheeses also ripen from the outside-in. Young cheeses are repeatedly "washed" with brine, beer, wine, or brandy (specifically marc, which is fermented from the leftover grape pomace, very much like Italian grappa) which creates the perfect environment for Brevibacterium linens to grow on their surfaces. This is the same bacteria found on all human skin (don't think too hard about it). This type of rind often matures into a beautiful burnt-orange color, and despite this whole process sounding somewhat repelling, it actually produces some of the most amazingly complex and delicious cheeses—and they really do smell good when you've developed a taste for them. Inside they can have wonderfully gooey textures and rich, meaty flavors.

Washed rind cheeses offer some of the most complex and interesting flavors in the cheese world and pair beautifully with a wide variety of beers. LtR: Epoisses de Bourgogne, Chimay Grand Cru, Taleggio, Munster, and Langres.

PASSIONATE PURVEYORS: THE ROLE OF A GOOD CHEESE SHOP

Kristin Sande and Bob Howald have run Valley Cheese and Wine in Henderson, Nevada since 2006. Pulling up to the front of their shop situated in the corner of a nondescript strip mall, very typical of the Las Vegas area, I was not expecting to find an exceptionally fine gourmet specialty shop. There are older, bigger, and fancier shops in some lucky communities around the country—Kristin keeps roughly 150 cheeses in their two cases, and Bob stocks around 400 different bottles of boutique wines and craft beers in their 2,400-square-foot store—but what makes this place so special is Bob and Kristin's total dedication to friendly service, to the highest-quality hand-selected artisanal products, and to passionately educating their customers. They know the story behind every item in the store, and very often they know the people who produced them as well. Bob conducts weekly educational seminars in the shop and regularly sends out a substantial newsletter. Every sample of cheese Kristin offers comes with a detailed description of its provenance. Each nibble leads into another until I'm powerless to resist buying the five-or-six-cheese tasting that I just experienced so I can take it home to share.

This is the way to REALLY learn about cheese. Reading about cheeses in books is great fun, and a good way to work up the confidence to ask some questions about the slightly fuzzy, blue-gray pyramid in the back corner of the cheese case (Valençay, ash-coated goat's milk made in France's Loire Valley,

from affineur Jacquin—now one of my favorites) or the little lopsided orange wrinkly one in the round wooden box (Langres, washed-rind cow's milk from the Champagne region, by Fromagerie Germain—again, so delicious), but it's no substitute for tasting and talking with enthusiastic experts. I thought I knew my cheeses pretty well, but over the course of our relationship Bob and Kristin helped me develop my own deep sense of the role artisanal cheese could play in my culinary career. They knew my tastes and made insightful recommendations, and not just about cheese: they introduced me to many other new products that have changed the way I cook today. They even invited me to prepare their annual anniversary dinners, with many of their suppliers in attendance. So get to know your local, independent cheesemonger(s). Visit often and foster a relationship. It's likely to result in the most delicious education you'll ever receive.

CHEESE'S ROLE IN THE MEAL

Cheese is a highly versatile food. It works well as both a meal unto itself and as an ingredient in other dishes. Just as there is a craft beer for every point in the meal, there too is a cheese for every culinary occasion. The traditional ploughman's lunch is probably the most classic example of cheese filling in as a meal. Consisting of a generous portion of hearty farmhouse cheese along with crusty bread, butter, and pickles, it's a simple meal that can satisfy any appetite, and demands a pint of ale to wash it down. Variations on this, perhaps with the addition of a dry salame, can make up an excellent picnic; pack in a chilled bomber of craft beer and you'll have a memorable event in store. This is cheese playing the starring role.

The cheese board is another very popular way of enjoying artisanal cheeses as the focal point of an event. Composing a progression of several cheeses is an excellent way to explore the effects of different combinations of beers and cheeses together over the course of a gathering. Different themes or collections of cheeses can be composed to accompany a selection of craft beers. You can explore whatever aspects of cheese or beer you're curious about or in the mood for. Bites of various cheeses along with sips of selected beers can offer a lot of insight into different pairing principles that you may want to pursue. Compose boards with a few cheeses and condiments, select a few beers, and see what happens as you enjoy them together.

But cheese is just as well-suited to playing a supporting role in a larger meal. A composed cheese course within a meal is one of my favorite ways to showcase a beer and cheese pairing. Combined with a few selected accompaniments, this is the most precise way to present the close flavor calculations of a thoughtful pairing. A single cheese paired with a single beer, along with some simple accents, can convey a very thought-provoking taste experience. Additionally, a composed plate can be designed to fit in at different points within a meal: as an amuse bouche, appetizer, intermezzo course, or dessert, for example. (Perhaps the most memorable amuse bouche I ever had was a quenelle of fresh local sheep's milk ricotta on top of a plain crostino, with a drizzle of local olive oil, alongside a few lucques olives at Chez Panisse in Berkeley, California.)

Cheeses with lighter, more delicate flavors, such as certain soft-ripened and goat cheeses, are best suited to an appetizer presentation. Their nuances are best experienced by fresh, unfatigued palates, and many of the best accompaniments to these cheeses work for an appetizer plate as well. A few delicate, lightly dressed greens, carefully cut seasonal crudités, or a small prepared item such as a slaw or roasted root vegetables, fit in nicely on an appetizer plate at or near the beginning of a meal. It is also quite convenient, and visually appealing, that many of these types of cheeses are offered as small, individual pieces that can be served either whole or halved. Additionally, the types of beers that pair well with these cheeses are lighter beers appropriate for the beginning of an evening.

Very distinctive washed-rind cheeses require special attention if served as the focal point of their own course. A few bites can regenerate the senses as they encounter aromas seldom encountered at the dinner table—edible smelling salts if you will. For fans of these cheeses, this experience is readily welcomed. For others, it could have a chilling effect on the appetite. That being said, there's nothing scary about these cheeses, which hold a special place in my heart. Just know your guests. Accompany these cheeses with contrasting flavors, aromas, and textures—and a great, distinctive beer. The complex interactions of the pairings will draw people in and really focus them on what's at work on the plate, in the glass, and in the mouth, instead of being distracted by the potentially unfamiliar flavor of a "stinky" cheese. A plate with some sweet-tart chutney, spears of bitter, crunchy Belgian endive, or a shave of dry-cured

ACCOUTREMENTS

Though not an absolute necessity, filling out a cheese board with the right accompaniments can add a lot to both the enjoyment of the cheeses and the visual appeal of the presentation.

Very creamy or runny soft-ripened cheeses usually benefit from being served with **bread**, which I prefer over crackers. Crusty baguettes work very well, as do rustic tartine-style breads. I generally avoid breads with herbs or flavorings that compete with the cheeses, though a raisin nut-bread can be very good with blues or other cheeses for dessert. If you do prefer crackers, I recommend very simple ones with good texture and not a lot of oil in them.

Adding an element of sweetness can really set off saltier cheeses, especially blues. **Honey** (seek out local examples) is an excellent companion. Although I love the look and idea of serving honeycomb, I find that chewing on wax disrupts my enjoyment of the subtle textures of the cheeses. **Chutney** has both sweetness and acidity that contrast with some simple, yet robust, cheeses. Other types of **preserved fruits** or **jams** can be very interesting with cheeses too, especially homemade preserves. But **membrillo** is my favorite. This sweet paté of quince fruit not only goes very well with Spanish cheeses, where this condiment originated, but with a great many other cheeses as well. Buy it and serve it in small slices. To avoid covering up the subtleties of your

cheeses, all of these sweet and tart accompaniments should be used sparingly to contrast with and enliven drier, salty cheeses.

Nuts are a classic too, complementing the flavors of many firm cheeses. **Marcona almonds** are another Spanish treasure. **Pistachios**, **pecans**, and **walnuts** are always welcomed.

Pickles are an excellent addition as well. Tangy cornichons are classic, but I also like pickled eggplant, turnips, green beans, and okra in addition to traditional cucumbers. Good **olives** also contribute a lot to the cheese board. Like pickles, their brininess provides a contrasting bite to many cheeses.

Lastly, **charcuterie** is often served alongside cheeses. While this transforms a cheeseboard into more of a meal unto itself, the right combinations of salami, cured ham, bresaola, pâtés, rillettes, and other artisanally produced meats, can make for a dramatic presentation.

ham—along with the right beer—can convert almost anyone to a devotee of these fine cheeses.

Strongly flavored, salty cheeses are best enjoyed at or near the end of a meal. Their assertive characteristics can revive tired palates and, given waning appetites, small amounts of them go a long way. Strong blues, pungent alpine-style cheeses, nutty-sweet aged goudas, and sharp traditional cheddars spring to mind. Accompany them with a few nuts, pieces of fresh or dried fruit, and a gastrique or some local honey. Occasionally, depending on the other foods that were served, I find that a luscious *triple-crème* can provide a counter-intuitive restorative effect at the end of the meal.

The purpose of these explorations is to show what a natural, versatile role cheese can play in all types of meals, and to foster as many opportunities as possible for showcasing the marvelous matchups that craft beer and artisanal cheese provide. A great beer and a great cheese together is perhaps the simplest way to explore the deep, complex sorts of pairings we discussed in the previous chapter. The complementary and contrasting "combination" beer and cheese pairing should be a well-used option in your culinary repertoire.

THE RIGHT BEER WITH THE RIGHT CHEESE

Having surveyed the affinities of beer and cheese, and the many ways in which cheese can be incorporated into snacks and meals, it's time to fashion specific pairings and courses. Again, there are few hard-and-fast rules to follow. I wouldn't, however, think of pairing a big coffee-infused Russian imperial stout with a fresh, tangy goat cheese. But, hey, you never know what may be just the right thing for the mood of your group. The point is that I want to share with you the principles that I use for constructing pairings that I have found to be most useful. I certainly have formed some rules for pairings that are based on my personal tastes, but my goal is to not pass these on verbatim, but instead to set up some grounding principles of flavor matching that can be used to form your own internal guidelines. So, thinking back to the general discussion of food and beer pairing, those same principles are at work here, but focused now through the narrower lens of artisanal cheese.

NOTABLE "BEER CHEESES"

Here we begin with cheeses that will enhance your enjoyment of beer. This list represents some of my favorite, iconic examples of each style, which are taken from both the Old World and America. Classic cheeses often serve as the inspiration for modern artisanal cheeses. In this way the artisanal cheese movement in the United States is analogous to the craft beer renaissance. And, like craft beer, artisanal cheeses often reflect the characteristics of the region they're from. Exceptional cheeses of all milk types and in many classic styles are produced in this country today. Eating local or regional cheeses can be as fun as exploring locally brewed beers— though the two are even more fun together.

When cheeses from a specific producer are mentioned they represent an example of the highest quality. (Colston-Bassett Stilton, and its raw-milk sibling Stichelton, reign supreme over all other Stiltons.) Consider them as more specific recommendations within their category. Substitute freely. Exploring the nuances of different artisanal cheeses and craft beers within the same styles of each is a fun way to discover the intricacies that make up what could be your new favorite.

Old World classics:

5-Year Aged Gouda (cow, Netherlands)

Gruyere (raw cow, Switzerland)

Parmigiano-Reggiano (raw cow, Italy)

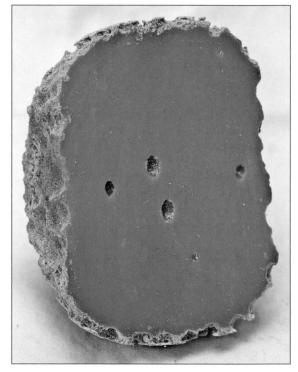

Mimolette (cow, France)

HARD CHEESES

Alpine-style cheeses make up a large part of this category. Their pungent, concentrated milk flavors, often with spicy undertones, are very beer friendly.

American originals:

Uplands Pleasant Ridge Reserve
(raw cow, Wisconsin)

Thistle Hill Tarentaise (raw cow, Vermont)

Winchester Super
Aged Gouda (raw
cow, California)

These cheeses go well with hop-driven beer styles, including spicy pilsners made from Saaz hops. Other types, such as a nutty, butterscotch-tinged aged gouda are beautiful with beers that have caramel malt flavors like porters, stouts, Scotch ales, barleywines, and RIS. Some even stand up to 2IPAs. The dry, salty, grassy notes of Parmigiano-Reggiano cry out for crisp, hoppy beers.

Old World classics:

Montgomery's Cheddar
(cow, England)

Berkswell (raw sheep, England)

Manchego (sheep, Spain)

Garrotxa (goat, Spain)

Fontina d'Aosta (raw cow, Italy)

Ossau Iraty (sheep, France)

SEMI-FIRM CHEESES

The sharp, precise flavors of traditional clothbound cheddars are perfect pairings with fruity and grassy aromatic pale ales and IPAs. The right 2IPA can also find its equal among these gorgeous cheeses.

Indeed, the whole category of British farmhouse cheeses should be extensively explored for their beer friendliness. Begin with the above and branch out to ESBs, stouts, porters, and Scotch ales.

American originals:

Cabot Clothbound Cheddar
(cow, Vermont)

Fiscalini Bandaged Cheddar (cow, California)

Vella Cheese Co. Monterey
Dry Jack (cow, California)

Tumalo
Tomme
(raw goat,
Oregon)

Bellwether
San Andreas
(sheep,
California)

The sheep and goat milk Pyrenees and Basque-style cheeses in the Ossau Iraty family, and those similar to them, possess a characteristic nutty sweetness, and can be paired with a wide variety of hoppy and malty beers. All those mentioned above, as well as ambers, browns, and barleywines can work very well with the wide variety of semi-firm cheeses. Experimentation is the key to this broad and satisfying category.

Old World classics:

Brie de Meaux/Brie de Melun (cow, France)

Camembert (cow, France)

Robiola *Tre Latti* (cow, goat, sheep; Italy)

SOFT-RIPENED CHEESES

This group, with its intense creaminess and delicate earthiness, shows best alongside light, effervescent beers such as delicately spicy saisons and bières du garde, as well as fruity hefeweizens and witbiers. The right Belgian-style golden or strong ale can also counter the creaminess with a bit of alcohol-driven oomph.

Brillat-Savarin (cow, France) Bucheron (goat, France) Selles-sur-Cher (goat, France)

American originals:

Cowgirl Creamery Mt. Tam
(cow, California)

Jasper Hill Constant Bliss (raw cow, Vermont)

Vermont Butter & Cheese Co.
Bijou (goat, Vermont)

Vermont Butter & Cheese Co.
Coupole (goat, Vermont)

Cypress Grove Humboldt Fog
(goat, California)

Capriole Wabash Cannonball
(goat, Indiana)

Aged goat cheeses are some of my very favorites, but they can provide some challenges for beers. Strong roasted malt flavors can easily overwhelm the cheeses' tangy, milky flavors; but certain dry stouts can be fun. Hops may fare better—especially those with crisp, vibrant citrus flavors. Wheat beers with fruity esters can be delicious with these cheeses, as well as the highly versatile saison and Bière du Garde styles.

However, I have had the greatest success with sour ales, gueuzes, and lambics. The light body and acidity of these beers—and especially their gamey fermentation notes—pair beautifully with the "goaty" tanginess of these cheeses.

Old World classics:

Epoisses de Bourgogne
(cow, France)

Munster (cow, France)

Langres (cow, France)

Taleggio
(cow, Italy)

Chimay Abbey
cheeses (cow,
Belgium)

WASHED-RIND

To me, these are the most fun pairings. The prominent fermentation aspects of certain beers perfectly complement the strong "fermented" aromas that washed-rind cheeses develop. Funky, sour ales from America, along with Belgian Flanders reds, lambics, and gueuzes—including examples that are fermented with fruit—are far and away the best matches for these intense, wild cheeses.

American originals:

Cowgirl Creamery Red Hawk (cow, California)

Meadow Creek Grayson (raw cow, Virginia)

Crave Brothers
Petit Frère (cow,
Wisconsin)

In another direction, saisons, bières du garde, and some Belgian golden and strong ales contribute just the right contrasting elements to make a great pairing.

Hops can be tricky. While their aromas can contrast nicely, their bitterness can sometimes become metallic with these cheeses.

Old World classics:

Roquefort (raw sheep, France)

Bleu d'Auvergne (cow, France)

Colston-Bassett
Stilton (cow,
England)

Gorgonzola
(cow, Italy)

BLUE

Here we can break out the big guns. IPAs and double IPAs can be fantastic with the "milkier" blues made in America. The floral and grassy aromas of the hops are especially well-suited for the musky, spicy blue characteristics.

American originals:

Rogue River Blue (raw cow, Oregon)

Maytag Blue (cow, Iowa)

Jasper Hill Bayley Hazen
(raw cow, Vermont)

Pt. Reyes Original Blue
(cow, California)

Sweeter barleywines and Russian imperial stouts pair extremely well with drier, "nutty" blue cheeses. The strong malt and alcohol profiles of these beers temper the rich, biting, saltiness of the biggest blues. The complex dark fruitiness of Belgian dark strong and abbey ales also work very well. These are the most serious blues to pair with brewers' most serious beers. The complexities that play out in these combinations can be astounding.

"Fresh" Cheese

Nearly any fresh, crisp, light-bodied beers will work here. Pale ales, wheat beers, pilsners, and IPAs are great. Dishes made with these cheeses, often salads, can be fine companions to beer as well. Fried cheese curds demand a beer with a malt and alcohol presence.

Laura Chenel Goat Log (goat, California)

Mt. Vikos Feta (sheep, goat; Greece)

"Cheese Curds"—various producers (cow, United States)

Burrata (water buffalo, Italy)

NOTABLE "CHEESE BEERS"

Here we begin with but a few beers from selected styles central to your enjoyment of cheese (and perhaps to food at large). Some of the best examples of Old World beer styles still come from their country of origination, while American ingenuity has, arguably, improved on others. Additionally, many much-loved craft beer styles have been developed here in the United States. The beers presented here represent specific examples in each style that I have had good luck in pairing with artisanal cheeses.

Certainly craft beer's regional availability will necessitate some substitutions, and though sometimes there may be no real substitute for a particular beer, the pairing principles expressed here can generally be applied to many of your own local craft beers. Start with your favorites, see where they take you, and expand as you come across others farther afield. The same goes for both beers and cheeses: one can make generalizations about beer styles and their pairing ability with different types of cheese, but the individual characteristics of each, and your personal preferences, will serve as the best guide to your explorations.

AMERICAN AMBER

Green Flash Hop Head Red
Bear Republic Red Rocket
Bell's Amber Ale
AleSmith Winter YuleSmith

I enjoy the more flavorful interpretations of this style. An amber is not a brown ale, and it's not a pale ale. It has good roasted malt and citrusy hop aspects—in precise balance. Some of these examples even push into the double red category. But more flavor is good, and these beers fill a niche. They go very well with a wide variety of rich cheeses with a lot of flavor, but are also not too strong or edgy. Experiment with hard and semi-firm cow and sheep's milk cheeses.

PILSNER

Old World classics:

Pilsner Urquell (Czech original)

American originals:

Victory Prima Pils
Avery Joe's Premium American Pilsner
North Coast Scrimshaw

I'm a bit reluctant to mention Pilsner Urquell, which is owned by SABMiller. Only the freshest product, on draught, preferably in the Czech Republic, which hasn't been light-struck through its green bottles, is the quintessential Bohemian pilsner. It goes great with mild cheeses. Victory's Prima Pils is a classic in its own right, and well-worth seeking out for pairings.

WHEAT

Old World classics:

Weihenstephaner Hefeweizen (Germany)
Hoegaarden (Belgium)

American originals:

Dogfish Head Festina Pêche
Allagash White

The best wheat beers are light, refreshing, and fruity with distinctive fermentation profiles. German hefeweizens are the classic, but Belgian wits are terrific too, which have lighter esters and phenols. Dogfish Head's Festina Pêche Berliner weisse-style beer made with peaches strikes a great balance between sour fruitiness and refreshing lightness. These beers go well with creamy bloomy-rind cheeses, semi-firm and soft-ripened goat milks, and mild farmhouse styles.

AMERICAN BROWN ALE

Bell's Best Brown
Big Sky Moose Drool
Smuttynose Old Brown Dog

Browns by nature are good all-around beers. Their very high versatility can also mean very simple pairings—which is not all bad. Low hops and moderate nutty malt profiles complement a huge variety of semi-firm and hard cheeses.

AMERICAN PALE ALE

AleSmith X
Three Floyds Alpha King
Anchor Liberty Ale

AMERICAN IPA

AleSmith IPA
Bear Republic Racer 5
Russian River Blind Pig
Bell's Two Hearted Ale
Ballast Point Sculpin

DOUBLE IPA

Russian River Pliny the Elder
Alpine Pure Hoppiness
Victory Hop Wallop
AleSmith Summer YuleSmith
Port Brewing Mongo

The panoply of hop-driven styles begins with pale ales and explodes from there. The vibrant aromatics and clean, crisp bitterness of the most lush examples are made for the creamy richness of cheese. Depending on the strength of the cheese and your tolerance for hops, pale ales, IPAs, and 2IPAs are all very compatible with cheeses. The best matchups consists of sharp, savory traditional Cheddars—like Montgomery's, the gold standard of English Cheddars—and

Rogue Ales and Rogue Creamery, both named for the same river in Oregon, have collaborated for years. To commemorate Rogue Creamery's seventy-fifth year of operation, Rogue Ales created a special hearty brown ale to pair with the creamery's cheeses, including Caveman Blue.

salty, piquant blues, both young and old. The increased hop levels in IPAs gives them an edge needed with such full-flavored cheeses.

Double IPAs take it still further with greater malt and alcohol. These powerhouses can easily tame creamy, pungent gorgonzola—and Rogue Creamery's Rogue River Blue, one of America's finest blues—seems destined for a pairing with one of the regions hearty 2IPAs.

Pungent, hard, Alpine-style cheeses are also a natural match for hop-forward beers. Salty, nutty sheep's milk semi-firm cheeses also stand up well to these beers' crisp bitterness.

AMERICAN STOUT/PORTER

Bear Republic Big Bear Black Stout
Dieu du Ciel Aphrodite (Canada)
Great Lakes Edmund Fitzgerald Porter
Bell's Kalamazoo Stout

RUSSIAN IMPERIAL STOUT

AleSmith Speedway Stout
Bell's Expedition Stout
Deschutes The Abyss
Founder's Breakfast Stout

As with the variety among hop-driven styles, the emphasis on roasted malt flavors varies greatly among different interpretations of porters and stouts. Porters' cocoa-like roastiness and relatively low malt sweetness and hop bitterness make them quite versatile among hard and semi-firm styles of cheese—especially goudas, and Basque-style examples.

The same holds true for stouts and their slightly darker, coffee-like roasted malt character, along with more alcohol sweetness in some examples. These are good for stronger cheeses in the same or similar styles.

Russian imperial stouts' extreme roasted flavors, malt sweetness, pronounced bitterness, and alcohol are best to tackle extremely strong, nutty, salty blues. The occasional extra-aged gouda or funky mountain cheese can also be the perfect match.

BARLEYWINE

Old World classic:

J.W. Lee's Harvest Ale

American originals:

AleSmith Old Numbskull
North Coast Old Stock Ale
Sierra Nevada Bigfoot

Strong barleywines with well-balanced sweet caramel and toffee notes, combined with a fruity alcohol profile create an absolutely alchemic pairing with the world's biggest, saltiest blues. The combination is transformative for both beer and cheese, and is reminiscent of the classic companionship between Stilton and vintage port. Fine cheddars and farmhouse cheeses also provide great satisfaction with barleywines.

SOUR ALES

Old World classics:

Belgian Gueuze/Lambic Selected Producers:
    Cantillon, 3 Fonteinen, Giradin, Hanssens
Belgian Flanders Red/Oud Bruin:
    Rodenbach/Grand Cru/Vintage Grand Cru,
    Verhaeghe Duchesse De Bourgogne,
    Liefmans Goudenband

American originals:

Russian River Temptation, Sanctification,
    Supplication, Consecration
Lost Abbey Red Poppy, Framboise de Amorosa,
    Cuvée de Tomme, Duck Duck Gooze
Cascade Kriek
Captain Lawrence Rosso e Marrone

What pleasurable pairings these beers provide! Looking forward to drinking fine sour ales is only enhanced by adding artisanal cheeses to the occasion. If that weren't exciting enough, they're ideal partners to meaty, satisfying, washed-rind cheeses. These beers are incredibly cheese friendly, capable of handling almost anything you put with them.

Hard cheeses do less well than soft-ripened ones, and very young, mild examples of those could potentially be overwhelmed by stronger sour beers.

The owners of Russian River Brewing insist that their Temptation sour ale is the perfect pairing for Humboldt fog. I agree that it is a wonderful matchup, and exploring similar types of pairings will be very rewarding.

Sour beers with fruit add even more dimension, and can be very gentle to milder cheeses. One of my highest pleasures is Lost Abbey Red Poppy and Cowgirl Creamery Red Hawk. The names even work out.

Belgian Flanders reds are amongst the most complex, wine-like beers. Try them alongside rich, buttery triple crèmes and others like them.

Belgian Strong Ales

Old World classics:

> Trappist Breweries: Achel, Chimay, Koningshoeven, Orval, Rochefort, Westmalle, Westvleteren
> St. Bernardus
> Duvel

American originals:

> AleSmith Grand Cru
> Avery Salvation
> Jolly Pumpkin Oro de Calabaza

This is a very broad category, perhaps too broad. But many Belgian strong ales do share some important similarities: dark, fruity fermentation profiles with strong esters and phenols; significant alcohol profiles; and sturdy, malty backbones. Certain washed-rind cheeses make great partners with them. It should be telling that the monks at the Chimay abbey produce several washed-rind cheeses. Simpler rich semi-firm cheeses work well, as do bolder alpine examples. Some sheep's milk cheeses can be challenging for certain Belgian beers.

Saison/Bière du Garde

Old World classics:

Saison Dupont Vieille Provision
Fantôme Saison
Castelain Blond Bière

American originals:

Lost Abbey Carnevale
Upright Flora Rustica

These are finessed, graceful beers that complement a very wide variety of both simple and complex cheeses. These beers combine mild, yet intricate, nuanced fermentation profiles with soft spiciness and fruitiness. Often some sweet alcohol shows up in the body as well. These are a safe bet for a lot of otherwise difficult to pair cheeses. Try them with everything from washed-rind to soft-ripened to semi-firms. However, do exercise caution with certain very strong blues.

Scotch Ales

Old World classics:

Traquair House Ale

American originals:

AleSmith Wee Heavy
Founder's Backwoods Bastard

Scotch ales have hearty malt profiles without a lot of hops. Not as roasted as stouts, and not as sweet and darkly fruity as barleywines, they can possess strong dark caramel notes and often a bit of smokiness. They also have quite subdued fermentation notes. Pair these medium-high alcohol ales with hard or semi-firm, nutty cheeses with their own strong characteristics.

Specialty Beers

New Glarus Belgian Red
Anchor Our Special Ale
Alaskan Smoked Porter

Here I'll mention a few representative beers from uncommon styles that all can be amazing alongside the right cheeses.

New Glarus Belgian Red is a celebration of sweet red cherries that is amazing with sharp Cheddars, soft-ripened, and goat's milk cheeses (think Bucheron).

Anchor Our Special Ale is an excellent spiced winter seasonal that is simply delicious with all the cheeses that seem to show up in shops around the holidays.

Alaskan Smoked Porter is a New World interpretation of the classic rauchbiers from Bamberg, Germany (see also: Aecht Schlenkerla). Give this style a chance, even if you hate it at first. Some simple, hearty cheeses can really go nicely with the campfire-like maltiness of this distinctive style.

TRAPPIST BEERS AND CHEESES

The tradition of monastic brewing and cheesemaking stretches back for hundreds of years. Of the sixteen Trappist monasteries, seven produce beer, and three of those also produce cheese. The "Authentic Trappist Product" label is carefully regulated since it must represent the highest levels of quality, devotion, and integrity. Authentic Trappist products must be produced under the strict standards of the International Trappist Association, which dictates that the monks produce the products themselves, or supervise their production, which must take place in or near the monastery, and that the proceeds support the order, its charities, and the community.

All of the beer-and-cheese-producing Trappist monasteries are located in Belgium. The Scourmont-Lez-Chimay monastery produces the famous Chimay line of three beers and five cheeses. The Orval monastery produces a unique ale and a cheese that is related to the original Port du Salut abbey cheese. And the monastery of Westmalle produces two beers and a raw milk cheese, available locally only, made exclusively by the monks with milk from their own herd of cows. Certainly any of these beers and cheeses together would make pairings worthy of deep contemplation.

It is thought that the careful, deliberate work of brewing, cheesemaking, and the other day-to-day tasks of life in the monastery, conducted in as near silence as possible, forms a sort of simple, silent prayer for the monks.

4 The Philosophy of Craft Brewing

ALESMITH BREWING COMPANY AND THE CRAFT BREWING COMMUNITY

Commercial craft brewing is a phenomenon unto itself, and to understand what drives the current explosion in American craft brewing requires a close-up view of the passions and values that drive an exemplary brewery. The one I know best is Ale-Smith Brewery in San Diego and I can tell its story in revealing detail, but if circumstances were different I could accomplish my aims in this chapter with the biography of a number of other fine craft breweries in my home region or another part of the country. In chapter five, in fact, I profile sixteen of the finest craft breweries and brewmasters across the continental United States. But here I'll use the example of Ale-Smith to get at the essence of the craft brewing ethos and the devoted following it has inspired.

Malted grains, such as this barley, are roasted to different degrees to provide a range of flavors and aromas in beer.

I first learned about AleSmith brewing company in early 2005 while doing Internet research for my newfound obsession with trying as many different interesting craft beers as possible. I had recently discovered double IPAs, whose lush aromatics, refreshing bitterness, and alcohol bite had me enthralled. Also on my list were Russian imperial stouts and barleywines. My palate was reeling from the intense flavors and deep complexity that these big beer styles offer—something I have yet to tire of. AleSmith was consistently coming up as I browsed online forums and lists of top-rated beers. I took notice.

Having befriended a few of the bartenders at the one local craft beer bar in Las Vegas, my residence at the time, I was allowed to explore the extensive beer cooler in the back. There, on the top shelf, was a Champagne-style bottle topped with crinkled silver foil, and a blue anvil printed on the bottle along with the words "Old Numbskull Barleywine." I knew that AleSmith's beers were not distributed in Nevada, and that this beer, like others in the cooler, had been brought in from California in the trunk of the bar owner's station wagon, which helped me justify the 300 percent markup I paid for it. Beyond a doubt, the inflated price was worth it. The quality and craftsmanship evident in this beer spoke to my culinary sensibilities. Here was a tightly woven, complex beer at once both incredibly easy to drink and rewarding to the most intense evaluation. I knew that the people who had made this beer had sophisticated tastes and a great understanding of the brewing art. I needed to meet them.

I've since had the opportunity to work in the craft beer community and get to know the individuals who make many of the beers I've come to enjoy so much. They all have remarkable stories of creativity, innovation, challenges, and setbacks. Though they share much in common, each is unique in its approach to this craft. Since my first taste of Old Numbskull, through my deep exploration of AleSmith's beers in pairing dinners, to currently assisting as AleSmith's culinary director, I've developed a respect and understanding for this particular brewery and how it

Hops provide bitterness, flavor, and aromatics in beer and also serve as a natural preservative. Pelletized hops such as this retain their freshness longer and are easier to brew with than whole-flower hops.

The grains are steeped in precisely temperature-controlled water to extract particular flavors and fermentable sugars from them in a process called "mashing." Water is then used to rinse any remaining sugar from the grain during the "sparge." The resulting sweet liquid is called "wort."

Clear wort is transferred from the mash tun to the boil kettle. The clarity of the liquid can be viewed through special windows built into the transfer tubing.

Boiling the wort serves a number of purposes including sterilizing it, removing certain proteins and polyphenols (which can lead to haziness and astringency in the beer), creating desirable caramelized flavors in the beer (known as kettle caramelization), and concentrating the fermentable sugars. The concentration of sugars in the wort is known as its "original gravity," which will indicate the final strength of the beer after fermentation.

applies its craft. It is certainly not among the largest or wealthiest craft breweries, but a close look at AleSmith Brewing Company and its owner and brewmaster Peter Zien does provide key insights into a brewing philosophy and the development of a business which, together, have been very successful at producing exceptional beers of a singular quality.

The AleSmith Brewing Company in some ways is not a typical brewery. It has only twelve employees and produces ten year-round beers, four seasonal beers, one annual anniversary beer, and occasional releases of barrel-aged editions of several of its beers. It was awarded the "Small Brewing Company and Small Brewing Company Brewer of the Year" titles at the 2008 GABF and has won numerous medals at that festival, the World Beer Cup, and many other local and regional festivals. And, at sixteen years of age, it is already an older craft brewery in this ever-expanding field. AleSmith's distinction continues online: as of 2012, three of its beers reside in the top-ten highest-rated beers in the world, as tallied by the influential craft beer website RateBeer.com, and thirteen AleSmith beers rank among the top-ten beers on their respective style-specific lists on the same website, with three at the very top of their categories. Beyond this list of statistics, AleSmith's beers serve as benchmarks for many of the most popular craft beer styles brewed in America.

The craft of brewing benefits from being able to turn relatively low cost ingredients into a highly valued, artisanal product. This fact is of the utmost importance to the success of craft breweries. It very closely and directly links the creative force of a brewery's philosophy to its revenue. Yes, very high quality beers are more expensive to produce than lower quality ones. But, the translation of these production costs into final retail costs is disproportionately lower than the increase in quality they produce. In short, an experienced, talented brewmaster applying an uncompromising approach to quality can produce beers of distinction that will be very competitive across all sectors of the industry. In a large field of similar products, in which a popular style of craft beer is made by hundreds of different craft breweries, a beer's distinctive characteristics produced through the unique brewing methods developed by a brewery, are key to its success.

Brewing any type of beer, however, is very equipment-dependant and labor-intensive. Additionally, producing truly great beers requires a wealth of technical knowledge and experience plus artistic inspiration and creativity. In contrast with winemaking, which is primarily an agricultural endeavor, brewing is the processing of ingredients to produce beer. Therefore, great breweries can exist in many more places than vineyards, and great beers of any style can be produced anywhere. The vital factor in brewing the most distinguished beers, therefore, is the recipe. And the best recipes are developed by individuals who apply their passion and creativity to making beers that they want to drink themselves, and are reflective of the aspects of brewing that interest them the most.

Distinctive, high-quality recipes and the brewing values that drive them often are first developed through homebrewing. This is how most craft brewers I've spoken with, and every member of the AleSmith staff, became interested in the field of professional brewing. For an initial investment of under $200, and some practice, one can produce reasonable approximations of professionally brewed craft beers, or create new styles of one's own design. This makes brewing more immediately accessible to creativity than other equipment- and technique heavy occupations.

Although I have never met a craft brewer who told me that he or she had gotten into brewing for the money, bringing a quality- and creativity-driven brewing philosophy to life—and sustaining it—requires a viable business plan and financial acumen. But these factors remain subservient to the overriding creative philosophies of the best craft breweries,

Peter Zien adds hops to the boiling wort. Boiling the hops allows their bitter oils to be isomerized into the wort. The longer hops are boiled the more bitterness is extracted but fewer flavors and aromas are preserved. Therefore special hops for bittering and aroma are added at different stages of the boil.

Brewer Anthony Chen fills a special device called a "hop back" with whole-flower hops. After the boil is complete the wort will travel through these hop flowers and become infused with a powerful fresh hop aroma.

After all of the fermentable sugars have been extracted from the malt the spent grain must be removed from the mash tun by hand.

Senior brewer Bill Batten takes his turn shoveling out the spent grain, which will be taken away by a local farmer and used for animal feed.

including AleSmith, where money is regarded more as an inconvenient necessity than a motivating force. Though such an attitude may not result in the highest profitability, it has, fortunately for craft beer drinkers, kept AleSmith viable over its lifespan, financing two significant expansions, and delivering it into debt-free profitability for the last three years. AleSmith's financial achievements, from a purely business perspective, have not produced the large profits one might expect, given its collection of accolades. But soldiering through thirteen years of financial uncertainty, with the goal of making the very highest quality beer possible, takes grit and verve not often possessed by conventional business minds.

Americans are reacting positively to this dedicated and persevering application of the creative drive, as is evidenced by the strength and number of craft breweries that are in operation in this country. Additionally, this robust brewing climate has risen without craft breweries making large investments in marketing, which sets them quite apart from their distant, macrobrewing cousins. Indeed many craft breweries do not spend anything on advertising at all, and instead rely solely on the fervent support of motivated enthusiasts and loyal local markets, earned purely by the quality of their products. This is the case for AleSmith as well, which doesn't even employ sales representatives, yet still manages to sell all of the beer it brews each month.

The good will earned by many craft breweries' socially conscious and sustainable business practices also contributes to their growing market segment. Sustainability is playing a larger role in the operations of many different types of businesses today, but this fact is especially prominent among many of the nation's craft breweries. Numerous craft beer festivals raise money for charities while giving fans an opportunity to come together and experience the offerings of many different breweries not normally available to them. Environmentally conscious business practices appear as a key issue for many craft breweries today—especially when concerning water resources, which are obviously of special significance to breweries. And it is also very common for breweries, including AleSmith, to have arrangements with local farmers to take away their spent grain for use as animal feed.

While not all craft breweries are as consistent as the group's best citizens, none are exclusively focused on growing their business through changing package designs, advertising campaigns, and contributing to a legal maze to keep competitors' beers away from consumers, as the macrobrewing establishment is doing. Quite simply, craft beer is about producing a high-quality product, introducing consumers to its joys, and supporting local communities while doing so. What do we as loyal consumers get from this? We get a celebration of the diversity of beer styles, friendly competition—as well as collaboration—and access to an amazing, artisanal product that can enhance our appreciation of cuisine and broaden our conception of beer. What once was thought of only as a bland, low-brow beverage, can now be recognized as something that offers a great variety of intense experiences.

This is why I felt such exuberance when I first breathed in the incredibly fresh, luscious hop aroma of AleSmith IPA, and tasted its precisely calculated, dry malt body and crisp bitterness. This encounter occurred at Lucky Baldwin's—a renowned craft beer pub in Pasadena, California—during their annual IPA Festival, on June 19, 2005. Sitting outside in the beer garden I sampled it, along with many other of the over sixty different IPAs on draught, and began to recalibrate my palate to comprehend the unbelievably vibrant hops characteristics that AleSmith IPA and many of the others possess. My original tasting notes for the AleSmith brew read: "Straight up hop aroma, good citrus notes in the flavor with some malt, easygoing body with a nice finish—a paragon of IPAs—well-balanced, amazing hops characteristics, everything an IPA should be." It was an experience I will never forget.

⊰◈⊱

The seeds for Peter Zien's passion for craft beer were planted at an early age. Frequent family trips to Europe, beginning in

The wort is chilled after going through the hop back and is transferred to a fermenter where the yeast will be added, or "pitched."

his teens, shaped his philosophy of life and the development of a worldly perspective on food and drink. The Old World's classic brewing traditions were especially influential for him, and Peter fostered a deep respect for the beers of England, Belgium, and Germany, among others, as he experienced them in context. Back home, well before he turned twenty-one, he worked to acquire a collection of international beers through a variety of means. This included support from his mother, who preferred to have him and his friends at home savoring a German export than secretly bingeing at a party somewhere. Eventually the bottles of over three hundred beers lined the walls of his La Jolla bedroom.

Throughout his life Peter traveled with his father each summer on fishing trips to Sioux Narrows in Ontario, Canada. During the long journey from California they would often stop at breweries along the way, including the August Schell Brewing Company in New Ulm, Minnesota. Touring this historic brewery's beautiful gardens and experiencing the sights, smells, and sounds of the brewhouse firsthand was particularly inspirational for Peter. These memories remained catalogued away as he went on to graduate from law school, dabbled in accounting and real estate, and worked together with his father at their business helping people finance home repairs. Then, in 1994, at thirty-two, Peter bought a home-

As the yeast ferments the sugar in the wort alcohol and carbon dioxide are produced. During the most active stages of fermentation excess gas vents out of the fermenter along with yeast particles, known as the "blow-off," through a container of water. When fermentation is complete the strength of the beer is measured in terms of its "final gravity."

brewing kit as a birthday present to himself. As the smell of steeping malt and boiling hops from that first batch of beer, an IPA, filled his kitchen, he knew instantly that he was hooked; the blend of art and science that brewing offered appealed both to Peter's creative and analytical sides.

In 1996 Peter Zien joined San Diego's preeminent homebrewing club, QUAFF (QUality Ale and Fermentation Fraternity), primarily to take advantage of the BJCP (Beer Judge Certification Program) seminar they were offering. This seminar is an intensive course designed to train beer tasting and evaluation skills for use in brewing competitions. Over the next several years, with barely three years of brewing experience, Peter took home over 300 medals at various homebrewing competitions. As he continued to amass awards and judged more and more competitions, he worked his way up to become QUAFF's vice president in 1998, alongside its president Tod Fitzsimmons, who would come to play a key role in Peter's brewing future. In 1999 Peter became president of QUAFF. He led the organization to a state championship in 2000, followed by a national championship in 2001. In 2005 he became the first Grand Master level beer judge in Southern California, the highest level of recognition the BJCP organization awards.

Head brewer Ryan Crisp fills kegs with AleSmith beer.

Shortly before Peter and QUAFF won their state title, Peter's father passed away at the age of eighty-eight. The thought of running the finance business without his father seemed impossible to Peter—he wanted to do something he could pour his creative passions into, something at which he could truly excel. This would not be accounting, it would not be a legal practice, and nothing else piqued his creative and competitive sides like brewing. And at just this moment he learned that Skip Virgilio intended to sell his small brewery, AleSmith.

Skip had founded AleSmith Brewing Company in 1995 with business partner Ted Newcomb. Within a few years Ted was out of the company, but Skip continued on with marginal success through contract brewing and with AleSmith Golden Anvil, a middle-of-the-road American golden ale. Skip slogged on, keeping afloat for seven years until he made the decision to sell the brewery in 2002.

Bolstered by his successes in homebrewing and QUAFF, and fueled by a mixture of what he admits to have been hubris and naïveté, Peter decided to save AleSmith, make it his own, and brew the best beers in the world. In a fortunate coincidence, the asking price for AleSmith was almost exactly the amount Peter had received from the sale of the finance business. On the condition that

Tod, who was AleSmith's lead brewer of at the time, would remain on staff, Peter purchased AleSmith Brewing Company on July 16, 2002.

The earliest days were grueling. With fewer than 40 cases of beer remaining to sell, the tanks dry, and no grain to brew with, Peter invested heavily in the company to once again begin producing beer. Bill Batten, then a volunteer at the brewery, was officially hired on, and remains with AleSmith today as a vital part of the team. Rather than double-down on the brewery's contract accounts and its Golden Anvil Ale—AleSmith's main sources of revenue at the time—Peter ceased existing production. The future of AleSmith would depend upon the passions of the brewers. Recipes were re-worked, the portfolio was expanded, and the packaging was standardized. Slowly the team—Peter, Tod, and Bill—began to build the brewery that exists today.

Such trials would continue as AleSmith slowly established itself as the premium craft brewery in San Diego, a region already known for its quality beer. AleSmith's lineup of high-alcohol beers, sold in 750-mL foil-topped bottles for about ten dollars each, really stood out amidst the lower-priced six-packs and 22-ounce brown bombers other breweries were producing. Initially it was far from clear that having the upper end of the market to themselves was an

Bottles are automatically rinsed, sanitized, filled, and capped.

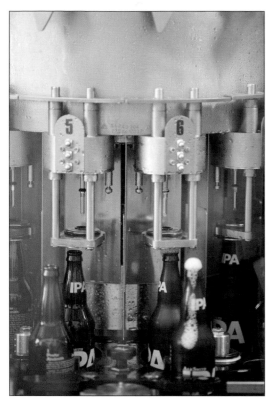

AleSmith's new state-of-the-art Prospero bottling line ensures that a minimal amount of oxygen remains in each bottle. Oxygen degrades a beer's aroma and can cause it to age prematurely.

advantage. Would the customer take a chance on the fancier, higher-priced bottle of beer beside the other familiar, low-risk offerings? They would. As Ale-Smith's reputation for quality and value increased, along with their production, the rest of the field began expanding their high-end offerings as well.

This is not the customary way a craft brewery gets off the ground, if any generalizations can be made on this topic. While founding a brewery is never easy, it has been done in easier ways than this. But despite these challenges, the goal of producing the very best beer these brewers know how to make has been achieved, and the fans have been gathering round to support them. AleSmith did benefit from being in a brewery-friendly locality—if also quite a competitive one. They did not, for instance, need to fight to change legislation forbidding its existence, as Delaware's Dogfish Head did. They did not need to train a distributor that craft beers need to be sold differently than macrobrewed beers; Stone Brewing Company of nearby Escondido has a distribution arm that specializes in regional craft beers. What is customary, and a fact that AleSmith shares with many excellent craft breweries, is their unwave
ring faith that their community will support their efforts to provide unique, high quality beers that are the direct product of an unbridled pursuit of creativity in their field.

CRAFT BREWING METHODS —THE STORIES OF TWO BEERS

Anvil ESB was the first beer brewed by AleSmith and became its flagship offering early on, though it has since been eclipsed by four of their other beers. It is modeled after the traditional English extra special bitter, a style not often brewed by American craft brewers, but Anvil ESB expresses distinctly American sensibilities. Historically brewed with stronger malt and noble hop characteristics than English pale ales, AleSmith's American version did replicate those aspects but with a bolder use of English aroma hops and a more forward caramel malt profile. The original recipe brewed before Peter's tenure was significantly modified during the brewery's transitional process, like all of the beers in AleSmith's current portfolio. But the new recipe for Anvil was locked-in early on as Peter saw his aspirations for the beer clearly reflected in the first few test batches. The Anvil that exists now resides between some commonly recognized style guidelines, and crosses aspects of a classical English ESB with influences from the modern American craft brewing climate. It is also the AleSmith beer Peter remains most fond of today.

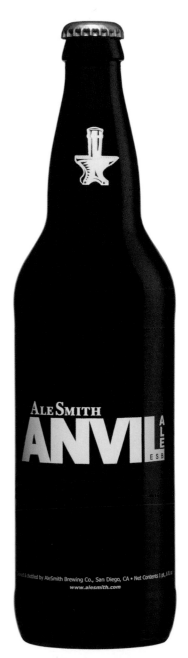

AleSmith Anvil ESB

San Diego brewers, and AleSmith in particular, are often thought of as only being known for their high-gravity and highly hopped beers. In contrast, Anvil is an unassuming beer. It's not a hop bomb or a malt monster; it's a nuanced session beer with a complex recipe that expresses the brewer's craft delicately but acutely. Probably because of these characteristics, Anvil hasn't won any major brewing awards. Nonetheless it offers both extreme drinkability and intellectual stimulation when thoughtfully contemplated. It is an example of careful recipe calculation, and the result of a concerted dedication to a flavor ideal. "We don't brew it for glory, and we don't brew it for money," says Peter.

The Anvil ESB that is brewed today is an example of a beer designed in reverse. Using the original concept of Anvil brewed by AleSmith's former owners as a template, Peter sought to adapt it to his tastes and brewing sensibilities without a jarring change to a completely new formula. Peter's idea for Anvil ESB began with the concept of a clean, malty beer with an assertive, aromatic hoppiness—giving it a sense of place in the San Diego brewing scene, but at the same time still retaining its identity as an adaption of a classic British-styled ale made with English ingredients. Many ingredients and techniques were modified to shape the beer to his vision. Adjustments were made to produce more nuances and complexity in an otherwise straightforward beer style. A higher percentage of specialty malts was incorporated into the recipe—much higher than conventionally used in commercially brewed beers. An extended boil time is employed to encourage more kettle caramelization, which creates a richer malt sweetness and gives the beer its dark, coppery amber hue. A new yeast strain was used, along with a unique, counter-intuitive fermentation temperature manipulation system—in addition to much higher than normal pitching rate (the amount of yeast used to make the beer)—to provide a cleaner, more precise fermentation profile. All of these mindful tweaks and careful coddling resemble the methods employed by many homebrewers as they shepherd their batches of beer from initial idea through finished product. This attention to minute details is not unique to Anvil ESB, but is applied to every batch of AleSmith beer. Such beers are an extension of an artist's sensibility, and a chemist's or engineer's technical prowess.

In this way AleSmith is very much a home brewery on steroids. Each complex, ingredient-driven recipe calls for only the highest quality components, with no consideration of cost—the way most homebrew recipes are formulated. A laborious trial and error process is used at the five-gallon batch level to formulate recipes for production beers. Extended boils for big beers are employed to create more malt richness—a homebrewing-inspired process. A "hop back" filled with whole-flower hops, a device frequently employed in homebrewing but seldom seen in a commercial brewery, is used to introduce fresh and vibrant, albeit expensive, complex hop aromas to almost every AleSmith beer as it travels to the heat exchanger to be cooled before fermentation. Finally, the sensory evaluation skills honed in the homebrew judging circuit are constantly employed to closely evaluate each batch of beer. This is done to maintain quality control and determine if any additional adjustments to the recipes or procedures are necessary.

All of these factors combined constitute the opposite of an industrial approach to brewing beer. At AleSmith there is no automation. No efficiencies are implemented that might alter the final quality of the product, and the result is labor-intensive brewing practices. Every aspect of the brewing process is carefully attended to with years of hands-on experience guiding a watchful eye as the brewer decides when each step is complete. Peter explains that having a physical connection to the brewing process—manually stirring the mash as the grain is added and slowly introducing the hops by hand, for instance—provides essential feedback during brewing and creates a deeper connection between the brewer and his or her art. Rigorously applying the homebrewing mentality proved essential to the success of AleSmith. The homebrewing community has always been free to experiment with beer styles, ingredients, and methods in ways that conventional breweries could not. Since AleSmith's team consists entirely of homebrewers, this mentality carried directly over into the ethos of the brewery. They were beholden to no one, and were exclusively guided by their integrity and by their creative vision of craft beer's future. This is the ethos of American craft beer.

⬥

Beginning in 2005, to commemorate AleSmith's tenth year of operation, the brewery inaugurated a series of anniversary ales called "Decadence." The recipe changes every year, and it's always fun for the brewers to decide what style to brew for each edition. It offers an opportunity to explore pet projects or experiment with new recipes and techniques. But the recipe for the first batch of Decadence needed no deliberation. Rather than modifying an

AleSmith Decadence
Anniversary Ale

existing production beer, Peter decided that they would brew a beer that he had designed from the ground up—a classic English-style old ale derived from his most highly decorated homebrewing recipe. It would represent the purest expression of homebrewing creativity and underscore AleSmith' brewing philosophy. The old ale is a traditional British style. It is a high-gravity beer, and its big, bold flavors would age very well in AleSmith's signature foil-capped Champagne-style bottles. The 2005 Decadence, in contrast with Anvil ESB, would go on to become one of AleSmith's most decorated beers.

This was a very personal beer for Peter. He won his first home-brew medal with an early version of his old ale. A subsequent version, which later would become the first AleSmith Decadence, advanced to the American Homebrewers Association's National Homebrew Competition, the largest and most prestigious home-brewing competition in the world. After taking first place in the Regional Competition, it also became the first homebrew of Peter's to advance to the second round of the National Competition, winning against 20 other finalists in that style category from around the country. (Some of Peter's other beers would go even further in AHA National Competitions.)

This is very high praise for an oft-misunderstood style. Frequently conflated with English-style barleywines, the old ale style is similar, but with some important distinguishing characteristics. Its distinctive malt profile tends towards a sweet, balanced dark toffee—with slightly less alcohol than a barleywine—and often expresses some aged oxidative characteristics as well. In Peter's words, "It takes some finesse to distinguish it in a competition."

In designing his original homebrew batches Peter used only the very finest traditional English ingredients, some of which were so specialized that the companies that produced them no longer exist today. Maris Otter, the gold standard of British malts, was used as the base malt. Crystal malts from the most prestigious maltsters were used to layer in caramel, toffee, and dark fruit flavors. Peter favors the 40–60 degrees Lovibond range of crystal malts (Lovibond being a measure of the color the product contributes to the beer).

Belgian aromatic specialty malts were employed to add toasted barley aromas. Three specialty sugars (a rare demerara sugar, and both Lyle's golden syrup and treacle) added color, darkly sweet flavors, and built up the alcohol body. All of this was constructed upon a water profile specifically designed to match that of the English brewing city of Yorkshire. More kettle caramelization deepened the flavor, and traditional noble hops—Ultra, Bramling Cross, and First Gold—provided a subtly herbaceous, spicy bitterness to balance out the robust malt sweetness. Lastly, a British ale yeast strain added the classic earthy, autumn fruit notes, with an almost wood-aged fermentation characteristic, to the finished beer.

Such is the detailed attention to style, ingredients, and technique characteristic of the finest American craft brewers.

Adapting this recipe for full-scale production created many challenges. Most beer recipes cannot simply be scaled up to make much larger batches. The cost of using such specialized ingredients for a large batch could prove cost prohibitive for some. Each brewing system contributes unique characteristics during the brewing process as well. But these issues were handled with aplomb; new ra-

Certain batches are aged in used bourbon barrels to infuse the beer with rich, complex flavors including caramel, toffee, vanilla, and oak.

The filled barrels age for at least one year. During this time some exposure to oxygen through the wood creates desirable oxidized characteristics in the beer.

The time and attention AleSmith pays to their beers has earned them numerous awards including medals from the Great American Beer Festival.

tios, methods, and adjustments to the recipe were carefully incorporated, and the first batch of AleSmith Decadence went on to win gold medals at both the GABF and the World Beer Cup in 2008, validating AleSmith Brewing Company and vindicating Peter's brewing philosophy.

The story of 2005 Decadence does represent an ideal that many craft brewers strive for, and achieve. The GABF awards new honors each year to many different exceptional beers and breweries, recognizing new contributions to American craft beer. The fact that an inspired homebrew recipe can move up into full production, reach a wider audience, and win recognition for its quality represents the ideal scenario for creating a handcrafted, artisanal product that can enrich people's lives. The passions expressed through such efforts cut to the core of what is fueling the artisanal food and craft beer movements—you can truly taste the dedication in these products, and the creative communities surrounding them represent positive, vibrant groups of people taking pride in what they do and offering their generous hospitality to all who wish to partake. Participating in this warm and welcoming scene offers a rewarding sense of kinship among fellow enthusiasts, and encourages constant mind- and palate-expanding explorations of the latest developments and achievements. The craft beer community is intoxicating in more ways than one, offering both good drink and good cheer.

THE BREWPUB RESTAURANT—ON THE FRONTLINES OF CRAFT BEER
STONE WORLD BISTRO AND GARDENS AND PIZZA PORT RESTAURANTS

The brewpub has become quite common as a successful model for running a restaurant. Fresh beer, casual food, and a convivial atmosphere are certainly attractive characteristics. Brewing beer on-site, usually in relatively small batches, provides very fresh beer to guests while allowing an establishment the freedom to experiment with lots of new beers and to create a direct link to the food being served. Beer and food pairings can be tailor-made and promoted to restaurant guests. Enticed by a fun dining atmosphere, the brewpub very often might be many people's first encounter with truly local craft beer. It also provides an opportunity to expressly consider the notion of pairing beer and food together.

The Stone Brewing World Bistro and Gardens, attached to their brewing headquarters in Escondido, California, is much more than a brewpub, and takes the concept leaps further. Only local, seasonal, and organic produce is used. All meats served are naturally raised. Every ingredient is vetted for sustainability and artisanal quality, with no artificial components (high fructose corn syrup is anathema). This is no easy feat for a busy 12,000-square foot restaurant. Sourcing the sheer volumes of such specialty ingredients necessary to operate the restaurant proved challenging in the beginning. So did the requisite high prices, as well as (to some patrons) Stone's trademark high-minded attitude. But I can't help but admire the gusto

of their full-blown dedication to the "Slow Food" culinary ideal. Such a whole-hearted commitment to educating people on the virtues and importance of this type of eating by such an influential player in the craft beer scene is an indication of the significant role craft beer can play in shaping the culinary climate in America.

Stone recently purchased a struggling local organic farm to help supply the restaurant with produce. They're also planning to construct and operate a boutique hotel adjacent to their brewery in a move to model sustainable practices to the business community beyond beer and food. In addition to all this, the gardens are simply one of the most beautiful and serene places anywhere to enjoy a pint of local beer.

Another side of the brewpub phenomenon is embodied by the local San Diego County chain of Pizza Port restaurants. After opening in 1987, the original Solana Beach location began serving its own craft beer in 1992 along with its straightforward menu of pizzas, salads, and wings. Three more locations have followed in Carlsbad, San Clemente, and Ocean Beach in San Diego. The atmosphere inside is the epitome of casual and family friendly with their signature blocky picnic table seating and close proximity to the beach. You're just as likely to encounter a Little League team there as you are a seasoned beer geek. Styles brewed range from some of the biggest double IPAs made anywhere to milk stouts and English-style brown ales. Each location, under the direction of its own head brewer, brews beers that have become iconic examples of American craft beer and have helped to shape the vibrant Southern California beer scene. Collectively, Pizza Port's beers are a powerful force at the GABF, winning multiple medals each year, with Carlsbad earning the prestigious Large Brewpub of the Year for an unprecedented three straight years—2009, 2010, and 2011—and each other location having won the Small Brewpub of the Year award at least once. This is world-class beer at the neighborhood level.

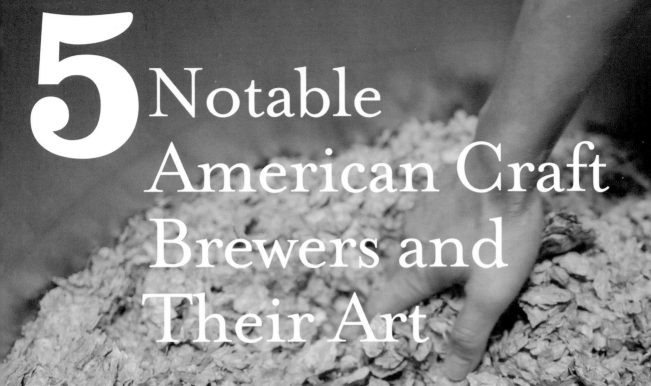

5 Notable American Craft Brewers and Their Art

THE 10 MOST IMPORTANT AMERICAN CRAFT BEERS

These are my ten most *important* beers made in America, not necessarily the ten *best*. I have chosen them because of their significance in the American craft beer movement. Each has played a significant role in the development of today's craft beer environment and represents an important facet of this diverse and ever-expanding field of passionate artisans and dedicated drinkers.

1. SAMUEL ADAMS BOSTON LAGER—THE BOSTON BEER COMPANY

Sam Adams is probably the most widely available craft beer in America and its brewer, The Boston Beer Company, is the nation's largest craft brewery. In fact, The Brewers Association recently revised its definition of a craft brewery in part to accommodate their projected growth. Created in 1984 at the very beginning of the craft beer era, it has become available in almost every gas station and grocery store in the country, and it's still good. It has distinctive malt, hops, and fermentation flavor characteristics. Although it is a lager, the unique yeast strain used is fermented at a higher temperature than usual, which creates ale-like flavors. It has often been the saving grace of craft beer fans who find themselves drinking in an anonymous sports bar with nothing but macrobrews and . . . Sam.

2. ANCHOR STEAM BEER—ANCHOR BREWING CO.

Anchor Brewing is often credited with reviving the craft beer industry in America. Fritz Maytag purchased the company in 1965, saving it from closure, and continued to brew its traditional signature Steam beer. This American classic, which has been around since 1896, represents the commitment to quality that has led the craft beer movement into its current success. The brewery has continued to be an innovator and has added many more great beers to its repertoire over the years and has added an artisanal distilling arm to the company as well.

3. SIERRA NEVADA PALE ALE—SIERRA NEVADA BREWING CO.

Their flagship beer, the widely available Pale Ale, is many Americans' first introduction to American hop flavors and aromas in beer. The Cascade variety of hops, the darling of American craft brewers, is celebrated in this beer, which showcases its characteristic orange zest and pine needle qualities. Sierra Nevada in many ways has defined America's expectations of the pale ale style. It continues to be the go-to craft beer for many enthusiasts around the country.

4. ARROGANT BASTARD ALE—STONE BREWING CO.

Hitting the Southern California beer scene in a huge way in 1996, Stone Brewing Company has done much to spread awareness of the craft beer movement's goals. Its in-your-face, "You're not worthy" marketing campaign issues a challenge to would-be drinkers: "You probably won't like it." Arrogant Bastard Ale, a cross of several American-born styles, has served as an entry point for many to the world of craft beer and has successfully converted them to its cause. Stone has also constructed a cathedral to local food and craft beer at their headquarters with the Stone World Bistro and Beer Garden, where everyone leaves at least a little bit more educated. They also faithfully distribute the beers of many other craft breweries to local markets.

5. ALESMITH IPA—ALESMITH BREWING CO.

The American IPA style is the golden child for an enormous number of craft beer enthusiasts. The style expresses a distinct sense of place through its use of domestic hop varieties and delivers a bright, crisp, intense drinking experience that can convert nearly anyone into a "hophead." San Diego is arguably the Mecca of IPAs, and is famous for them. Nearly every brewery produces one or more example, and it is always one of the most competitive categories in beer competitions (it was the largest category in each of the last eight GABFs). The AleSmith IPA is the pinnacle of the style, and is ranked as the world's top IPA on RateBeer.com. This brewery practices a no-compromises approach to quality. Hundreds of dollars worth of hops are added to each batch at the end of the boil and in a special "hop back" to infuse the beer with its lush, tropical fruit aromas. These techniques add no additional bitterness to the beer, which is usually the standard by which breweries tout the extremity of their IPAs. Incredibly balanced, complex, and flavorful, this is *the* American IPA.

6. PLINY THE ELDER—RUSSIAN RIVER BREWING CO.

American brewers are known for pushing styles to the extreme. The double IPA style typifies this, and is purely American. Vinnie Cilurzo is often credited with producing the first commercial example of the style at Blind Pig Brewing in 1994. Today, his Pliny the Elder double IPA from Russian River Brewing Company is viewed by many hard-core hopheads as the benchmark of the style. It represents a masterful balance between extreme hop aroma, flavor, and bitterness, and an astonishingly drinkable, mainly dry, malty 8% ABV. Its painfully limited availability only adds to its cult-like status.

7. PRIMA PILS—VICTORY BREWING CO.

The American pilsner lager has been the anti-beer of the craft beer movement. Few craft brewers even produce lagers because of their increased difficulty and production time. The pilsner lager, hallowed in its native Czech Republic and Germany, gets very little respect from the American macrobreweries that produce millions of gallons of it using adjuncts and do their best to market it as the official beer of America. Enter Prima Pils, the craft beer answer to insipid American light lagers. At the very top of many "Best Pilsners in America" lists, it has genuine flavor, including hops! This is the craft beer that fights directly back at every stereotype of American pilsner lagers.

8. DUCK DUCK GOOZE—THE LOST ABBEY

Barrel aging is the norm in Belgium for the production of many traditional ales such as lambics. These beers utilize naturally occurring yeasts and bacteria in the barrels to produce the complex, funky, and sour beers that, when blended, are known as geuze. American craft brewers have recently begun to delve into this world as well, inspired by such legendary Belgian producers like Cantillon and Drei Fonteinen. Few have done so as vehemently and successfully as The Lost Abbey. Their sour-styled beers are amongst the most coveted bottles in America, and are at the center of an ever-growing sour beer craze. They also represent an amazing adaptation of traditional Belgian methods into the American craft beer environment. Duck Duck Gooze, a pun on the children's playground game, is their interpretation of the geuze style, which is a blend of young and old lambics from multiple batches aged in different barrels. This beer is a testament to the particular balance of highly complex flavors and aromas that a can be achieved through the fine art of blending.

9. UTOPIAS—THE BOSTON BEER COMPANY

In the continuing quest to create "extreme" beers and expand the definition of what beer can be, The Boston Beer Company created Utopias. It is a unique blend of beers that were brewed with maple syrup and then aged in a variety of oaks barrels including bourbon, sherry, brandy, Cognac, and Portuguese moscatel casks. It is not carbonated and is packaged in elaborate decorative copper flasks. The first edition, released in 2002, contained 24% alcohol, making it the strongest beer in the world at the time. New editions are now released every two years and are blended from an extensive library of barrels, some of which still contain beer from the original 1994 batch. I described my first experience with Utopias as "like drinking alcoholic crème brulée from a wooden spoon." It is delicious, highly complex, and unlike any other "beer" ever sold. It is an intellectual after dinner sipper of the highest order. It redefines the boundaries of what beer is—indeed it is unrecognizable as beer—and marks an important moment of innovation for craft beer in America.

10. DARK LORD—THREE FLOYDS BREWING CO.

The Russian imperial stout is consistently the biggest, darkest, thickest, most intense beer style brewed in America, and one of the most lauded. It drives beer geeks crazy. Dark Lord Russian imperial stout is the highest rated beer brewed in America according to RateBeer.com. The single day per year on which it is available for sale to the public is the basis of a festival called Dark Lord Day. In 2010 the event drew an estimated 12,000 attendees to an industrial park in Munster, Indiana. Twenty-two-ounce bottles of the beer were presold over the Internet for the event; the sales website experienced so much traffic that it crashed within seconds. "It's not normal," is the motto of the Three Floyds Brewing Company. Indeed. Many devotees who have waited for hours in line to receive their bottle limit agree that it's mainly about the hype. Yes, the beer has its rabid fans. But, its intense, syrupy sweetness and incredibly dense roasted malt profile makes it drinkable mainly as an intellectual exercise. It is a phenomenon that represents the enormous power that a beer can hold over its worshippers, driving them to huge lengths to get a bottle to brag about in online chat forums or sell for hundreds of dollars on eBay. It is a cautionary tale of hype and hyperbole, and represents yet another extreme in the craft beer phenomenon.

CALIFORNIA

BEAR REPUBLIC BREWING CO.—CLOVERDALE, CA

Richard G. Norgrove, Brewmaster & COO

I visited Bear Republic's new brewery in Cloverdale, California, on a rainy February afternoon to meet with Richard G. Norgrove, the brewmaster and COO. I had arranged the meeting via email with his father, who handles publicity for the brewery. His mother met me inside the front door at reception. I would later meet Tami, Richard's wife, who runs the financial side of the business. Together they are all co-owners of Bear Republic Brewing Company in the heart of Sonoma wine country. I was there to learn about the brewery and make plans for a future beer dinner at my restaurant, and what I found was one of the most hospitable and friendly groups of beer people I would ever meet. I have since tried to keep in touch with Richard and Tami as their business continues to grow. Their dedication to making quality craft beer with a worldly awareness and firm roots in their community serves as an inspirational model of a family-run brewery.

Sonoma County—synonymous with wine—is a world-class wine region whose products have earned acclaim around the globe. It is less known for its equally impressive beers. Though not necessarily as dependant on the particular local climate as Sonoma's vineyards, the beers brewed by Bear Republic certainly have solid foundations in the local community. As fourth generation Sonoma County residents, the Norgroves are steeped in the region's culture. Richard is an avid amateur stock car racer on the local circuit and his enthusiasm for the sport has carried over into the names of several of his beers. He is also a volunteer firefighter and serves the community on several panels and boards. This sense of place informs the brewer just as it does for the winemaker. "I have to know where I've been to know where I'm going," says Richard. "Sonoma County is such an epicurean center—I resisted that notion for a while with our beers and kinda got beat up about the brewery. There are 84 wineries nearby and beer is finally catching up to those folks. We've blended into the community, we provide them with beer, and now they're beginning to understand what they've got."

What Bear Republic offers is a solid lineup of classically styled ales produced with meticulous craftsmanship that are now serving as Sonoma County ambassadors to the larger beverage world. Richard describes his philosophy of brewing in this way: "We brew beers that we like. We research a traditional style and develop it in the 'Bear Republic style,' which is a house style that has naturally evolved around applying our personal preferences to traditional methods." If Bear Republic's house style can be distilled down to its essence, it would have to be described as representing an unflagging attention to detail resulting in highly consistent beers with precisely crafted complexities.

A perfect example of this is demonstrated by Hop Rod Rye. Long before the hybrid style of the black IPA became vogue, this beer offered both a rich maltiness and a big citrusy American hop presence. This beer slips in between standard style designations but demonstrates the most positive aspects of each. Calculated levels of caramel malt, fresh hops, and toasted specialty grains give Hop Rod Rye the vibrant pungency of an IPA and the structured malt backbone of an imperial red along with the added interest of spicy rye. As unconventional as this particular combination of characteristics may be, according to style guidelines, the final impression of Hop Rod Rye is one of a purely classic balance of flavors and textures.

Another combination of traditional styles can be found in Red Rocket Ale. Richard has a special fondness for this beer and had originally intended for this robust amber ale to become the beer Bear Republic would be best known for—"our beer," as he puts it. It was developed during his homebrewing years as malt-driven Scottish-style ale with a West Coast influence in the form of a significant American hops profile. Red Rocket bears the peaceful motto "make beer, not bombs" and reconciles in one beer all of the characteristics Richard loves across several styles. It is an excellent beer, is very food friendly, and has won two GABF silver medals, but its sales have been eclipsed by the ascendency of the IPA as the dominant craft beer style. Bear Republic's signature IPA, Racer 5, was later developed, "and really took off with the public," says Richard.

In a crowded field, Racer 5 IPA, now the brewery's flagship offering, stands out as one of the best American IPAs found anywhere. It has won numerous awards including two gold and two silver GABF medals, and in 2006 helped Bear Republic win the competition's highest honor, the Small Brewing Company of the Year award.

What has led these deceptively straightforward beers to such high levels of success? "We are continually developing our own unique techniques and methods. There's a certain exclusivity to our products; we're not trying to make something that's unsustainable. Our growth is determined by being able to maintain the same level of quality and consistency. We always want to be true to our process," says Richard. "We could produce a beer in seven days and make more money on it, but instead we produce it in 21 days to make it just the way we want it to be. Our vision for the beer and our house styles determine the process we use for the beer."

Hops are the basis for Racer 5's distinctive characteristics. And the process used to infuse this beer with such unique and vibrant qualities involves going back to the hop fields themselves. Each year Richard takes two trips to Washington's Yakima Valley, one of the largest hop producing regions in the world, to meet with growers, sample the harvest, and secure a consistent supply of the highest quality hops. This hands-on approach, with particular attention given to the individual growing regions, allows for a carefully controlled hop element in each of Bear Republic's beers. Richard directly likens this to the importance of grape growing regions: "In Sonoma County understanding all of the microclimates is a pretty big deal. We have a very particular terroir there as a wine-producing region. I needed to find the same level of detail regarding where our hops were coming from." He has found that fostering relationships with individual growers, each operating within different microclimates, and each practicing individualized cultivation methods, is crucial for maintaining a consistent supply of high-quality hops. "The supply chain is the key to our success," says Richard. "There are seven major growing regions for cascade hops in the Yakima Valley. The bitterness and aromatic ranges [of the hops] can vary widely based on where they are grown," he explains. Even though Bear Republic is a sizeable brewery by craft beer standards, its production is miniscule when compared to the largest players in the field. But the mentality doesn't change. "You've got to think like you're a bigger brewer," says Richard. "Meet with your suppliers every year. Get to know what's going on in their world and experience different aspects of the hop growing season. It's important to know your growers and what they're facing." In addition to the work of growing hop vines, their flowers must be processed and dried before they can be used to brew beer. This phase of production is important as well. "You really have to monitor suppliers' production methods and understand their processes to circumvent any vulnerability in the supply chain to maintain consistent supplies and quality."

In 2006 his careful approach paid off. A devastating hop warehouse fire destroyed huge stores of product—4 percent of the entire country's harvest by some estimates—and created major hop shortages and price hikes. In response, some breweries changed their formulas. But Bear Republic was minimally impacted. Years before, Richard had secured his supplies of Centennial hops, an essential component of Racer 5, through long-term contracts with independent producers. His commitment to those growers ensures that they can maintain their diligent production methods and supply him with the highest quality hops.

Though the warehouse fire tragedy sent shockwaves through the beer community, a larger threat now faces the hop supply. "The hop farming industry is changing. Hop varietal production levels are shifting all the time. Certain varietals are becoming niche within the hops growing industry," says Richard with concern. "Moxee, Washington, for instance," in a prized sub-region of the

Yakima Valley, "is known for growing aromatic hops, which are less profitable than varieties with higher alpha acid levels, (a measure of the level of bitterness they can contribute to a beer) which are better for hop oil production." Hop oils are concentrated extracts that only add a non-distinct, generic bitterness to beers. The increased use of these "value-added" hops products by less scrupulous brewers puts pressure on the growers in the best regions to switch to new higher-yielding, but less aromatic, flavorful, and distinctive hop varieties. "Developing better-yielding hops is counter to the process of getting better aroma hops," says Richard. "And the finest aroma hops are essential for making great craft beer." I asked him if we're now entering into an era of "heirloom hops," similar to the current effort to preserve or recover diversity in food crops. Thankfully, he doesn't feel that we are at that point just yet. But Richard stresses that the success of craft beer depends upon building and maintaining good relations with suppliers, including hop growers. "The producers have become our friends. Without them we couldn't have a business. I want to make sure that they also understand how their business decisions affect us as a brewery."

Such mindfulness results in community-oriented products which, in the case of Bear Republic, consistently demonstrate all of the hallmarks of the finest classic beers.

Bear Republic's year-round lineup includes Racer 5 India Pale Ale, Red Rocket American amber, Hop Rod Rye IPA, Big Bear Black Stout, Peter Brown Tribute American brown ale, and XP American pale ale.

Bear Republic also brews a wide variety of seasonal and special edition draught-only releases that include (among others) Racer X double IPA, Apex double IPA, Olde Scoutter's barleywine, Crazy Ivan Belgian-style ale, Black Raven robust porter, Double Rocket imperial red ale, and Heritage Ale wee heavy. They also experiment with barrel-aged beers which are occasionally available at their brewpub.

Bear Republic's beers are distributed in Arizona, California, Colorado, Delaware, Illinois, Kansas, Maryland, Massachusetts, Michigan, Missouri, Montana, New Jersey, New York, North Carolina, Ohio, Oklahoma, Oregon, Pennsylvania, Rhode Island, South Carolina, Texas, Utah, Virginia, Washington, and Wisconsin.

RACER 5   Bright copper with a thin, fine off-white head. The aroma is full of bright orange, fresh grassiness, and soft resinous hops, followed by hints of earthy spice and toasted malt. Bitter orange peel, dried grass, and pine resin flavors from the hops are supported by a dry malt backbone with a bit of alcohol—classic West Coast IPA flavor profile. The very well-balanced medium body comes across as both light on the palate and full-flavored in the mouth. Hops take center stage but are backed-up by a solid malt framework.

RED ROCKET   Clear dark amber with a flash of dark bronze at the rim and a thick, medium-fine light brown head. Citrusy American hops ride above a basis of nutty roasted malt with cocoa and soft caramel in the aroma with a slight fruity fermentation note. Significant bitterness from both the hops and roasted malt in the flavor with dry grain notes alongside more caramel and bitter cocoa. Resin and orange zest hop characteristics round out the flavor profile. The medium-full body delivers a lot of flavor without being overly heavy. It is very well-balanced with good alcohol integration that supports each flavor element well.

HOP ROD RYE   Clear mahogany red with a thick, rocky light tan head. Big citrus hop aroma with a significant caramel malt component along with a bit of bitter cocoa and alcohol in the background. Dark fruit, alcohol sweetness, and a spicy nuttiness linger in the aroma as well. Strong, dark bitterness in the attack is surmounted by a spicy roasted malt character bolstered by some alcohol. Citrus and pine resin hop flavors arise mid-palate. This is a full-bodied beer with a lot of flavor that manages to not be heavy. The mouthfeel is both sharply bitter and well-rounded and creamy. The roasted malt fades in the finish as multidimensional hop bitterness lingers with a bit of alcohol warmth.

WET HOP BEERS

Enjoying foods in season is a very familiar concept. Though we may associate certain beers with different times of the year—pumpkin beers in the fall and dark strong ales for the winter holidays, for instance—these beers can really be brewed and enjoyed anytime. However, a truly seasonal beer style has been gaining a lot of popularity among American craft brewers in recent years: wet hop ales. These beers, also known as "fresh hop" or "green hop" ales, are brewed with freshly picked "wet hops" that must be used immediately after harvest before they begin to degrade, making them intensely dependant on the seasonal hop harvest. Wet hops are generally used in low-malt, hop-driven styles, such as pale ales or IPAs, in order to showcase their unique aroma and flavor characteristics. Wet hop beers possess herbaceous, leafy, and grassy flavors along with unique earthy and spicy qualities which are different from those imparted by dried hops.

Drying hops makes them more stable and concentrates their essential oils, which allows brewers to impart more bitterness to their beers by using greater amounts hops. But the drying process can also drive off some of the delicate, volatile aromas and flavors of wet hops. When using wet hops brewers generally need five times more hops by weight to achieve the same bitterness levels that dried hops provide.

Some beers labeled as "fresh hop" ales actually contain freshly harvested and dried hops. Though not made with "wet hops," these seasonal beers are also worth seeking out and convey the more traditional fresh, vibrant flavors and aromas of dried hops at their very best.

Look for wet hop ales to appear around September and October. Like the wet hops themselves, these beers should be enjoyed right away and not aged. If you live in a hop-producing region, such as the Northwest, look for fresh local examples on draught.

Sierra Nevada brews and bottles several excellent seasonal fresh hop editions. Their Estate Homegrown Ale is made with organic wet hops and barley that are grown at their brewery in Chico, California. Northern Hemisphere Harvest Ale is made with wet hops harvested in Yakima, Washington within 24 hours of brewing the beer. Spring brings their Southern Hemisphere Harvest Ale, which uses distinctive New Zealand hop varieties whose harvest occurs at this time of year. The hops are picked, dried, and flown to Sierra Nevada's brewery within one week of harvest.

THE LOST ABBEY/PORT BREWING—SAN MARCOS, CA
TOMME ARTHUR, BREWMASTER

The first people arrived in the darkened parking lot of The Lost Abbey Brewing Company in San Marcos, California, at three in the morning. They were waiting for the chance to purchase a beer that they knew almost nothing about, except for its cryptic title, Veritas 009, and its price, $35 for a 750-milliliter bottle. It had never been released before and would never be again. The only indication of its contents was a blurb posted on the brewery website the week before:

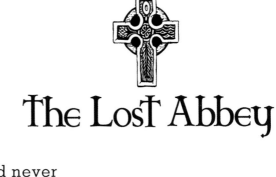

The most complex and time-consuming beer released by the brewery to date, Veritas 009 took more than three years, with periods in bourbon and wine barrels, to create. Begun in late 2007 as a dark base beer, it was sent to freshly emptied bourbon barrels from Kentucky's Heaven Hill Distilleries. The beer aged for 15 months before it was moved into French oak barrels previously used for wine (primarily Syrah). Sour cherries were added and the beer was left to rest for another year and three months. Finally, in mid-2010, it was pulled from the barrels, blended, bottled and sent off to condition for an additional 11 months.

This was enough to cause hundreds of people to gather in that parking lot and, when the sale finally began at ten o'clock, purchase all of the 1,200 bottles available within one hour. This was a very special event in the craft beer world. The Lost Abbey, under the direction of brewmaster Tomme Arthur, produces some of the most sought-after beers in the world, though it was established just a few years ago in 2006. I met with Tomme at the brewery on the day of the special release, just as the last bottles were being sold.

My first question to him was how he felt about the cult-like phenomenon that has arisen around many of the special editions brewed by The Lost Abbey. "It's hard for me to wrap my head around it," he said. "I'm not sure I'll ever completely understand it. I don't struggle with it. I push for us to be creative and complex. That's part of our desire as brewers. It's what we do. We take some big risks with some of our beers. Some are rewarded and some are not." But Tomme definitely is proud of the following the brewery has achieved and feels a lot of commitment to its devotees. "I appreciate it. We have a responsibility to them to keep doing what we do so that they are rewarded when they choose to spend their time in line."

Despite only being able to acquire these limited editions at the brewery, the beers are openly available. At 100 cases, Veritas 009 was by far the largest Veritas release ever. "If this was a winery with a 100-case release," Tomme explains, "the product would never hit the market beyond the wine club or reserve list. Now there's an opportunity for consumers to get in line and be rewarded. We're very mindful of that. We don't want this to be an elite 'you-just-can't-get-this, nanner nanner' type thing."

But it cannot be denied that there is something elite about the Veritas series. These beers come out of The Lost Abbey's pure brewing experimentation—when the brewers deem one worthy of public release. Previous batches have achieved legendary status in corners of the craft beer community and are regarded as benchmarks for American barrel-aged blended beers. Tomme stresses that they are in no way meant to be commercially oriented beers. "There's no timeline," says Tomme. "They are one-time, one-place beers. They are never produced with salability in mind." He has just a few guidelines for Veritas beers: "They are oak-aged, have some level of sourness, and are made with a fruit component." But The Lost Abbey's creativity is guided by solid brewing principles as well. "I don't want to be esoteric for its own sake," says Tomme. "I think it's very easy to say we use bat guano in a beer and maybe it tastes OK or it doesn't—that's shock value. I'd rather there be a reason for it."

The Veritas series is just a tiny part of the brewery's barrel program, which in turn represents only a small part of their overall brewing portfolio. But it is the barrel-aged sour beers that Tomme is most proud of, and for which The Lost Abbey is best known. Indeed, fans' fervor is certainly not limited to the infrequent Veritas releases. Sour beers like Red Poppy, Framboise de Amorosa, Cuvee de Tomme, and Duck Duck Gooze are also very highly prized. There is something about the complexity and dimension of these beers that cast a spell on people. The inspiration for these beers are traditional Belgian examples, but The Lost Abbey's interpretations take them further by brewing them in its own way. "We're not pushing the pure homage button," says Tomme. "Red Poppy is an homage to the beers of Flanders, as seen through our travels, but it is also an expression of our place and our experiences." Tomme explains that, "Our palates define our sour beer program. We draw from our knowledge of what is out there in sour beer—what we've tasted along the way. We then choose how to spin that back into our beers according to our 'house character.' We've found our niche and I think we do a good job of following it."

Red Poppy is a Flanders-style ale made with sour cherries that is released once every year in quantities large enough for most people who want it to be able to buy it at the brewery and at certain specialty shops within the local market. Tomme believes that the 2011 edition "is far and away the best batch of Red Poppy we've ever released. It's also the biggest batch we've ever released," he adds. "I see a lot of success here in that we were able to do both." This is very good news for beer fans. Producing beers of this type is not an exact science. "There are some real difficulties in making a 5% alcohol beer with that much texture and that much finesse," says Tomme. "We've really nailed how to achieve these characteristics through the blending process." How large a batch of blended beer will be all depends on the characteristics of the individual barrels. If many of them don't age as planned then a smaller batch will result. "We never blend to a specific case total," says Tomme. "We never want to dilute what we can accomplish [in terms of flavor]. We'll make a 500-case batch instead of 1,000 if it means it'll be a better beer. Our goal is to never 'water down' the product based on adhering to a certain level of sales."

Framboise de Amorosa is a recent addition to The Lost Abbey's annual sour beer portfolio, and is in many ways a raspberry counterpart to Red Poppy. After initial trials within the Veritas program, it was first released in its current form in 2010 and quickly became a fan favorite. Offering sweetness from the raspberries, complex sour fermentation flavors, and unique barrel-aged characteristics, it is another must-have special release in the craft beer community.

Though not as rare as the singular Veritas releases, Duck Duck Gooze is still only released every three years. It is modeled after the Belgian geuze style, which is a blend of one-, two-, and three-year-old barrel-aged sour beers. Unlike traditional Belgian geuzes, Duck Duck Gooze is not spontaneously fermented. Instead, portions of beer from barrels of previous batches are added to newly filled ones to reproduce similar flavors. Tomme explains that the final blend represents "the essences of each of the different-aged barrels. Some might have more brett, more oak, or more acidity. Balancing these complexities is what makes this beer unique." Duck Duck Gooze is a landmark beer. It is perhaps the finest blended beer produced in America, and represents the best aspects of Belgian brewing traditions combined with a unique expression of American terroir. This quality was recognized at the GABF in 2009 where Duck Duck Gooze won the gold medal in the "Belgian-Style Lambic or Sour Ale" category.

Beyond these special releases, the availability of The Lost Abbey's standard year-round and seasonal releases is very dependable. Beers like Red Barn, Lost & Found, and Avant Garde are flavorful, nuanced, and balanced classically styled offerings. Tomme greatly admires these beers as well, but feels that they tend to get overshadowed. "For all the glory and accolades we've acquired through our experimental, 'wild child' projects—if you treat this as a family of beers, the middle children don't get the same attention for just really behaving like they should." One of the most "well-behaved," yet still very expressive and unique beers is 10 Commandments, their widely available spring seasonal. It is a Belgian-style strong ale that is brewed with caramelized raisins, rosemary, and a touch of brettanomyces. "Dumping raisins into a brew kettle isn't 'thinking outside the box,'" says Tomme. "Taking the raisins and altering them through a cooking process—taking that extra step [with our beers] is something we're very proud of." The result of this extra process is a rich, complex, multidimensional beer that offers up more layers of flavor the longer you ponder it.

Tomme also brews another lineup of beers at the same facility under the Port Brewing brand that features non-Belgian craft beer styles such as IPAs, stouts, and experimental lagers. Both The Lost Abbey and Port Brewing brands represent the highest quality craft beers. This was reflected in 2007 when The Lost Abbey/Port Brewing won the GABF's prestigious Small Brewing Company of the Year award. No, you can't buy these beers everywhere. And yes, it is really helpful to live close to the brewery. But the effort and the wait are worthwhile. Any opportunity to open one of these excellent, unique beers is its own special occasion. Tomme is satisfied with what The Lost Abbey and Port Brewing are contributing to the craft beer landscape. "We're not a grocery store brand. We're not an everyman brand. We are looking to grow like everybody else, but we never look at what the guy next to us is doing. We don't look at trends. We don't believe we have a natural competitor. We don't feel like we're missing any opportunities."

The Lost Abbey's year-round portfolio of beers includes Avant Garde bière de garde, Devotion Belgian-style pale ale, Inferno Belgian-style strong ale, Judgment Day quad, Lost & Found dubbel, and Red Barn saison.

Their seasonal offerings include Carnevale saison with brettanomyces (spring); 10 Commandments Belgian-style strong ale with caramelized raisins, rosemary, and brettanomyces (spring); Witch's Wit Belgian-style witbier with grapefruit zest and honey (Summer), Gift of the Magi bière de garde with frankincense and myrrh (fall), and Serpent's Stout Russian imperial stout (winter).

Annual special-release barrel-aged beers include Cuvee de Tomme sour dark strong ale with cherries, Red Poppy Flanders-style red ale with cherries, The Angel's Share bourbon and brandy barrel-aged barleywines, and Duck Duck Gooze Belgian-style geuze (triennial release). Additionally, The Lost Abbey blends a batch of Cable Car sour ale each year for sale only at the specialty beer bar Toronado's two locations in San Francisco and San Diego.

Port Brewing's year-round portfolio of beers includes Mongo double IPA, Old Viscosity Russian imperial stout, Shark Attack imperial red, and Wipeout IPA.

Their seasonal offerings include Hot Rocks dark stein lager brewed with heated granite (spring), Anniversary IPA double IPA

(Spring), SPA (Summer Pale Ale) American pale ale (Summer), Hop 15 double IPA (Summer), Panzer Pils imperial pilsner (fall), High Tide wet hop IPA (Fall), Midnight Expression schwarzbier (winter), and Santa's Little Helper Russian imperial stout (winter).

Port also releases two special bourbon barrel-aged versions of their Russian imperial stouts annually: Older Viscosity (Spring), and Barrel Aged Santa's Little Helper (Summer).

RED POPPY Cloudy medium mahogany brown with a very fine, thin, off-white head. Pleasant horse blanket and barnyard brett aromas along with sour top-notes and a very subtle, soft sweet malt background with cherry pit, wood, and spice. These aspects are also present in the flavor along with more overt, but dry cherry characteristics and lactic fermentation sourness. The oak barrel aging integrates the bold flavor characteristics together into a tight, coherent flavor profile and softens the body, which is light but nonetheless perfectly asserts the many dimensions of this beer as a straightforward presence in the mouth. The alcohol is appropriately mild and hardly noticeable making this a refreshingly complex and funky drinking experience.

FRAMBOISE DE AMOROSA Clear bright rosy red with a fine, light pink head. Quite a beautiful and sensual beer. Tart fresh raspberries are immediately apparent on the nose along with bright lactic fermentation and barrel-aged characteristics. The flavor of the raspberries is preserved very well and comes across quite fresh in the beer. There is a lovely faint toasted malt lift in the finish just as the sourness fades. The multilayered flavor profile delivers a great impression of depth. This leads into a superbly balanced body that conveys both strength and delicacy. Not strictly sweet or dry, this beer strikes the perfect balance between fruitiness and sour complexity.

VERITAS 009 Opaque brown-black that thins out to a dark bur-
nished bronze at the rim. Virtually nonexistent head. Dark caramel malt aromas with strong vanilla and oxidative notes followed
by softly sweet alcohol notes and spice. Dark fruit tannins in the
very background. Showcases a true melding of complex dark malt
notes and a delicate yet prominent tartness with very dark fruit flavors. Sweet malt core is surrounded by a dense, dark malt profile.
Bourbon barrel aging aspects are very strong with notes of caramel,
vanilla, and booze. Big body—massively full with balancing tartness
and oxidative complexities with a long, warm alcohol finish.

COLLABORATION BEERS

The spirit of the craft beer community has always been one of friendly competition and collaboration. This ethos directly manifests itself in the frequent collaboration beers that are produced throughout the country between two or more breweries working together. These special brews often represent a hybrid of each brewery's specialization, or sometimes a completely different sort of beer than either brewery makes. Whatever the beer, collaboration ales represent the powerful camaraderie shared between craft brewers.

One of the most interesting, and delicious, collaboration projects I have come across was produced by Garrett Oliver of the Brooklyn Brewery and Hans-Peter Drexler of the historic Weissbierbrauerei G. Schneider & Sohn in Kelheim, Germany. Garrett traveled to Germany to brew Schneider & Brooklyner Hopfen-Weisse, an 8%+ alcohol pale weizenbock heavily hopped with the regional Bavarian Hallertauer Saphir variety. And two months later Hans-Peter traveled to Brooklyn to brew Brooklyner-Schneider Hopfen-Weisse, which is nearly the same beer except that it is made with American Amarillo and Palisade varieties of hops. Garrett said in a press release, "Essentially, I brewed a beer in Germany to celebrate Schneider's hop terroir, and now Hans-Peter is brewing a beer in Brooklyn to celebrate our hop terroir." Born out of the men's ten-year friendship and mutual respect for each other's beers, this was the first collaboration project in Schneider's 400 year history.

Another beer that represents the cooperative spirit of craft beer is produced each year by Avery and Russian River Brewing Companies. Both breweries brew a beer called Salvation. Rather than battling each other for the trademark rights in court, brewmasters Adam Avery and Vinnie Cilurzo created Collaboration Not Litigation Ale, a blend of each of their versions of Salvation, which released by Avery. Regarding the spirit of collaboration Vinnie says, "I think the fact that most of us in the craft beer industry are friends is very exciting. There are very few industries out there where the competitors are friends and will help each other."

But perhaps one of the most exciting collaboration ales ever produced was Isabelle Proximus, a blend of barrel-aged sour beers from the breweries of Tomme Arthur of The Lost Abbcy, Rob Tod of Allagash, Sam Calagione of Dogfish Head, and the aforementioned Adam Avery and Vinnie Cilurzo, which in many was a harbinger of the enthusiasm for sour beers in America. The final blend was bottled by The Lost Abbey, about which Tomme said, "I'm extremely proud of the Isabelle Proximus project because I think that when someone sits down and catalogues all of the collaboration beers that have been done Isabelle will be in the top five. It was not a fluff beer from five guys who said 'let's get together and screw something up.' It was a beer that worked out really really well."

RUSSIAN RIVER BREWING CO.—SANTA ROSA, CA
Vinnie Cilurzo, Brewmaster & Co-Owner

Craft beer fans throughout the world are known for their dedication. Whether to a particular beer style, a favorite brewery, or a single beer, the enthusiasm embodied by its fervent followers can run to extremes. Perhaps no single brewery generates as much excitement and passion as Russian River Brewing Company in Santa Rosa, California.

Originally founded in 1997 by Korbel Champagne Cellars in Guerneville, the company hired Vinnie Cilurzo as their brewmaster, and he led Russian River to a GABF Small Brewing Company of the Year award in 1999. When Korbel decided to get out of the beer business they sold Russian River to Vinnie and his wife Natalie in 2002, and they moved the brewery to Santa Rosa. Their reputation has since been built on specializing in an unusual but prescient combination of beer styles: ultra-hoppy IPAs and barrel-aged sour beers, both of which have grown into darlings of the craft beer community. Vinnie simply brews what he is passionate about. "We usually don't focus too much on what other breweries are doing," he says. "We tend to stay very focused on our own beers and are always working towards making them better."

Before moving to Sonoma County Vinnie began his professional brewing career as a co-owner of the now defunct Blind Pig Brewing Company in Temecula where he was very likely the first to brew what is now recognized as the double IPA style. One of Russian River's main regular production beers today is Blind Pig, an aggressively hopped IPA based on his early recipes. The influence on the craft beer community of using hops in this unique way has been immense, and now the double IPA is a standard bearer of American craft beer innovation. The strikingly bitter, full-flavored characteristics of American hop varieties are showcased in these intense, powerful beers. And there is no better example of this style than Russian River's flagship beer, Pliny the Elder.

Pliny the Elder is a remarkable achievement in beer. Named for the ancient Roman naturalist who first catalogued wild hops in his famous historical work *Naturalis Historia,* it contains 40 percent more malt and more than double the amount of hops used in Blind Pig. At 8% alcohol and 100 IBUs, it is a massive beer that still manages to come across as bright and refreshing. It redefines the term "balance" when applied to flavors in beer. Pliny the Elder is through and through a hop-driven beer, but these flavors are supported by a dry, crisp malt body that conveys the beer's power while giving deference to its focus on hops. Creating this sort of positioned balance requires a high level of technical mastery. Vinnie explains that "for our hoppy beers our primary focus is on creating the most explosive hop character while keeping the dissolved oxygen at the lowest level possible. Keeping it as low as possible enables us to make a beer that has a long lasting hop character." This is a beer that simply must be tasted to be believed.

And many have heard its call. Pliny the Elder has achieved cult status in the craft beer scene. Though it is brewed year-round, demand still well-exceeds supply. "Our brewery is unique in that our number one selling beer is Pliny the Elder," says Vinnie. "There are not too many breweries whose top selling beer is a double IPA." While filling a niche and creating cachet is great for business, many remain frustrated at Russian River's lack of availability in wider markets. The brewery has steadily grown each year, but Vinnie's focus is not on simply making more beer. "For us, we have a continued focus on bringing the quality of our beer up to an even higher level than it is at the present time, as opposed to growing the business by volume," says Vinnie. "Growing through innovation is more important to us than volume." In the meantime, craft beer fans not in select areas of the country must practice the "drink local" mantra while they plan a pilgrimage to Russian River's brewpub.

Early February is a popular time to embark on such a mission. Each year hundreds of people line the sidewalk for blocks outside of the brewpub on the release day of Pliny the Younger, the decidedly over-the-top nephew of Pliny the Elder. This draught-only "triple IPA" clocks in at 11% alcohol with a level of hoppiness that defies belief. It is without question the Holy Grail for hopheads. The entire 2010 brewpub release, anticipated to last for a week or more, sold out in a mere ten hours. In 2011 and 2012 kegs were rationed to ensure some availability each day for two weeks. On the first day there were some reports of people waiting three hours or more to get inside. After opening at eleven each morning the beer was often sold out by three. But a great many people had a chance to enjoy ten ounce pours of this legendary beer for the exceedingly reasonable cost of $4.50.

Enjoying a glass of a Pliny the Younger is about more than just bragging rights or checking a box on a beer "life list." Tapping a keg of it creates an instant event. Standing in a bar where nearly everyone is drinking the exact same beer gives you the satisfying sensation of participating in a larger shared experience. While crowds, lines, and a raucous atmosphere may not be ideal for contemplating this complex beer, such a scene perfectly expresses the sense of camaraderie and community that craft beer can create.

On the other end of the spectrum are Russian River's pioneering barrel-aged sour beers. Vinnie developed a deep connection to Belgium's wild brettanomyces-fermented beers while visiting traditional breweries there in the early '90s, and has since developed this inspiration into "a full time barrel-aged sour beer program." He uses the term "sonambic" to describe beers spontaneously fermented with wild Sonoma yeasts in a method similar to that used for Belgian lambics. Other beers are dosed with a concoction of brettanomyces and saccharomyces yeasts combined with lactobacillus and pediococcus bacteria to create distinctively sour fermentation profiles. Vinnie utilizes an abundant local resource to age his beers while the microorganisms go about their work. Emptied barrels from Sonoma County wineries impart an American twist to his sour Belgian-style beers. Each beer sees time in barrels that formerly held wines of different varietals including chardonnay, pinot noir, and cabernet sauvignon.

Temptation was his first barrel-aged release. A blonde ale aged in French oak chardonnay barrels, it offers delicate wine-like complexities along with its pointed sourness and oak influences. Sitting across from Vinnie and Natalie in their lively brewpub one evening, I sampled some unblended Temptation straight from one of the barrels. It possessed a bright, citrusy tartness with a delicious lightly toasted grain finish. Vinnie pondered his small glass of still, golden liquid and said that he thought it could be approaching readiness. According to Russian River's philosophy of barrel aging, "There is no real formula when aging beer in barrels; the beer tells us when it is ready, not the other way around." But, generally speaking, it usually takes between one and two years for each barrel to fully develop. Each barrel possesses its own unique complexities, which are then blended together to form a finished batch of beer. And when it comes to the art of blending, Vinnie has another philosophy: "Usually blending is a dirty word in the beer industry. Big breweries making 'industrial lager' blend batches all the time to ensure that every batch tastes the same. We often blend barrel-aged beers, not for consistency, but to develop unique flavors." Each new release offers drinkers an opportunity to sample a unique expression of Russian River's creativity and its terroir.

One of the more recently developed additions to their sour beer portfolio is Consecration, a dark, strong sour ale aged in cabernet sauvignon barrels with currants. I was fortunate to be able to sample batch number one on draught at the brewpub when it was first released and have since enjoyed noting the subtle distinctions of each batch. At 10% alcohol, Consecration is a marked departure from the generally much lighter-bodied sour beers of Belgium, and a unique beer among American sours as well. Its dark, subtly sweet fruity characteristics, combined with some tannic complexities, results in a highly structured beer that is as comfortable alongside food as any wine.

Each beer in Russian River's sour beer portfolio is regarded as being among the best in its class, and collectively they have garnered numerous awards at major festivals like the GABF and the World Beer Cup. This reputation reached the highest levels of recognition in the culinary world when renowned chef Thomas Keller commissioned Russian River to create a special beer to serve in his restaurants. The result of this collaboration is White Apron, a substantially hopped pilsner designed as a beer that "a line cook could drink several of after an eight-hour shift on the line."

Vinnie downplays the near legendary status his brewery has reached in the craft beer world. He's certainly pleased with the reputation Russian River has achieved but reserves his greatest pride for the personal goals he has accomplished within the brewhouse.

"We have never gone out and laid an agenda," says Vinnie. "Our brewery has been very fortunate to be recognized for some innovative brewing practices and styles, but we have never gone out looking for props. Things happen organically around Russian River." When asked to pinpoint one beer in particular he's most proud of, Vinnie responds with an enticing teaser for a yet unannounced project: "If I had to nail one down it would probably be one of the beers I am working on right now on our pilot R&D system that will be released sometime late next year—most likely." I suggest getting in line early.

Russian River brews and bottles Blind Pig IPA and Pliny the Elder double IPA year-round. Draught-only releases for the brewpub and select markets include Pliny the Younger double IPA, Russian River IPA, Aud Blonde blonde ale, Happy Hops pale ale, OVL Stout on nitrogen, Hoptime Harvest wet hop ale, and Beer Esteem California common.

Their lineup of bottled barrel-aged beers, released when each batch is ready, includes Temptation chardonnay barrel-aged sour blonde ale, Supplication pinot noir barrel-aged sour brown ale with cherries, Consecration cabernet sauvignon barrel-aged sour dark strong ale with currants, and Beatification, a blend of spontaneously fermented beer aged in neutral oak barrels. Framboise for a Cure is a limited brewery-only release made with raspberries from which all the profits go to breast cancer research. Compunction barrel-aged sour blonde ale with pluots is occasionally brewed as a draught-only release.

Russian River also bottles a series of traditional Belgian-style beers that are released throughout the year and includes Damnation strong golden ale (produced year-round), Sanctification fermented with 100 percent brettanomyces, Redemption blonde ale, and Salvation abbey quad. Additional Belgian-style beers are produced throughout the year as draught-only releases including Perdition biere de garde, Deification pale ale with brettanomyces, Benediction Belgian-style abbey ale, Erudition saison with brettanomyces, Rejection Belgian-inspired black beer for Valentine's Day, Defenestration Belgian-style IPA, and Little White Lie Belgian-style witbier.

Russian River's beers are distributed in California, Colorado, Oregon, Pennsylvania, and Washington.

PLINY THE ELDER   Clear medium gold with a fine, creamy white head. Possesses an arresting, intense fresh hop aroma with citrus, resin, earth, and grass. Deeper analysis reveals notes of yuzu, pine needles, and eucalyptus leaf. The aroma carries directly over into the hop-driven flavor profile whose mouth-coating bitterness is supported by a dry, restrained maltiness and well-balanced alcohol. Medium-full body packages everything together in just the right balance to make this a highly drinkable, extremely complex celebration of American hops. The finish is long and lingering with a subtle reminder of alcohol.

TEMPTATION   Brilliant clear bright yellow-gold with a fine, medium-thick white head. Lovely fresh tart aroma with yellow fruit and green strawberry notes over a soft spiciness and wood-aged oxidative characteristics. The fermentation character shows nicely in the flavor with focused well-balanced sourness and darker "animal" characteristics set against a light, yet sturdy, golden malt profile. Some alcohol comes through faintly in the light, well-structured body which gives way to a long multidimensional finish. This is a finely crafted, delicate, and somewhat understated sour ale that slowly reveals itself in a rewarding way.

CONSECRATION   Clear dark reddish brown-bronze with dark garnet highlights and a thin, superfine off-white head. Aroma first presents dark sour fruit with a slightly sweet grapiness. Earthy and woody undertones emerge and combine with a softly tannic, spicy vinous character. Flavor begins with bright sourness in the attack that leads into a deep, multilayered dark fruit profile that is surrounded by complex secondary fermentation flavors, oxidative notes, and subtle oak wine barrel influences. The body is lithe and refreshing and completely hides the significant alcohol. Its force is instead delivered through the huge variety of sensations on the palate—good weight, bright sourness, sweet fruit, dark wood, and earth. It is simultaneously juicy, rounded, edgy, firm, and voluptuous, with a clean, mostly dry finish.

THE PACIFIC NORTHWEST

CASCADE BREWING CO.—PORTLAND, OR

Ron Gansberg, Brewmaster

As the popularity of craft beer continues to grow, so does people's awareness of the variety of styles produced and the array of flavors each offers. But even among craft beer devotees, the sour ale style still remains elusive to many. "Sour" is an adjective not normally associated with beer in most people's minds, but the traditional sour beers of Belgium have been produced in the Senne River valley and Flanders for centuries. In recent years more American craft breweries have been experimenting with sour ales, and their niche popularity has been steadily growing. Even so, they often represent a very small percentage of the total volume of beer brewed by a brewery, and are often only released as experimental side projects. That is what makes the Cascade Brewing Company of Portland, Oregon, whose main focus is on the production of sour beers, so unusual.

Ron Gansberg has been the brewmaster at Cascade for thirteen years, and has been brewing sour beers there for the last six. Ron considers the title of "brewmaster" to be convenient "shorthand." "It's more like we are brew-mastered," he says. "A brewmaster may work in some large breweries where they bend the beer to their will," says Ron. "We are just here to steward and shepherd [the beers] along." This admission gets to the core of the challenges that face the sour beer brewer. The many microorganisms at work to give sour beers their flavor (predominantly the wild yeast brettanomyces and the lactobacillus and pediococcus bacterium) can be unpredictable and difficult to control. To combat this, Cascade uses only lactobacillus in its sour beers, which generally produces moderate sourness and leaves some residual sweetness. These beers must age for long periods of time in oak barrels to develop their characteristic complexities. Ron likens this fermentation process to an intrepid sea voyage: "When we put a beer into oak it's like laying it down in the keel of a nineteenth century vessel. We try to forecast where it's going and what it's going to undergo," but its final destination, while anticipated, is unknown. "The next batch is put into keel slightly differently. We analyze the effects of tweaks to each recipe to see what the end results are."

Ron stresses the importance of blending as the other key method to producing consistent beers. Each barrel may develop slightly different flavors during the aging process. Blending funkier, highly aged batches with younger, tart batches is the traditional method used to produce Belgian gueuze. Through blending, the brewer can exert a bit more control on what the final product will be like by emphasizing varying amounts of certain aspects from particular barrels. But Cascade purposely does not try to recreate the classic Belgian beers that result from the unique climate there. They instead strive to make beers that embody their own beer *terroir*. Cascade ages much of their beer in emptied wine barrels from Oregon wineries. Each different type of barrel imparts the beer inside with different flavor characteristics. As a result, Cascade produces a vast array of traditional-styled and completely original ales, creating as many as thirty new beers per year. "Our staff is highly creative," says Ron. Everyone at Cascade is allowed "a lot of freedom to give creative input. That's why we're all in this business," he explains. "Freedom and creativity are key." Ron describes himself and his brewing team as "strong-willed and creative individuals," who are engaged in "controlled chaos" at the brewery. "It's along that ragged edge where we get the greatest creativity, the highest level of satisfaction, and produce very good beers," says Ron.

Fruit is a traditional ingredient in many sour beers, and the local availability of seasonal produce plays a role in Cascade's creative process and help gives their beers a sense of place. The Pacific Northwest is known for its cherries, and Cascade uses both Bing and sour pie cherries in its Cascade Kriek, one of their most commonly available sour beers. Goldrich and Rival varieties of apricots are also sourced locally for use in their Cascade Apricot Ale that is also generally available. Wine grapes, raspberries, and blackberries have all been used in various editions, as have more unconventional brewing fruits, such as cranberries. Since cranberries are generally in season in the fall, and these sour ales takes many months to produce, Ron planned a year in advance to brew his Cranberry Wheat ale to be available for the next year's holiday season.

The time and attention that is necessary to produce these uniquely acidic beers seems at odds with the fact that sour beers remain somewhat divisive among people. One the one hand, their complexity and acidity makes them stand out amongst nearly all other craft beer styles, and also gives them extreme versatility in a wide variety of food pairings. On the other hand, these flavor aspects and their characteristic funkiness are a drastic departure from most people's conception of what "beer" should taste like. Trying a sour beer for the first time can bring about either elation or revulsion in different people, and it often takes a little while to develop a real appreciation for the style. Nevertheless, Cascade is actively trying to recruit drinkers to what they call the "Sour Beer Movement." "We try to make the sour beers to be predominantly food friendly," Ron explains. But occasionally "some are an event unto themselves," and others "push the edge of conviviality."

The combination of using only high quality specialty ingredients, time intensive barrel-aging methods with unpredictable microorganisms, and the resulting higher prices that are necessary to keep this production model sustainable creates some big challenges for a brewery like Cascade. Ron is acutely aware of these challenges, but he's confident that sour beer's popularity will continue to expand. He likes doing things differently. "We despaired of being part of the hops arms race," says Ron. "What we once saw as a hoppy beer is no longer hoppy. An increase in the level of sensory experience was required. We wanted to increase that sensory experience without using the effects of hops and make it approachable," he says. "After twelve-plus years of hoppy beers, people are looking for a new experience. If we are getting tired of them, then others must be feeling that way as well and are looking for something different."

The task then becomes creating a perception of value for these high-end sour craft beers. Aside from the many reasonably priced small batch beers served on draught, a 750mL bottle of 2010 Cascade Kriek sells for $16.00 at their Barrel House brewpub in Portland, well below the price of some popular supermarket wines, yet significantly above the per-ounce price of most other craft beers. (Other bottled special edition beers command higher prices.) And Cascade's local beers are often cheaper than the imported Belgian examples of similar styles. Ron repeatedly asks himself if "what we're doing is contributing to the bottom line and making us a healthy and viable business [which can last] into the future?" He notes that "our margins have improved above attempting to sell regular micros to a distributor, but are still razor thin, especially for a small producer," like Cascade. But a clear answer did come from a powerful force in the craft beer world: in 2008 Cascade Kriek earned a bronze medal at the GABF, and in 2009 Bourbonic Plague won gold and Vlad the Imp Aler took silver. Though sour beers may only ever make up a niche in a niche market, they represent an essential part of the diversity of flavors that are found in craft beer. They are in many ways one of the most complexly flavored beverages produced, and an intensely artisanal facet of the craft brewing industry. And, if Cascade's continued success is any indication, sour beers are winning the wider following they deserve.

Cascade produces many beers each year with varying availability. Its core lineup consists of Cascade Apricot Ale, Cascade Kriek fermented with cherries, Sang Royal blend of sour ales aged in red wine barrels, The Vine sour ale fermented with white wine grape juice, Bourbonic Plague blend of sour porters aged in wine and bourbon barrels, and Vlad the Imp Aler blend of sour blond and quad ales aged in Bourbon barrels with spices.

Cascade's beers are distributed in California, Florida, Massachusetts, New York, North Carolina, Oregon, Pennsylvania, and Washington.

KRIEK

Clear pale red with a large, rocky light pink head. Full sour aroma with cherry tartness and a lot of lactic fermentation notes. Very bright as well as funky. The flavor is bracingly tart—complete with salivary gland cramping on the first sip. Light cherry notes are entwined with a complex barrel-aged, multi-faceted fermentation profile. Very light body whose intense

sourness makes it seem to float above the tongue on the way down while stimulating the soft palate. This is a good one.

Vlad the Imp Aler

Medium orange-gold color with a thin, very fine white head. Aroma possesses of deeply complex toasted malt with significant oxidative notes and bourbon barrel aging characteristics consisting of soft caramel, vanilla, and oak spice. A trailing of a faint, ripe wine-like fruitiness can be detected. Highly complex, multilayered, and multitextured flavor profile conveys a light yet densely constructed mélange of tastes. Brightly sour and spicy flavors with bitter top notes come on at first, and are followed by a light toasted malt presence interwoven with a vinous fruitiness. Spice, vanilla, and soft caramel characteristics contribute delicate, well-balanced nuances while downplayed bourbon notes fill a secondary role. A cloak of sourness gently envelops everything. Very well hidden alcohol notes create a structured, light body that remains subservient to the flavor profile it supports, but pokes through with some sweet fruitiness at the very end. Some well-integrated, slightly sweet maltiness lifts into a delicately textured, multilayered finish.

Sang Royal

Hazy dark chestnut with a thick, very fine tan head. Mouth-watering sour aroma with pleasant balsamic-like acetic notes, dark sour fruits—including a dark grapiness, and a soft spiciness along with a bit of bready toasted malt in the background. The flavor offers a piquant sourness on the attack that supports tart under-ripe fruits notes before transitioning to a dry toasted maltiness that is combined with a hint of earth and hops spice. The medium-weight body gives the impression of lightness from the tart characteristics and finishes long and slow with a bit of lingering spice.

DESCHUTES BREWING CO.—BEND, OR

Larry Sidor, Brewmaster

I spoke with Larry Sidor, the brewmaster of Deschutes Brewing Company in Bend, Oregon, in the summer of 2011. For the past eight years, under his direction, Deschutes has grown into a significant player in the West Coast craft brewing scene, making some very highly regarded beers. Larry had just announced that he would leave the company at the end of the year to found his own brewing company, but his mark on the Deschutes's brewing philosophy will continue to be felt.

Larry Sidor has a long and varied history in the industry. After graduating with a degree in fermentation science he went to work for Olympia Brewing, which made generic light American lager. When that company was purchased by Pabst in 1983 Larry found himself part of a huge enterprise that sent him around country to brew in many locations including Newark, Milwaukee, St. Paul, San Antonio, and even abroad to China. Working for such a large conglomerate exposed him to the industrial and corporate sides of brewing. He worked on enormous brewing systems with teams of chemists, engineers, and support staff, and consulted closely with the powerful Pabst marketing department. He describes these experiences in three phrases: "great people, good equipment, failing endeavor."

Larry eventually left Pabst, went to work for a hop company in the Yakima Valley, and purchased a vineyard to explore the other side of fermented beverages. He supplied grapes to commercial wineries while saving the best parcels for his own wines. Though he enjoyed tending the vineyard and making wine, brewing remains his true passion. When the Deschutes Brewing Company offered him a position, after he had been selling them hops for several years, he gladly accepted.

Deschutes is a large craft brewery that produces over 200,000 barrels of beer each year, but it's tiny in comparison to macro-brewing operations. The most significant difference for Larry, however, was the commitment to quality and creativity that Deschutes represents. He describes the company's brewing philosophy as seeking to create "layered beers that are well-constructed and not just hitting you in the face with one particular aspect."

Deschutes's flagship beer is a good example of this philosophy. "We started with Black Butte Porter. We began our existence through a dark beer," Larry says, noting the distinct difference in that approach from anything in the macro world. "It was the second beer ever brewed in the Deschutes brewpub twenty-three years ago; we pay a lot of attention to that beer." Black Butte is a flavorful, light-bodied porter with well-integrated notes of cocoa and American hops. "It's a great representation of what Deschutes is about," say Larry. It is a solid interpretation of a standard style that is broadly appealing to many craft beer drinkers. But pushing the envelope creatively is another important element of Deschutes's philosophy, and it is in this area where Deschutes's larger size really becomes an asset.

As brewmaster, Larry brings a unique skill set the company. He has the technical, high-volume experience to ensure production quality while also having the passion and knowledge to provide the brewing team with a well-honed creative discipline. He first began by adding more layers of control to the brewing process to improve consistency. He encountered some resistance at first from his brewers, but they soon realized how much it affected the achievement of their ultimate goal. "I'm kind of a grumpy guy," Larry says playfully, "a very driven, demanding, 'retentive person.' I demand excellence from the brewing staff while allowing them freedom with their brewing endeavors." He goes on to explain, "I cannot be the sole creative source of the brewery. I support them with equipment, ingredients, techniques, and my experiences from travelling the world." Larry also uses Deschutes's resources to provide all of his brewers with extensive training and educational opportunities. "We have the highest educated brewers per barrel of any brewery in the world," he says proudly. In this way Larry prepares fertile grounds for his team's creative explorations.

When Larry first began at Deschutes "the formulation they had was very loose," he recalls, so he took a page from his Pabst playbook. "I made a structured [formulation] with a place for pricing on the brewery sheet." Larry stresses that pricing "means everything when you're making a light American Lager." In the macrobrewing environment, he explains, "the sales and marketing people dictated how the beers were brewed," but at Deschutes, "I eventually deleted [the pricing] column. The raw material cost really didn't matter." Deschutes's size allows it the freedom to experiment and create new beers without having to "pay attention to how much it costs," says Larry. "We do what it takes to make what we want. I dictate to finance and sales what they have to charge to get a return on that product." This arrangement is the complete opposite of his previous brewing experience. Now creativity rules the day.

Deschutes's uncompromising approach to brewing means that they can be very particular about the ingredients they use. "We don't ever do anything the easy way," Larry says. For example, Deschutes uses only whole flower hops in all of their beers, goes directly to local farms to acquire fresh cherries for The Dissident barrel-aged sour ale, imports genuine Seville bitter oranges from Spain for Black Butte XIII anniversary edition, and sources specific French oak and Bourbon barrels for aging The Abyss Russian imperial stout. Larry has great admiration for these beers. The Dissident "is a beer that we put out there when sour beers weren't all that popular," he says. It went on to win a gold medal at the GABF in 2008. And "The Abyss truly represents the ingenuity of our brewers." Its recipe includes licorice and molasses and one third of each batch is barrel-aged before being added to the final blend to create a host of rich, deep complexities.

Again, the contrast with macrobreweries is striking. Looking at hops usage alone, Deschutes uses an amount of hops each year equivalent to what a macrobrewery producing over 1 million barrels of light American lager would use. But Larry does credit macrobrewing with helping craft beer to some degree. "The marketing machine has created the light American lager, but is also responsible for the craft beer industry." I pressed him for clarification. "To make light American lager is a very challenging issue. You're always pushing the system to make the best beer you can," he says. "The thing that is most gratifying is, who are your customers? What are they expecting? [Macro drinkers] didn't want Abyss or Dissident, they wanted lager." Larry credits the ubiquity of bland beers with creating a craft beer revolution in favor of unique, locally produced options. "Now our customers are pushing us to produce new, flavorful beers."

One interesting example of a new long-term project Deschutes has been working on is an *heirloom* Cascade variety fresh-hop beer. "The flavor of Cascade hops has changed over the years," notes Larry, who has been brewing with this classic American variety since 1974. As a result of continued propagation through cuttings for commercial hops production, "the stock has been diluted over the years," he explains. To recreate that taste that first propelled American craft beer forward for today's fans, Deschutes has leased four acres of hop fields in the Willamette Valley that it replanted with "the original rhizomes that everything has come from." For two years Deschutes contracted farmers to slowly divide the original rhizomes until the entire fields are filled with plants. The first beer to feature these heirloom hops was a 1,000-barrel batch of Fresh Hop Mirror Pond Pale Ale, which was released in the fall of 2011 as part of their Bond St. series of special edition beers.

Deschutes's portfolio of year-round beers includes Black Butte Porter, Mirror Pond Pale Ale, Inversion IPA, Green Lakes Organic Ale amber, Obsidian Stout, Cascade Ale blonde, and Bachelor ESB.

Their seasonal releases include Red Chair Northwest Pale Ale (January–May), Twilight Summer Ale blonde (May–September), and Jubelale strong ale (October–December). Reserve Series ales are released periodically throughout the year and include The Abyss Russian imperial stout, Jubel 2000 and 2010 strong ale (brewed once a decade), Black Butte XX–XXIII anniversary reserve porter (numerical designation increases each year), The Dissident barrel-aged sour ale, and Mirror Mirror barleywine. The Bond St. Series Ales are experimental ales inspired by their original Bond St. brewpub and consist of yearly releases of Hop Henge IPA, Hops in the Dark Cascadian Dark Ale, Hop Trip fresh hop pale ale, and the occasional other special release.

Deschutes's beers are currently distributed in Alaska, Arizona, California, Colorado, Hawaii, Idaho, Minnesota, Montana, Nevada, New Mexico, North Dakota, Oregon, South Dakota, Texas, Utah, Washington, and Wyoming, with plans to begin distribution soon in Kansas and Missouri.

Fresh Hop Mirror Pond Pale Ale

Medium amber-gold with a medium, dense white head. Fresh hop aroma consisting of damp earthiness, soft spice, delicate pine, and freshly cut grass along with lightly toasted grain in the background. The flavor follows directly from the aroma with a soft, well-balanced bitterness that resides alongside crisp grain notes. It is difficult to determine the specific difference of the heirloom Cascade hops used here being that this beer is made with wet hops and standard Mirror Pond is not. Considered on its own, the subtle, complex hoppy nuances of this beer make for a highly enjoyable historical drinking experience.

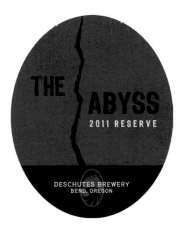

The Abyss

Pure opaque black with a dark brown rim and a fine, thin chocolate-brown head. Complex aroma of dark chocolate, coffee, treacle, and a slight milky roasted malt character with hints of dark spice, anise, and bourbon barrel aging. The flavor presents bitter coffee and chocolate, sweet molasses, and dark bitterness that rises and then fades over a backdrop of subtle spice, licorice, and wonderful oxidized characteristics. A very deft hand with the malt balance is evident here. Each element is well represented in a way that is complementary to one another. Each flavor peaks at a different moment so that none is overpowered and each can be discerned both individually and in combination with the whole. The body is exquisitely balanced with the 11% alcohol present only in the structure and not in the aroma, flavor, or finish as any harshness. Only a slight warmth accompanies the bitter roasted finish. The mouthfeel is disarmingly light despite the massive, dark flavor profile. This is a meticulously crafted beer.

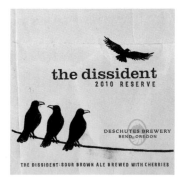

The Dissident

Dark orange-amber with a thick, medium-fine off-white head. Dark caramel malt aroma with earthy and spicy hops and deep citrus notes. Strong malt presence with both nutty caramel and cocoa top notes. Full-flavored hops and malt profiles deliver copious amounts of bitterness with herbaceous hops and roasted caramel malt. Caramel and toffee flavors are evident in measured doses without being sweet along with candied quince, orange zest, and dark muskmelon flavors. The body is very full but maintains a balance among all of the intense flavor characteristics. The long finish phases though both hops and malt complexities.

THE ROCKIES

AVERY BREWING CO.—BOULDER, CO
Adam Avery, Brewmaster & President

Adam Avery has an agenda. He wants you to drink good beer. The team at Avery Brewing Company in Boulder, Colorado, brews beer that they want to drink, and they hope you like it too, but that's largely irrelevant. "We're not trying to fill a hole. We're trying to change the demand," says Adam. He founded Avery in 1993 with the intention of brewing big, hoppy beers, and concedes that their products were perhaps "a little before their time." The word he uses to best describe Avery's beers is "aggressive." The style that best represented brewing in Colorado then was the American amber, a style that Avery wasn't that interested in. "We didn't make money for nine years," says Adam. However, he does feel that those years were very well-spent educating the public on the type of beers he believed they *should* be drinking. In 1996 "we produced the first bottled IPA in Colorado." It didn't sell well initially, but being the first one in the market helped build a familiarity that is now paying off. Avery IPA, their flagship beer, currently accounts for 35% of their business. "We are cutting-edge and always trying to push it, for the right reasons." One such reason, according to Adam, is: "We never make a beer to sell a bunch of it."

Adam describes Avery Brewing Company as "a brewer's brewery." Even if the general public isn't quite ready for a particular style, and it doesn't succeed commercially at first, he's satisfied knowing that he and his brewers and others in the industry appreciate it, and that it may help to free up the brewing climate and promote more experimentation. "We can influence other local breweries to be adventurous as well," says Adam. "They may not like it, but they respect it. Everything we make resonates with people in a different way." He sums up his mission succinctly: "We're not trying to switch everyone from light lager to a wimpy amber." Like Avery's beers, Adam is aggressive about exposing people to serious flavor. "We've got to have people out front with spears driving people forward to bigger, more diverse flavors . . . We're trying to pound this down their throats: 'Hey, this is something you should like!'"

"We've been brewing a style that others are just now beginning to brew," says Adam. "I think that we are industry leaders." He lists a string of "neat little sayings": "'innovative,' 'pushing the envelope,' 'brewing outside the box,'" call it what you will, "we're about huge flavor," says Adam. Avery's first big break came in 1998 with Hog Heaven, a dry-hopped American barleywine, the brew that Adam considers "our most important beer." "It was a gamble," he says. He wanted to create a "hugely hoppy ale to see what people would think. We needed to do something to set ourselves apart." Adam gives "big props" to Ken Grossman at Sierra Nevada Brewing Company and their Bigfoot Barleywine, the inspiration for Hog Heaven. While admiring that classic American craft beer and lamenting "the raspberry-wheat craze of the mid-90s," Adam thought, "we can make our own big, super-hoppy barleywine." Using a single hop variety, Columbus (his favorite), and a simple grain bill consisting of crystal 75 and two-row malts, he created a beer that he describes as "super simple in its recipe, but not at all simple in the mouth." With Hog Heaven, he had succeeded in creating the "overtly aggressive, very hop-driven beer" that he had envisioned. Hog Heaven captured the attention of beer geeks online and several out-of-state distributors. "It got us started with out-of-state distribution," he says, "and led us down the road of big, massive, flavorful beers."

Such risk-taking is not uncommon for Avery. In fact, it best describes their brewing philosophy. "We're not afraid of flavor," Adam says. He recalls Avery's fifteenth Anniversary Ale, brewed in 2008, which was a 100% brettanomyces-fermented beer made with black mission figs, hibiscus flowers, and white pepper: "We got equal love and hate mail . . . perhaps a bit more hate mail," regarding that beer. He paraphrases one memorable bit of feedback they received: "Though I didn't like it, I'm glad you guys had the balls to put out a beer that tastes like that." "Nobody brews 100% brett beers," says Adam, let alone a 400-barrel batch of it. "It was not a success, financially," he notes. "It was too polarizing." But it certainly did further Avery's mission. It was very successful in "promoting a conversation about what beer is and what it can be. 'I hated that beer' is always the beginning of the best conversations with beer drinkers," says Adam. "I love to have that interaction. Some are really cool about it, some are not. Their palates are not ready for these beers. It's fun to almost talk people into understanding the beer. They respect it even if they didn't necessarily enjoy it." In this way Adam considers a beer like that to be a great success on a personal level, and appreciates the attention it brought to the brewery. "It embodies our core values. We did what we wanted to do and consumer demand be damned. That's why we're small," says Adam. "We're not interested in being 'mainstream,' even among craft brewers. We are successful if nobody's telling us what to do."

Pushing people out of their beer comfort zones has become a successful business model for Avery, which has recently experienced a 60 percent growth rate and is set to max-out its capacity by the end of 2011. Adam is amused by the fact that many of the larger breweries are now adopting some of the same principles he began with. "You can't *not* make big and interesting beers now in the craft brewing environment," he says. "Now it's kind of funny to see the reversal—[brewers are] reminding themselves about the soul of craft beer. There's now a market for all of these crazy beers that we've been wanting to do. It's now viable. You can make money producing these small batches." This is perhaps most evident in the public's reception of Avery's ongoing series of eccentric, limited edition barrel-aged beers. With titles ranging from coyly suggestive to nonsensical, these are beers which defy any categorization more specific than "wild ale." The release parties at the brewery are well attended and these thought-provoking ales—many of them sour—spark impassioned conversations among their fans and detractors.

This confrontational spirit certainly is not limited to Avery's one-off beer releases. The over-the-top attitude is powerfully embodied by their "Demons of Ale" series of strong ales which consists of Samael's Oak-Aged Ale (14.5% ABV), The Beast Grand Cru (14.9% ABV), and Mephistopheles' Stout (15.1% ABV). These powerfully flavored beers contain some of the highest alcohol levels to be found among craft beers.

Avery also brews a variety of traditional styles, each with a non-traditional twist. Joe's Premium American Pilsner is much more substantially hopped than usual interpretations of the style. Even Adam needs to take a break from double IPAs once in a while. "I'm 45 and can't drink as much as I want to and feel good the next day," he says. "I needed to make a beer that I could session on . . . [Something] hoppy with a lot of flavor and low alcohol." Avery's New World Porter is everything one would expect from a traditional porter, but is dry-hopped with American hops for an added kick.

Another popular beer for Avery is The Maharaja Imperial IPA. Adam describes this beer as a "hop monster—super-aggressive in the West Coast style of imperial IPAs. We wanted to make a sledgehammer." No expense is spared for its hop additions. "We're almost positive that we waste hops in that beer, using more than we can extract the bitterness from," he says. He remarks that "almost every single flavor that you can get from American hops is in there: orange, grapefruit, lemon, topical fruit, melon, pine, gange, everything." "We add malt to give it a semblance of balance," he adds. Adam is a huge fan of this style, and feels that "they should be kind of hard to drink—challenging." Which brings us to Dugana, another double IPA that "took us two years to develop into what we wanted." Why another high-gravity IPA? "We had room," says Adam. "I wanted a different flavor profile than Maharaja—more to the point, with a drier flavor in the mid-alcohol range." That would be 8.5% ABV. So, between Avery IPA, Hog Heaven, The Maharaja, and Dugana, "We have all of our bases covered—four hop bombs with varying flavor profiles. We just ask ourselves 'What do we want to drink today?' It's fun own-ing a brewery."

Adam is very grateful for the craft beer fans that have stuck with him. "It's fun to watch people trying to educate their friends. Craft beer fans take it very personally and take a lot of ownership in it." He thanks the brewery's fans "for understanding our quirkiness and fighting the battle with us against bland, flavorless beer." His only request is to keep the movement going: "Make your friends drink it. Make sure your kids drink it when they turn 21."

Avery's year-round lineup of beers includes: India Pale Ale, White Rascal Belgian-style witbier, Ellie's Brown Ale, Out of Bounds Stout, and Joe's Premium American Pilsner. Also avail-able year-round are "The Holy Trinity of Ales," consisting of: Hog Heaven American barleywine, The Reverend Belgian-style quadru-pel, and Salvation Belgian-style strong golden ale.

Three seasonal six-packs are released including: New World Porter (Jan.-April), Karma Belgian-style pale ale (April-Aug.), and Old Jubilation English-style old ale (Sep.-Dec.). The sea-sonal releases making up "The Dictator's Series" include: The Maharaja Imperial IPA (Summer), The Kaiser Imperial Oktober-fest Lager (one batch each Aug.), and The Czar Russian Imperial Stout (Nov.-Feb.). The seasonal "Demons of Ale" series in-cludes: Samael's Oak-Aged Ale English-style strong ale (variable yearly release), The Beast Grand Cru Belgian-style dark strong ale (one batch each Aug.), and Mephistopheles' Stout (one batch each Dec.).

Occasional one-off batches of "Barrel-Aged Series" are re-leased periodically throughout the year. A different one-off an-niversary beer is released each May named for the number of the anniversary (nineteen in 2012). Collaboration not Litigation Ale is a collaboration ale brewed with Russian River Brewing Company with a variable release schedule each year.

Avery's beers are distributed in Alaska, Arkansas, California, Colorado, Florida, Georgia, Illinois, Kansas, Kentucky, Massa-chusetts, Michigan, Minnesota, Missouri, New Jersey, New York, North Carolina, Ohio, Oregon, Pennsylvania, South Carolina, Texas, Virginia, Washington, and Wisconsin.

IPA

Bright, clear copper-orange with a fine, medium-dense white head. Lots of fresh orange in the aroma along with pine needles, earth, and an intriguing honey-like floral sweetness beside a bit of nutty toasted malt. The flavor is dry and crisp with bright hoppiness and resinous bitterness. Citrus zest, honeyed malt, and the suggestion of chamomile flowers are also present. The body is fairly light and quite dry, which delivers the hop bitterness clearly and cleanly. Only a bit of alcohol is evident in the finish. Extremely refreshing and drinkable.

Hog Heaven

Dark orange-amber with a thick, medium-fine off-white head. Dark caramel malt aroma with earthy and spicy hops and deep citrus notes. Strong malt presence with both nutty caramel and cocoa top notes. Full-flavored hops and malt profiles deliver copious amounts of bitterness with herbaceous hops and roasted caramel malt. Caramel and toffee flavors are evident in measured doses without being sweet along with candied quince, orange zest, and dark muskmelon flavors. The body is very full but maintains a balance among all of the intense flavor characteristics. The long finish phases though both hops and malt complexities.

Maharaja

Dark amber with a fine, medium-dense white head. Dark caramel malt aroma supports powerful notes of candied citrus, resinous hops, and dried flowers. A slight suggestion of cocoa powder follows in the back-end. The flavor is strongly malty with both caramel and toffee aspects along with significant alcohol sweetness. This is balanced by a huge, resinous hops profile with dark citrus and deep piney characteristics. The big, thick body delivers a counter-punch of malt and alcohol that makes for a surprisingly drinkable, very full-flavored beer.

GREAT DIVIDE BREWING CO.—DENVER, CO
Brian Dunn, Founder

The name Great Divide is very suggestive of the huge rift between the aspirations of artisanal craft breweries and the macrobrewing companies that have long defined the American beer scene. The name is also suggestive of the iconic Rocky Mountain peaks visible from nearly everywhere in Denver, CO, the home of Great Divide Brewing Company. Brian Dunn, the brewery's founder, definitely feels that "the geographic diversity of the state is reflected in our beers." Though the Denver area, and the Rocky Mountains, have long been associated with the Coors Brewing Company, Colorado is now home to many regional and microbreweries as well. But perhaps none embody the rugged spirit of that range like Great Divide.

When asked which beer best represents the brewing philosophy of Great Divide Brian names Yeti, a robust Russian imperial stout. This beer is opaque black, full of dark roasted malt flavors, possesses a high level of bitterness, and contains 9.5% alcohol. This is undoubtedly the furthest thing possible from the light lager that has historically flowed from this region. Beers as strong and densely flavored as this can even be divisive among craft beer drinkers. But Yeti is delicious. Brian describes Great Divide's mission as an attempt to make "assertive and challenging beers that are a lot of fun, but with a sense of balance as well." He does go on to add, "Yeti is pretty edgy though."

This liquid challenge has been met by droves of craft beer fans, and Great Divide has been steadily growing at a rate of 40–50 percent per year for the last several years. Brian describes the biggest challenge facing the brewery as "keeping up with the growth in an organized fashion; it can be a challenge to keep the infrastructure and organizational aspects growing at the same rate." Their desire to reach what he calls, "a comfortable size through managed growth" has even included retracting out of some markets to better serve local ones. But at this same time, their portfolio of beers has continued to expand.

Yeti has been brewed in nine different variations including: Whiskey Barrel-Aged Yeti, Belgian-Style Yeti, Yeti with Brett, Oak-Aged Yeti, Chocolate Oak-Aged Yeti, Espresso Oak-Aged Yeti, Vanilla Bean Yeti, and Chocolate Oak Aged Yeti with Cayenne and Cocoa Nibs. None of these beers are for the faint of heart. These derivations, many experimental, are much like the explorations of a chef working on a new version of a classic favorite. Brian described to me how the culinary arts have affected his explorations in beer, "We use ingredients that we all like—that we've learned about from eating. We love chocolate and spice, why not add it to beer? We all drink a lot of espresso . . ." he trails off. Why not? The cost of the 880 pounds of espresso that Great Divide uses per year to brew one beer might be a reason for some brewers, but Great Divide isn't concerned. Brian puts it simply: "It costs what it costs; we only use ingredients that we like to use."

This philosophy extends to all of Great Divide's beers. Some offerings are equally bold, such as the popular Hercules double India pale ale, an early entrant in this cult style that brewers often stumble over, producing examples with syrupy maltiness and flat hop bitterness. Hercules, however, is precisely constructed despite its outsized nature. Brian considers it "one of the more balanced beers we make." Great Divide makes another double IPA, which it ages on oak: Anniversary Wood Aged Double IPA (the "18th Anniversary" edition was released in 2012). Traditional English IPAs were originally shipped from England to India in oak barrels. Their pitch linings would have kept those early beers from picking up much flavor from the wood during their voyage. But the American double IPA, with its significant malt backbone and alcohol presence, along with a huge hop character, could stand up to the type of barrel aging applied to many of the other big craft beer styles. This type of experimentation blends old and new ideas together to create original, contemporary craft beer styles.

The inspiration for these types of craft beer explorations is very often the result of continually drinking a lot of different beers.

"Being in the business, we're tasting new types of the beers all the time," Brian says happily. But he takes equal satisfaction in drinking old, classic beer styles. Great Divide's spirit of ingenuity results from a combination of these old and new brewing traditions on the American craft beer frontier. Sometimes a gap in the portfolio calls for the addition of a classically styled beer. This was the case for their spring seasonal, Colette, Great Divide's first saison-style beer. Other times Brian likes to "put a twist on a style by doing our own thing to it." This notion is often borne out of drinking a lot of different examples of a style that then inspires them to brew something original, with a combination of characteristics that none of the others possess. This is the case for their many tweaks on their barleywine, Old Ruffian, and their explorations of using Belgian yeast strains in non-Belgian styles, as in Belgian Yeti and Belgica, a Belgian-style pale ale, among others.

But sometimes there's no substitute for just looking out your front door to see what inspires you. "We get a lot of inspiration from the state that we live in," Brian says as he recalls fondly creating the original recipe for their first English-style strong ale in 1995. "I can remember just where I was when I sketched out that recipe," he says. Despite the fact that it's name, Hibernation Ale, evokes thoughts of the long, mountain winters, it was a warm summer day in Denver and Brian was sitting outside on his porch, the bustle of the city nearby, "in flip flops and shorts, drinking a beer, and thinking about one that will be brewed for an October release." The hearty 8.7% alcohol winter seasonal he designed was probably very unlike the beer he was drinking at the time, but his inspiration held strong and they immediately put it into production. "We didn't do any test batches," he noted, "We just brewed out a full batch" and it remains one of his favorites today.

The sense of place Great Divide's beers convey is reinforced by the fact that the majority of the base malts used in their beers are grown and malted in Colorado. Maintaining these supply lines can be challenging, and Colorado is relatively new to the malting industry, but Brian feels very strongly that it's important to utilize these local products in Great Divide's Beers as often as he can. Additionally, the glass for bottling is produced 60 miles away and the cardboard for their packaging is also made and printed locally.

The ways in which Great Divide Brewing Company can support the local community are some of the most exciting aspects of the business for Brian. In addition to the charitable projects Great Divide participates in, including an effort to rejuvenate the neighborhood surrounding the brewery, he is witnessing a trend among the locals he encounters in the taproom and at special events: "People are becoming more and more accepting of locally brewed beer and their level of knowledge about the beers is increasing," he says. "Beer drinkers are becoming quite savvy and that's great to see," he adds. Brian only wants to encourage this adventurous spirit among people through Great Divide's Beers. One way they do this is by listing multiple beer and food pairing suggestions on the label of every bottle of Great Divide beer. "It's a personal mission of mine to promote beer and food," Brian says. "In the last five years more restaurants are starting to carry great beer—it's starting to resonate with people," he notes. "Chefs and restaurant owners have been on our side for a while, but now regular drinkers are on our side as well."

The efforts of breweries like Great Divide to harness the spirit of their community and embody it in a product that brings people together and share local pride are doing much to shape the quality of life offered through the appreciation of great local beer. In this way the rugged spirit of the Rockies, and the beers it has inspired, is uniting people in good taste and good cheer.

Great Divide Brewing Company brews nine year-round beers including Claymore Scotch ale, Denver Pale Ale, Hoss Rye Lager, Hades Belgian-style ale, Hercules double IPA, Samurai unfiltered rice ale, Titan IPA, Wild Raspberry Ale, and Yeti Russian imperial stout. They also brew 13 seasonal beers which include Belgica Belgian-style IPA (Jan.–April), Belgian Style Yeti (July–Sep.), Chocolate Oak Aged Yeti (April–July), Colette saison style ale (Apr.–July), Espresso Oak Aged Yeti (Jan.–Apr.), Fresh Hop pale ale (Oct.–Dec.), Grand Cru Belgian-style dark ale (Jan.–Mar.), Hibernation Ale English-style old ale (Oct.–Jan.), Oak Aged Yeti (Oct.–Jan.), Old Ruffian barleywine (Dec.), Rumble American IPA (July–Oct.), Smoked Baltic Porter (July–Oct.), and an annual Anniversary Wood Aged Double IPA (Apr.–July).

Great Divide's beers are distributed in Alabama, Arizona, California, Colorado, Florida, Georgia, Illinois, Kansas, Maryland,

Minnesota, Missouri, Nebraska, New Jersey, New York, North Carolina, Oklahoma, Oregon, Pennsylvania, South Carolina, Texas, Virginia, and Washington.

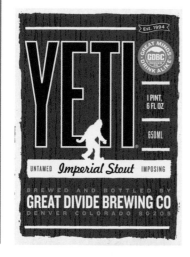

YETI

Thick opaque black with medium-fine, creamy, chocolate-colored head. Sweet aroma of molasses, toffee, dark chocolate, coffee, caramel, and a hint of red berry fruits. The flavor is intensely bitter with hops and roasted malt over a thick sweetness with coffee, dark toffee, roasted grain characteristics along with some alcohol as well. Thick and syrupy in the mouth with an assault of bitterness and sweetness. Intriguingly intense.

OAK-AGED YETI

Thick, opaque black with a thin, medium-fine dark tan head. Sweet aroma of dark roasted malt with caramel, dark toffee, coffee liqueur, and vanilla. Bittersweet chocolate and alcohol notes round out the dense aroma profile. Strong dark chocolate flavors with bitter coffee and a touch of milk-like creaminess. Well-balanced malt sweetness in the background with a well-integrated alcohol character. Vanilla and caramel oak notes are intermingled throughout and add a rounded fullness to the flavor profile. The full body maintains good dimension on the palate where the heavy flavors are evenly conveyed. The bitter finish fades into soft alcohol sweetness.

HIBERNATION ALE

Dark chestnut brown with a thin, creamy light tan head. Aroma of sweet roasted malt, subtle cocoa, earthy hops, and a bit of toasted bread, with hints of alcohol and dark candied fruit. More dark malt in the flavor with a dry nuttiness and softly spicy and herbaceous hops. Roasted bitterness and some alcohol sweetness assert themselves in the finish which follows from a hearty, well-rounded body.

THE MIDWEST

BELL'S BREWING CO.—GALESBURG, MI

Larry Bell, Founder & President

"Absolutely thrilling," is how Larry Bell, founder and president of Bell's Brewery, Inc., describes working in the craft beer community. When he founded his original homebrewing shop in 1983 in Kalamazoo, Michigan, he hardly realized he would become one of America's craft brewing pioneers. Now he operates the oldest craft brewery east of Boulder, Colorado, which produces 180,000 barrels of beer annually. "I'm just a homebrewer whose hobby has gotten out of control," says Larry. "I'm a homebrewer at heart."

This grand hobby got its start rather unromantically. "My dad made homemade wine. I was a beer can collector so I enjoyed trying different kinds of beer. I realized I could make beer and just started brewing it in the basement." He subsidized these early efforts by illegally selling his homebrews, but he eventually "got scared that I was going to get busted." Larry recalls, "I had nothing else to do so why not start a brewery?"

He invested a $200 birthday present from his mother into opening a homebrew shop and incorporated a brewery on paper in 1983 so he could begin "selling stock to unsuspecting homebrewers that came through the door." In 1985 he gathered his investments, secured a loan, and bought a big homebrewing setup with a 15 gallon soup kettle and started brewing in a dilapidated warehouse with $39,000 of seed money. "I didn't know that I was a nano-brewery in 1985," says Larry, in reference to a new term in the industry describing today's similarly tiny upstarts.

Larry brewed 150 barrels in 1986 and patiently waited for the public's tastes to catch up to the robustly flavored beers he was making. Today is another story. Fifty percent of Bell's production is a seasonal wheat beer called Oberon, which is has a light, fruity flavor and a delicate, refreshing body. "I never imagined that Americans would drink so much cloudy wheat beer," says Larry. "It's fascinating to see the education of the American public and how they have really grabbed onto craft beer."

Another 33 percent of production is IPAs and double IPAs. Two Hearted Ale, named for a river in Michigan's Upper Peninsula made famous by an Ernest Hemingway short story, is a classic American IPA made with 100% Centennial hops. The beer has a very loyal following, and the trout on the label is a nod to the excellent fishing conditions the Big Two-Hearted River offers. In the early nineties Two Hearted Ale was a completely different beer. Brewed as a pale ale, "it was made with English malts and Wisconsin hops, which represented the two hearts of that beer," says Larry. But, "the original project had some issues and was shelved." The brand eventually returned as an IPA. The massive popularity of Two Hearted Ale has made Bell's the single largest buyer of Centennial hops in the world. Larry lovingly describes this beer as forming a "one plus one equals three" equation. "The Centennial hops and our yeast management match up so well to bring out some wonderful aromas. It's not all hops—there's a lot going on with the yeast as well. The aromas combine in a magical way that's just one of those great things about brewing," says Larry.

Bell's Hopslam is a huge, full-bodied double IPA whose popularity is growing so rapidly that the brewery cannot keep up with demand. "Somebody flipped a switch on Hopslam this year," says Larry. "We made 40% more and it felt like we made 40% less. I wish I could get more hops."

The rest of the brewery's production consists of the seven other year-round beers, 12 other seasonal beers, and dozens more specialty releases each year, including a large number of stouts. "We still are idiots enough to make 14 different stouts in November," says Larry. "A big brewery would cut out all those other brands. But we don't because we like doing those other things. A lot of people think of us as a stout brewery because of all the stouts we make."

One of the first stouts brewed by Bell's, and still one of their most popular, is the Cherry Stout, which Larry first made in 1988. "It really seems to galvanize people. They either love it or hate it," says Larry. The recipe was modeled after what many of his home-brew customers were doing with local Michigan cherries. When he decided to produce it commercially, the previously unseen combination of beer and fruit confounded the label approval board. "The government didn't know what to do with me," says Larry. "It took four months to get it approved." With its superb balance between roasted malts and darkly sweet cherries, this beer has an amazing resemblance to chocolate-covered dried cherries.

If Bell's is beginning to sound like an unconventional craft brewery, then Larry's goal has been achieved. The overall eccentric feel of the brewery is well recognized. Bell's operates a brewpub at the original Kalamazoo site called The Eccentric Café. Many one-off draught-only beers are tested out here including fan favorites such as Pawpaw Hefeweizen, made with the obscure local banana-like pawpaw fruit. But the biggest event of the year for Bell's is Eccentric Day, held each year in December. The day before the party a batch of Eccentric Ale is brewed to be served at the party *the following year*. The recipe for Eccentric Ale changes each year but past recipes have been made with a variety of herbs, spices, and syrups including, birch bark, hawberry syrup, juniper berries, elderflowers, popcorn, and malted milk balls. It is generally brewed to a strength of around 11% alcohol. The event creates quite a buzz in the community. Larry says he is often asked, "How do you guys do it? How do you get everybody so excited?" His answer: "We're just regular folks who know how to let our hair down and have a good time. The public feels that fun and they want to be a part of it." It surely also helps that Eccentric Day is a massive dress-up party. "Not in costumes like Halloween," Larry specifies. "You come dressed up as someone that you're not. It's a freak show."

But in addition to all the fun and games, Bell's is a major force in American craft beer. "We have history. That's one thing," says Larry. "But we still like to play and experiment." Over the years Bell's has amassed a portfolio of beers that provides a unique opportunity to explore a wide variety of flavors in beer, all within the framework of their own unique style. "It's our house flavor," says Larry. "It's the yeast that's in most of our beers that people have come to recognize and love." Whether complex and eccentric, or simple and classic, "There's fun, and then there's brewing consistent quality beers." Larry feels Bell's is best defined by its "quality, attention to detail, and personality. We're eccentric and fun. People are looking for that kind of fun in a product." And Bell's is eager to give it to them.

Bell's year-round lineup includes Amber Ale, Two Hearted Ale American IPA, Pale Ale, Porter, Kalamazoo Stout with brewer's licorice, Third Coast Beer American pale ale, Bell's Lager Beer, and Oarsman Ale American wheat.

Bell's seasonal lineup includes Consecrator Doppelbock (spring), Oberon Ale American wheat (summer), The Oracle DIPA double IPA (summer), Octoberfest Beer (fall), Hell Hath No Fury . . . Ale Belgian-style dubbel (fall), Best Brown Ale (Fall), Hopslam double IPA (winter), Winter White Ale Belgian-style witbier (winter), Cherry Stout (winter), Special Double Cream Stout (winter), Java Stout with coffee (winter), Expedition Stout Russian imperial stout (winter), Third Coast Old Ale (winter), and Christmas Ale Scotch-style ale with 100% Michigan barley (winter).

Bell's also produces many variable release special edition beers that are primarily draught-only with limited distribution. Bottled special releases include Eccentric Ale (variable recipe), Batch XOOO strong ale (currently on Batch 10000. The name and recipe change with each 1000 batch milestone), Thee Wild One barrel-aged sour ale, Quinannan Falls Special Lager, Rye Stout, and Sparkling Ale Belgian-style tripel.

Bell's beer are distributed in Alabama, Arizona, Florida, Georgia, Illinois, Indiana, Iowa, Kentucky, Michigan, Minnesota, Missouri, North Carolina, North Dakota, Ohio Pennsylvania, Puerto Rico, South Carolina, Virginia, and Wisconsin.

TWO HEARTED ALE

Light copper-gold with a thick, fine white head with excellent retention. Lots of fresh, fruity hops in the aroma, which suggests some sweetness. The light, grainy malt profile is very well integrated with the lemon and grapefruit citrus hops characteristics. The body is dry, tightly structured, and quite light on its feet while balancing all the flavor characteristics. The result is a highly flavorful, refreshing, and powerful IPA. Side note: this beer wins my award for the coolest label ever.

CHERRY STOUT

Opaque brown-black with a fine tan head. Sweet roasted aromas of coffee and chocolate alongside rich dark cherry notes. The flavor profile is largely a continuation of the aroma with the addition of sweet-tart cherry flavors and well-integrated hop bitterness. The entire mélange conjures up quality dark chocolate-covered dried cherries. The roasted malt aspects, combined with a vibrant cherry fruit profile makes for a balanced, multidimensional body that clearly conveys the depth of this complex beer.

ECCENTRIC ALE

2008 edition brewed with birch syrup, honey, maple syrup, spices, juniper berries, and elderflowers. Nearly opaque very dark brown with a thin, fine tan head. Strong dark spice and herbal characteristics with significant maltiness and alcohol sweetness. There is an intriguing root beer-like aromatic profile that borders on the complexity of an Italian amaro digestive liqueur. Sweet malt flavors serve as a foundation for the complex herbal and spice characteristics that make for a highly unusual drinking experience. Caramel and soft roasted malt notes round out the full body that presents the 10.1% alcohol component quite delicately. Eccentric is the perfect word for this original beverage.

FOUNDERS BREWING CO.—GRAND RAPIDS, MI
Mike Stevens, President & CEO

There are many types of professional brewers making beer in the United Sates. Some view it as an occupation or a simple business venture; others passionately strive to continually push the limits of their creativity and production to grow into a serious force. And then there is Mike Stevens, the president and co-founder of Founders Brewing Company in Grand Rapids, Michigan, whose philosophy of life directly informs his inspiration for brewing, and his craft brewing culture, in turn, helps shape the life he chooses to live. Mike's brewing inspiration "comes from life outside of work. There's inspiration from the fun and great things in life outside of what the 'serious' world is. Friendships, travel, things that open your mind and make you ask 'what if' all play a role in helping us make better beers." He describes this intertwined way of living and brewing as a process of "self discovery," saying "the more you explore in life the better you become at making beer." Founders' brewing philosophy "attracts a breed of person that looks at living life as the reason that we're here—beers, careers, and family," says Mike.

Such a holistic approach to brewing and life highlights the ability of a brewery and its products to enrich the social lives of both a local community and the greater craft beer community. "We create experiences. We create memories. We're people's weekends. We put smiles on people's faces at the end of the week. We're in a cool position to be a part of people's lives. I take that very seriously," says Mike. Though such enthusiasm is not just endemic to Founders, Mike expresses his beliefs on the power of craft beer in a particularly passionate way. "Live the dream," he says, "and we do believe that. We are creating a dream here and people look at us and what we're doing and it makes them smile and feel good. It puts a warmth in their hearts. We have a responsibility to respond to them, and accept that if we move forward together with that in mind it will make us both that much stronger." Mike's enthusiasm is infectious. "I'm excited about the whole industry," he says. "It goes beyond a couple of guys owning a brewery—you become somebody in your community. Hopefully brewers can see that and take advantage of that to do some good things. This industry can become something extremely powerful."

So what makes Founders beer such a powerful force? "We are in the minority in how we process our beer," says Mike. "We are much more focused on the creative-exploratory side. We're not going to put all of our efforts into *selling* our beer, but into *making* it. It keeps us focused on our craft." Mike thinks that the craft beer renaissance is a good thing, but that one can lose track of what's most important in brewing. Given craft beer's proliferation, Mike expounds on the importance of remaining dedicated to brewing exceptional beers: "It's easy these days to get caught-up in sales figures. If I was a betting man, I'd say that too much over-zealous brewing could lead to reduced quality. Sometimes brewers try to 'over-create,' or be something that they're not, as opposed to being true to their craft. The volume doesn't matter to me. I'm more focused on staying true to that craft, and wherever that volume goes, that is where it should be." This notion follows directly from the motto prominently displayed on Founders' website: "We don't brew beer for the masses. Instead, our beers are crafted for a chosen few, a small cadre of renegades and rebels who enjoy a beer that pushes the limits of what is commonly accepted as taste. In short, we make beer for people like us."

This rebel alliance is growing, however, and the demand for more flavorful beers is steadily increasing. "This is more than a movement," says Mike, "it's a sustainable movement. It will forever change the dynamics of beer in America. Craft is here to stay, and hasn't yet hit its top market share. We're changing people's tastes. People's taste buds are evolving. They're eating differently now," explains Mike. "Cuisine is becoming more and more important in our field. [Beer and food] are two separate industries, but the way they operate is akin to one another. Together they make a great piece," he says. Mike and Founders are acutely aware of how craft beer and fine food, especially when enjoyed together, can be socially unifying forces that shape and transform our shared experiences. In this way the craft beer movement is very relevant to America's growing whole foods movement. Within this movement, Mike says: "The breweries that stay true to their roots are the ones in this industry that will succeed—not in terms of barrels, but in terms of their quality."

Mike describes Founders as making beer in a "traditional homebrew style," meaning that its recipes and methods are created to fulfill the brewers' creative urges without any compromises to quality. He also notes that Founders is "known not for making one or two great beers, but many excellent beers across our portfolio of styles." He adds that "all of our recent medals have come across all different styles—not doubling up on any beer." What these beers share in common is that, "we are heavy-handed in our brewing process. I don't know if it's a Midwestern thing or what, with our cold winters, but we like our beers bigger, meatier, heavier, and with a thicker mouthfeel. We put a lot more of everything into our beers. We don't skew heavily to either a malty or hoppy side—we're going to put in all of the above. If there's going to be an exaggerated amount of hops the beer is going to be heavily malted as well."

Mike points to one beer that perfectly represents this type of brewing. "KBS to me defines what Founders is about. It satisfies that bigger beer notion, but also satisfies our exploratory side." A bit of back story is necessary here. One of Founders' most interesting beers is their seasonal Breakfast Stout, which is brewed with coffee, oatmeal, and chocolate. This beer serves as the base for Kentucky Breakfast Stout, or KBS to its friends, which has been aged for one year in bourbon barrels. Mike goes on, "Seven years ago we started pushing the envelope on ourselves—testing out staff. First came a double chocolate coffee oatmeal imperial stout. Next we're putting it into oak bourbon barrels. Then we find old gypsum mines to store it in. (The constant cool temperature and high humidity in the caves expands the wood, which creates very low losses from evaporation as the beer ages.) We kept getting more and more creative as we went along. This gives us the ability to take what simply seems like a beer and turn it into ten times more than what it started out as." KBS is definitely a huge, intensely flavored, nuanced beer, and is perhaps Founders' most celebrated and sought-after beer.

But the story doesn't end there. BLiS, an American artisanal food company, approached Founders about acquiring some the barrels that KBS had been aged in, which they would then use to age a gourmet maple syrup. Mike agreed, under the condition that the barrels be returned after they were emptied of syrup. Those barrels were filled with Curmudgeon, an old ale, and aged for an additional year. Mike likens the resulting bourbon-KBS-maple syrup-barrel-aged beer, called Kaiser Curmudgeon, to "drinking a Werther's Original candy." Unfortunately, but not surprisingly, this was a special edition draught-only release.

Regular Curmudgeon is itself quite a serious beer. Brewed with an enormous malt bill and molasses to a strength of 9.8% alcohol, then aged with oak, it offers "a lot of diversity in the flavor profile, more than any other beer we make," says Mike. "It's tiny in terms of our output," he notes, "but speaks volumes in terms of representing who we are."

Founders' sense of identity rests in its ability to maintain its "craft origins." Mike relishes this fact. "The beauty of craft is," he says, "that it's still an industry, but it's not built like the big guys are. We're flexible enough to be able to maximize our flavor profiles and satisfy more discerning consumers. We can afford to be nimble and keep satisfying a larger band of people that will only grow. That's what's so great about what we're doing—we can experiment with beers that are completely different from our 'house style' and be successful at doing it." As the success of craft beer's artisanal philosophy continues to grow and gather more devotees, Mike maintains his commitment to sustaining this bright future. "Hold on," he says, "it's only the beginning. Welcome to the show."

Founders' year-round portfolio of beers consists of Dirty Bastard Scotch-style ale, Centennial IPA, Red's Rye P.A. American pale ale brewed with rye, Pale Ale, and Porter.

Seasonal offerings include Double Trouble double IPA (Jan.-May); Cerise cherry-fermented ale (June-Aug.); and Breakfast Stout brewed with coffee, oatmeal, and chocolate (Sep.-Dec.).

Annual special releases include Imperial Stout (Jan.), Kentucky Breakfast Stout bourbon barrel-aged coffee oatmeal chocolate stout, Curmudgeon Old Ale (May), Devil Dancer Triple IPA (July), Harvest Ale wet-hopped American IPA (Oct.), and Backwoods Bastard bourbon barrel-aged Scotch-style ale (Nov.).

Founders' beers are distributed in Georgia, Illinois, Indiana, Kentucky, Massachusetts, Michigan, Minnesota, Missouri, New Jersey, New York, North Carolina, Ohio, Pennsylvania, South Carolina, Virginia, Washington D.C, and Wisconsin.

BREAKFAST STOUT

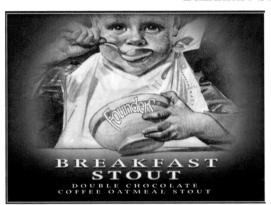

Pure opaque black with a thin, fine, dark tan head and a thick viscosity. Roasted grain characteristics are strong in the aroma but are not overpowering along with coffee, softly spicy hops, and a light milky quality. The aroma suggests some malty sweetness, which is in contrast with the flavor, which comes across as mainly dry. Not too much coffee or chocolate in the flavor—this is a good thing, as it lets the elemental flavors of the roasted malt take center stage. The coffee and chocolate play supporting roles here, along with a calculated hop character. There is some alcohol sweetness in the full body that contributes a good bit to the flavor profile as it flows into a long, warm finish. This is a beer of great power and great finesse. It possesses enormous flavor and strength but is thoroughly drinkable.

KENTUCKY BREAKFAST STOUT

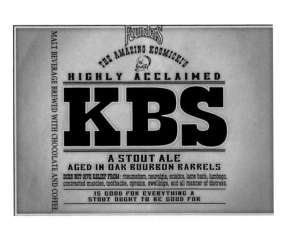

Opaque oily black with a very fine, thin, shimmering caramel head. Heady aroma of sweet coffee, caramel malt, dark dried fruit, and oxidized notes combined with a slightly smoky, almost metallic edge. The flavor consists of a balancing act between layers of sweet and roasted malt characteristics that support and complement one another. The initial level of flavors consists of dark roasted malt and significant hop bitterness followed by sweet dark toffee and vanilla-infused bourbon notes. Strong yet balanced coffee flavors, oatmeal creaminess, and wood-aged characteristics are present throughout. More flavors arise in the back palate—hints of black fruits and alcohol. The big body is very well-balanced and filled with smooth, mouth-filling expressions of bitterness, sweetness, and the complex range of flavors in between.

Curmudgeon Old Ale

Rich amber color with a thin, fine golden-tan head. Sweet, malty aroma with caramel, alcohol, a nutty graininess, soft earthiness, and a hint of red cherry. Bitter hops, a touch of malt sweetness, and great toasted grain notes fill the well-rounded, malt-forward flavor profile. Very classically styled old ale with a lot of subtle complexities. The medium-full, multidimensional body conveys all of the nuances along with soft alcohol sweetness and a very pleasant warming finish.

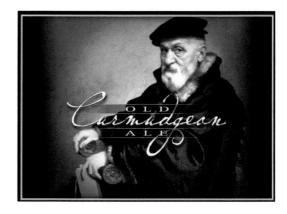

NEW GLARUS BREWING CO.—NEW GLARUS, WI

Deborah Carey, Founder & President

One of the most satisfying aspects of craft beer is the sense of place local breweries and their beers represent. There is perhaps no craft brewery more emblematic of its locality than the New Glarus Brewing Company of Wisconsin, whose motto reads: "Drink Indigenous." Wisconsin claims many ambassadors including cheese, cows, bratwursts, and beer in general. Milwaukee, for instance, is a city rich with brewing traditions (albeit mainly macrobrewing) and is often thought of as the capital of beer in Wisconsin. But the town of New Glarus, with its eponymous brewing company has become the leader of the craft beer movement in that state.

Native Wisconsinite Deb Carey founded New Glarus Brewing Company in 1993 and is its president. Her husband Dan Carey is its brewmaster and co-owner. New Glarus has since grown into the twenty-first largest craft brewery in the United States as of 2010, while exclusively selling its beer within its home state. But achieving this sort of prominence isn't what motivates Deb. She isn't interested in simply being big and distributing to a wide area. Her primary concerns are brewing great beer and improving the lives of her family of employees at New Glarus. "It's more important to be successful than to be big," Deb says. "Size is a guy thing. This is a girl brewery. We don't need to be in a lot of states."

Her personal goal is to change the way people think about drinking beer, to promote a shift of focus "from the cost to the flavors," she says. "People are getting tired of mass-produced beer. People really are looking for flavor. There're a lot of things going on right now with people and flavor [in the food and beverage world]. Where are they going to go?" Deb asks. She hopes that they will turn to craft beer. She's very proud of what New Glarus has achieved. "We are profitable and flavorful and something that consumers can turn to." She also notes that within the craft beer community, "there's room for everybody to be great. There could be a million wonderful breweries and all could do well, and maybe everyone would stop drinking mass-produced beer."

The key to achieving this goal, according to Deb, is to go about business in an original way. "I don't care what other people are doing. I don't care how much money I make. I just do things so differently," admits Deb. She has always possessed an entrepreneurial spirit. She started her first business at 16, became the first woman in America to found and operate a brewery, started the Wisconsin Brewers' Guild, and is constantly working on social and political advocacy projects to promote a progressive business climate in Wisconsin. Her company is often cited as a model of business success. "We've won a lot of business awards and are always flabbergasted by it. I guess they call what we're doing 'innovation,'" says Deb, incredulously. "Many of my math teachers would disagree with those honors." What Deb and New Glarus are doing is "a lot of regular old hard work—teaching people how to sell beer, pair beer with food, maintain draft systems—not big shiny ads." Running her business in a creative yet straightforward way "is what makes us successful," she says. "We're different. You have to be your own person. It's part of the fun of it."

This sort of independent thinking was present for the original purchase of the brewery itself. Dan was working an unsatisfying corporate beer job in Colorado while Deb was hatching a plan to start their own brewery when a used 10-barrel system came up for auction in Appleton, Wisconsin. Deb describes the rest of the story like this: "We negotiated for a good loan and bought used equipment at a hair-raising auction. We had $40,000 of seed money, rented a scary house, and traded stock to occupy an abandoned warehouse in New Glarus for a year. We packed up our stuff like the Beverly Hillbillies and started clearing out the warehouse."

The business success that followed drives home the point that the beers of New Glarus represent something special, including what Deb calls a "sense of local terroir." "We want our beers to be part of the fabric of Wisconsin," she insists. "It is important to me that the beer reflects us." Many factors go into designing one of the dozens of beers that New Glarus produces each year. In August an online "beer vote" is held to let the community decide some of the beers that will be released the following year. Other times they experiment with completely new beers, as in the case for their Unplugged series. "We think about families of flavors when designing a beer," says Deb. She and Dan begin the process with "a conversation about an idea of a flavor for a beer. The recipe comes next." Deb likens the flavor profile of a good beer to a piece of music: "something interesting in the beginning, something that builds throughout, and then finishes cleanly."

As the brewmaster, Dan is responsible for transposing these notions into a concrete recipe. How does he go about capturing the essence of a community in a beer? "It's hard to explain how he thinks," says Deb. "His beers are a very personal expression of himself, and it causes a great deal of anxiety when he goes about designing a new beer. He's a beer geek. He genuinely has a gift." Inspiration can come from many places, but it often comes from the bounty of ingredients that are close at hand in Wisconsin. "The first opportunity he had to get a hold of fruit he made a cherry beer." After visiting traditional breweries in Belgium, Dan purchased oak tanks and worked to develop a spontaneous fermentation method that he could employ in Wisconsin. After six years Belgian Red emerged—brewed with one pound of Door County, Wisconsin cherries per 750-milliliter bottle. It is now the beer for which New Glarus is best known.

It's difficult to overstate the fervor that surrounds Belgian Red. "Many people have tried and failed to recreate Belgian Red," Says Deb. "Lots of people want the recipe. People are always saying that they're going to do this, but nobody has yet." The exact production method is a closely guarded secret. They looked into patenting the unique brewing process, but decided against it upon learning that it would then need to be revealed to the world. What is known is that brewing Belgian Red is a tiring labor of love. "It's crazy around here when he makes it," says Deb. "The floor is covered with sheets of cardboard. Everybody [involved in brewing] changes their clothes; we have 'inside teams' and 'outside teams' so that there's no cross-contamination."

To describe the flavor of Belgian Red is to describe the flavor of pure, sweet ripe cherries uncannily translated into beer form. It is unlike any other "cherry beer" made. In a testament to its uniqueness, it was the first beer to be inducted into the Slow Food Ark of Taste, which is described by that organization as "an international catalog of foods that are threatened by industrial standardization, the regulations of large-scale distribution, and environmental damage." This distinction is in many ways a validation of the values that New Glarus is promoting through their beers. "We're hanging onto old world ways of making traditional foods. Wisconsin values education and hard work and we have been embraced for our transparency and the realness of our company in the same way that people embrace farmers' markets, homemade cheeses, and such." It simply feels good to drink beers like these.

Raspberry Tart—the raspberry counterpart to Belgian Red—is another benchmark beer for New Glarus. It captures the same headiness of summer in a bottle using fresh Wisconsin raspberries.

It's a little-known fact that Wisconsin produces more cranberries than any other state. In homage to this, New Glarus brews a cranberry lambic called Cran-bic as part of its "Thumbprint" series of small-batch special release beers. Wisconsin apples have also found their way into beers like Apple Ale.

Wisconsin, of course, also grows a lot of corn. Corn has been a traditional brewing ingredient in America since before prohibition, but today it is generally added to macrobrewed beers as an adjunct to reduce malt costs and lighten a beer's flavor. This is not the case for New Glarus's flagship beer, Spotted Cow, a golden farmhouse ale in which some Wisconsin corn is used to impart a light, fruity, faintly sweet character. Spotted Cow is a Wisconsin institution and has become the second-best-selling beer in the state after the macrobrew Miller Lite. This is no small feat. New Glarus's sales have steadily grown by double-digit percentages each year for the last fifteen years. "I never expected to be doing as well as we are," says Deb. She takes great satisfaction in what New Glarus has been able to contribute to her home state simply by following her goal of building a business that runs like a family and is true to the spirit of her local community. "This is where I've been dropped on the planet so I want to make things better where I am." And for the beer? "Our industry is maturing. We're not a fad anymore. Craft beer is moving into being considered simply 'beer.'"

New Glarus's year-round lineup of beers includes: Spotted Cow golden ale, Moon Man pale ale, Fat Squirrel brown ale, Two Women pilsner lager, Belgian Red cherry ale, and Raspberry Tart raspberry ale.

New Glarus also brews a rotating selection of seasonal beers which changes yearly. Current and past offerings include: Black Top black IPA, Laughing Fox kristal weizen, Snowshoe Red Ale, Uff-da German bock, Back 40 bock, Cabin Fever Honey Bock, Coffee Stout, Dancing Man Wheat Bavarian-style hefeweizen, Staghorn Octoberfest, and Totally Naked lager.

New Glarus also occasionally brews small-batch specialty beers as part of their "Unplugged," "Thumbprint," and "R&D" series of limited-edition beers.

New Glarus's beers are distributed only in Wisconsin.

Spotted Cow

Hazy yellow-gold with a fine white head. Soft fruity sweetness with a light graininess in the aroma. Flavor is very light and straightforward with the sweet fruity aromatic characteristics appearing here as well. The extremely light, crisp body leaves you refreshed. A very easygoing, drinkable, light cream ale.

Belgian Red

Beautiful clear, bright ruby red with a thin, fine light pink head. The bright, intensely ripe sweet cherry aroma is pleasantly candy-like while delivering the full range of cherry components—skin, flesh, and pit. The flavor is very sweet with intense cherry characteristics that are not at all cloying or syrupy, yet retains the power and focus of a sweet cherry syrup. It is remarkably well-balanced and structured with refreshing tartness and subtle fruit tannins. This tartness appears to come from both the sour cherries themselves and the fermentation. The body is appropriately light and nimble, delivering both the delicate nuances of the cherries at the same time as their more powerful overtones with balanced levels of sweetness, tartness, bitterness, and subtle malt underpinnings. This is truly a FRUIT beer.

Raspberry Tart

The appearance is nearly identical to that of Belgian Red. Striking raspberry aroma comes across as sour in multiple ways from both the acidity of the fruit and the fermentation agents. The raspberries are sweet, ripe, and juicy with some subtle floral notes and an underlying vinous character. The flavor is again full of sweet, juicy raspberries with an overriding tartness. The body is light and airy and delivers a tart prickle on the palate with the clear flavor of fresh raspberries along with very soft malt and hops. Drinking this beer immediately transports you to a mid-summer afternoon in Wisconsin.

THREE FLOYDS BREWING CO.—MUNSTER, IN
Nick Floyd, Brewmaster & Co-Founder

"It's not normal," says Nick Floyd, the brewmaster for Three Floyds Brewing Company. "Everything we make is a little outside the bounds of normal while still respecting brewing traditions," he says as he lists some unique aspects of Three Floyds' brewing philosophy. "The quality of the beer and our attitude about beer should be fun. Some people take themselves so seriously—trying to take beer to where wine is as the only way to get respect. Yes, beer deserves more respect, but we're tattooed, punk and metal-listening brewers that just like to drink really good beer."

Nick Floyd began homebrewing at an early age, eighteen, and his discovery of "imports and the true flavor of real beers," along with emerging classic American microbrews such as Sierra Nevada Pale Ale and Bell's Two Hearted Ale, were his initial inspiration. His English mother remained oblivious to the true motivation for her son's basement hobby: Nick found the warm, macrobrewed beer at the high school parties he frequented to be unpalatable, so he decided to make his own. At 21 he attended brewing school in order to turn pro. He's been a passionate brewer ever since.

Fast forward to 1996 when Nick founded Three Floyds Brewing Company with his brother Simon and their father, Mike Floyd. The original brewery, which he has described as a "kind of ghetto system," consisted of a wok burner-fired five barrel brew kettle and open fermentation tanks that were formerly used to produce Swiss cheese, all housed in a dilapidated warehouse in Hammond, Indiana.

In 2000, Three Floyds moved into a new, modern 15 barrel facility in Munster, Indiana. This facility still only brewed beer for draught sales, and the first bottles of their flagship beer, Alpha King pale ale, were contract-brewed and bottled until 2002, when they were able to purchase a reconditioned bottler and began to exclusively brew and bottle all of Three Floyds' beers. What bolstered them through the brewery's challenging beginning was their unique and uncompromising approach to shaping their image. They were brewing unconventional beers in a region that they themselves described as having a "bleak craft brewing scene." Their iconoclastic tattooed, punk, and metal-derived attitude demanded attention, screaming from the design of their tap handles and labels across the Rust Belt. Their distinctive beers and branding have attracted a loyal following of like-minded individuals, normal or otherwise.

Alpha King pale ale perfectly exemplifies this attitude. Its label features a grimacing green demon dropping hops into a smoking pint of ale. Alpha King "put the brewery on the map." Nick explains that the beer "came out at a time when American pale ales and IPAs weren't nearly as hoppy as they are now," so its aggressive hop and malt profiles made it stand out and garnered attention for the brewery. Its unique recipe is a combination of Nick's homebrewing inspiration and his later experience with commercial brewing methods. He appreciates its "balance between the malt and the hops. Most people," he says, "set out to make these hugely hoppy beers without the malt to back it up." Indeed Alpha King is an uncommonly malty American pale ale that captivated drinkers in the region from its initial release.

Another manifestation of Three Floyds' unconventional approach and their dedication to the "punk-metal spirit" is a series of special release beers paired to the particular tastes of some of their favorite bands. Examples include a collaboration ale with Amon Amarth, a Swedish group that brews meade back home. The beer created for them, named Ragnarok, was a smoky porter brewed with honey, in honor of their own brewing traditions, which included an inscription with allusions to Norse mythology: "When Heimdall sounds the Giallar-horn this is the beer to be hoisted by the gods in anticipation of the coming battle." Other such editions have been made in association with Chicago-area groups including Devil's Handshake Pale Ale, brewed to the tastes of Bible of the Devil, and Evil Power Imperial Pilsner, designed for the band members of Lair of the Minotaur to be able to slam while performing. Yet another unique collaboration beer was created to showcase the Floyds' interest in body art. The rotating labels of Blackheart English-style IPA feature artwork by their friends at

Black Heart Tattoo in San Francisco. All of these beers, along with every other batch, were doubtlessly brewed to the hard beats blaring from the "Nematron," the brewery's repurposed, oversized, mobile stereo system that resembles a crude vintage robot painted in battleship camouflage.

The success of this brewing philosophy has become a kind of double-edged sword for Three Floyds. Currently, the demand for its beers "greatly exceeds supply," says Lincoln Anderson, Three Floyds' sales manager. One of the biggest challenges facing the brewery is "controlling expectations about availability," Lincoln says. As the brewery's sales manager, it's clear that he fields a lot of questions about how to get a hold of Three Floyds beer. "We want to get the message out that we are growing, but at a rate where we can maintain our quality," he says. The brewery's twelve employees produce 20,000 barrels of beer per year, making Three Floyds a true "microbrewery." In addition to their five year-round beers, they also produce twelve seasonal beers, as well as their other occasional special editions.

It seems that the thrill of the hunt has only fueled peoples' enthusiasm for the brand. The single day each year on which Dark Lord Russian imperial stout can be purchased, has grown into a huge phenomenon in the craft beer world, making it Three Floyds' most famous brew. In 2010, an estimated eight to twelve-thousand people showed up to attend the release party, known as "Dark Lord Day." The resulting logistical chaos led them to restrict attendance to the festival in 2011. So Six thousand tickets were issued, with each attendee given the option of purchasing up to four bottles of Dark Lord. It's now the only way to purchase this beer though official channels.

Dark Lord's limited production is the result of a truce of sorts between a small brewery and a gigantic beer. Brewing Dark Lord is "ridiculously expensive and slows down the production of other beers," says Nick. "It's not feasible to brew more. We've reached an equilibrium—selling all the beer we make and not screwing over the people who are expecting beer year-round." Whether or not you decide to brave the lines to buy bottles, Dark Lord Day has become a major festival in which craft beer fans come together to share bottles from their collections, sample the many other craft beers served there from around the world, and enjoy live music and barbeque.

Even the story behind the first brewing of Dark Lord conveys the edgy attitude of the brewery. When a neighboring Illinois brewery kept winning State Fair gold medals for their Russian imperial stout, a style that Three Floyds did not make at the time, they decided to "crush the competition with a gigantic Russian imperial stout," Nick recalls. What does he think of Dark Lord? "It's not something I drink every day. It's a huge beer that should be aged for five to ten years at least. It's a beer to be cellared and forgotten about until a special occasion."

But Dark Lord is just one of Three Floyds' beers, and there are many others that are much easier to acquire. One is a new pale ale called Zombie Dust: an "incredible pale ale with citra hops that's going to quench a lot of thirst this summer." Despite Three Floyds' challenge to keep up with demand, they still want to attract newcomers to craft beer. Nick feels that beers like Zombie Dust do this best. Balanced, approachable, yet distinctive beers have the capability of turning people on to the joys of craft beer. He believes that there's a craft beer out there for everyone, they just have to discover it, and he relishes the occasional tasting room moment when that happens. "When someone gets just the right beer for that moment, the look on their face says 'Wow. Now I understand why people love craft beer.'"

Three Floyds' year-round beers consist of Alpha King American pale ale, Robert the Bruce Scottish-style ale, Pride & Joy American Mild Ale, Gumball Head American wheat ale, and Dreadnaught double IPA.

Their seasonal offerings are: Behemoth American barleywine (Jan.), Brian Boru Irish red ale (Feb.), Rabid Rabbit Franco-Belgian-style farmhouse ale (Mar.), Dark Lord Russian imperial stout (Apr.), Blackheart English-style IPA (May), Apocalypse Cow double IPA with lactose (June), Gorch Fock Franconian-style Helles lager (July), Munsterfest Bavarian-style Oktoberfest lager (Sep.), Broo Doo wet hop pale ale (October), Alpha Klaus Christmas Porter (Nov.), and Black Sun stout (Dec.). Three Floyds also occasionally releases a limited edition double IPA called Arctic Panzer Wolf into limited distribution.

Three Floyds' beers are distributed in Illinois, Indiana, Kentucky, and Wisconsin.

ALPHA KING

Dark orange-amber with a loose, medium-thick light tan head. Significant caramel malt aroma along with dark citrus and earthy pine resin notes. More of these components are present in the flavor with a substantial bitterness that coats the tongue and lingers on the palate with some malt richness. Orange peel, caramel malt, and zesty, dark hops spice flavors add complexity in addition to well-integrated alcohol. The body is full and well-rounded making for a big, though excellently balanced pale ale that is both assertive and distinctive.

GUMBALLHEAD

Slightly hazy yellow-gold with a medium-thick, loose white head. Fresh, light lemon and orange citrus hop characteristics in the aroma with a slightly tart, grainy edge over a soft sweetness. Light orange fruitiness in the flavor with a slightly sweet malt core and a moderately dense resinous hop bitterness. Fairly light, even body that's very easy to drink with a few distinctive flavor peaks.

BLACKHEART

Light orange-gold with a thin, fine off-white head. Light citrus hop aroma over a loose malt backdrop with faint fruity elements. More fruity malt characteristics in the flavor along with a significant hops profile that comes across as quite resinous. A backdrop of maltiness persists that showcases the dense orange and holiday spice notes which dart out in front of the alcohol base. The medium-thick body expresses both the malt and hops profiles quite prominently. A fruity, lifting quality to the alcohol provides a refreshing finish to this ale.

THE NORTHEAST

ALLAGASH BREWING CO.—PORTLAND, ME

Rob Todd, Founder

Allagash Brewing Company in Portland, Maine is one of the few American breweries that focuses exclusively on Belgian-styled beers. When Rob Tod founded Allagash in 1995 there weren't many American craft beer interpretations of traditional Belgian beers available. "It would have been a much easier road for us if we had focused on a style of beer that people were more familiar with or was more accessible," says Rob. But his rationale was, "Why go to all this work if we're going to do something similar to what someone else is doing? If it's already being done why bother doing it?" Indeed, the brewery's earliest years were a challenge. "We could barely give the beers away during the first few years. People didn't understand them," Rob recalls. His first brewing venture at Allagash was White, now their flagship beer, which he describes as a "traditional-styled wheat beer with a different twist."

Traditional Belgian white ales, also known as witbiers, are made with a high percentage of wheat malt, bitter Curaçao orange peel, and spices such as coriander and grains of paradise. "We wanted to push the style guidelines and do something different," says Rob. When White was released, "It was different in so many ways. It was hard to find beer that had this sort of flavor profile," says Rob. When compared to the ubiquitous American light lagers Allagash White's difference is immediately apparent. "Bartenders would ask what's wrong with it because of its cloudiness." The flavor profile is also distinctive. "It's spiced, made with a Belgian yeast strain, has a creamy mouthfeel—it was a unique experience for most people who first tried it." All of these characteristics put it in stark contrast with many people's expectations of "beer" at the time. Even among craft beer fans familiar with the witbier style, White presented them with something new. Rob says that "the general flavor profile of it is something I just haven't gotten in other Belgian-style wheat beers. It's got a lot of body to it. It's a very drinkable, refreshing beer, while still being unique."

But the drinking public soon came around to these new, flavorful offerings. Rob explains that, "Beer in Europe was beginning to become dumbed-down and commoditized, much like what had happened in the U.S." But now, as craft beer has continually gained more momentum and people's trust, their expectations are shifting towards more experimental beers. "One of the best aspects of the craft beer culture in the U.S. is that people are excited to try new beers. We're undergoing a renaissance and people are looking to have new experiences and try new things."

Allagash's success is quite dependant on this sense of exploration being acted on not only by craft beer consumers, but also by the brewers themselves. "We're not trying to duplicate the original styles. We're inspired by the Belgian originals, but we want our beers to be their own," says Rob. "Any employee can brew an experimental batch on our ten-gallon system." This approach fits appropriately within the nature of Belgian brewing traditions. "A lot of other cultures don't have such a tremendous variety of flavors to draw from," notes Rob. "You have sour beers—Flanders reds, lambics, fruit beers—all of these beers are tremendously different, even within the same family of beers. The Trappist ales provide another avenue still. The world is your oyster when you're brewing Belgian beers. You can use fruit, bacteria, wild yeast, spices, different grains, et cetera—almost anything."

Given that Allagash is at once both rooted in Belgian brewing traditions and has wholeheartedly embraced the sense of innovation embodied by American craft beer, maintaining a portfolio of innovative and often esoteric beers involves constantly working to educate the public on the unique pleasures that these types of beers offer. An important part of making this strategy work is highlighting situations in which these beers excel. For this reason Rob is actively dedicated to spreading awareness of the pleasures of enjoying craft beer and food together. "I've always been a believer in beer with food. We've been tied in with the culinary community for years. It's an important part of what we do." Why does craft beer, and Belgian-style beers in particular, go so well with food? According to Rob, "The family of Belgian-style beers in general lends itself particularly well to pairing with food due to the massive diversity which exists within it. If a beer's more complex it gives you something to explore through the flavors and aromas. In terms of a food pairing, the beer and the food interact with one another. Different foods can bring about difference experiences within the beer, and vice versa."

By investing time and energy into the shared success of craft beer and food Rob has positioned Allagash to be a leader not only in the craft beer world, but in the larger whole foods movement as well. He recognizes that the success of craft beer and artisanal foods are linked to one another. "Opening people's eyes to beer and food enriches their lives," says Rob with emotion. Promoting events that turn people on to these possibilities empowers them to take advantage of the growing bounty of culinary experiences available today. "In the past there was no opportunity to give people that [type of] experience. Now that it's right in front of them many people don't realize how fulfilling enjoying these products together can be." He and Allagash celebrate craft beer and food together in a variety of ways. "We've been doing beer dinners for years—well back into the mid-nineties," he says. Rob especially loves witnessing the "ah ha" moment when people's perceptions of craft beer shift: "One of the most fulfilling things at beer dinners is when someone says, 'Wow. I had no idea beer could taste like that. I always thought beer was beer.'" In addition to participating in regular craft beer dinners, Allagash has worked with the Institute of Culinary Education in Manhattan for ten years awarding culinary scholarships. "Students generate beer recipes and we hold a contest to select the finalists. We have a cook-off and award a scholarship to the winning chef."

Within Allagash's varied lineup of distinctive beers, a few in particular come up as especially interesting and well-suited to culinary applications. Curieux, now an Allagash staple, originally came about as the result of a fortuitous bottle shortage. Empty Jim

Beam Bourbon barrels had been ordered for an undecided future project and were sitting around the brewery. A fermentation tank holding a batch of Tripel needed to be freed up. When no bottles were available, "we decided to go for it, and filled the barrels." The result is a unique blend—both of beer, and of traditional and contemporary brewing methods. "It became a perfect marriage of flavor that we would have never guessed in a million years," says Rob. The characteristic fruity flavors and distinctive fermentation characteristics of a traditional Belgian-style tripel are combined with the non-traditional, very American influence of oak bourbon barrels that impart subtle vanilla and coconut flavors. "We had to erase our preconceptions of what we thought would work," says Rob. "Honestly, if we wouldn't have run out of bottles that beer would never have existed." After spending eight weeks in the barrels under cold storage, between 7 and 12 percent of freshly brewed Tripel is blended back in to bring out the complexity. "It actually brings out the wood," remarks Rob. Every batch of Curieux is individually blended to achieve just the right flavor profile. Despite its 11% alcohol content, Curieux comes across as surprisingly light. The bourbon notes are well-integrated, and the normally prominent honeyed fruit characteristics of Tripel become muted after aging. What remains is a beer with a lot of strength and character that can pair with a diverse array of foods from grilled swordfish to steak au poivre.

Another instance of chance playing a huge role in the development of a highly successful beer is found in the story of Interlude. Rob initially set out to make a saison, "but with a twist." That twist would turn into a drastic detour. Brewing went as planned, and a traditional saison yeast was added. "The fermentation started out great for three days, then stopped half-way through," Rob recalls. This would usually spell disaster for a batch of beer. But, as chance would have it, "we had the capacity to leave it in the tank, so we did. Then one day it just started fermenting again." This sort of spontaneous fermentation can also pose a huge problem for breweries. Naturally occurring wild yeasts, such as brettanomyces, can impart flavors that are undesirable in most types of beer. But this brewery was Allagash. In Belgium indigenous yeasts and bacteria are frequently utilized in the production of traditional beers. "We liked the flavor of where this was going, and brett is a traditional ingredient." says Rob excitedly. "So we let it ferment out over the next three or four months." But that is where tradition stops and modern innovation begins. Allagash purchased ten merlot and syrah barrels from Plumpjack Winery in the Napa Valley and aged half of the beer in them and the other half in stainless steel. The result is a part sour, part malty, part strong "farmhouse ale" with unique, tart fermentation characteristics and fruity vinous flavors. "The odd thing about that beer," Rob explains, "is that it has a ton of body and complexity but is completely bone-dry." He's very pleased with the results, and has been brewing an intentional batch each year since with the original wild yeast strain that they cultured from that first batch. "It's a unique, indigenous strain for the brewery. It opens the door to a whole new set of flavors. We plan on making a lot of new beers with that yeast."

Honoring tradition, taking creative license, and actively educating the public through the results has made Allagash a remarkably successful brewery that produces strikingly unique beers. They follow their brewing instincts and constantly push the limits of experimentation to discover new ways of expanding the world of craft beer to include as many people as possible. They've recently installed traditional Belgian open fermentation vessels called coolships and are using them to experiment with more spontaneously fermented beers. "Now we're brewing styles that didn't even exist thirty years ago," says Rob enthusiastically. Though much has changed in the American brewing industry, one thing has remained constant: "Whether it is over dinner, or at a pub, the craft beer movement is enriching peoples' lives."

Allagash's year-round portfolio includes: White Belgian-style wheat ale, Dubbel Belgian-style dubbel, Tripel Belgian-style tripel, Four Belgian-style quad, Black Belgian-style stout, and Curieux bourbon barrel-aged strong ale.

Their specialty lineup of limited annual releases includes: Odyssey oak-aged dark wheat ale, Confluence dry-hopped golden ale, and Interlude farmhouse ale aged in wine barrels.

Their Tribute Series limited annual releases beers includes: Victoria Belgian-style strong ale brewed with white grapes, Victor Belgian-style strong ale brewed with red grapes, Hugh Malone Belgian-style IPA, and Fluxus, an anniversary ale whose recipe changes each year.

Allagash also produces many one-off special editions through-out the year which are only available at the brewery or in select local venues.

Allagash's beers are distributed in California, Connecticut, Georgia, Illinois, Maine, Maryland, Massachusetts, New Hampshire, New Jersey, New York, North Carolina, Pennsylvania, Rhode Island, South Carolina, Texas, Vermont, Virginia, and Washington.

WHITE

Cloudy light yellow-gold with a thin, medium-fine white head. Aroma presents classic Belgian wit fermentation notes along with spice and orange. The complex esters are rounded out by a light malt background with a hint of sweetness. There is a significant spice character and soft fruitiness in the flavor as well as a crisp, dry maltiness. The light body delivers the complex yet clean flavor profile in a straightforward and refreshing way.

CURIEUX

Hazy light gold with a thin, very fine creamy white head. The aroma is very fruity with prominent orange zest notes along with sweet malt, alcohol, hops spice, and muted fermentation esters. The flavor brings more of the same, but with vanilla, oak, and soft oxidative notes from bourbon barrel aging. The body is surprisingly light and nimble. The alcohol is evident with some warmth, but isn't heavy or overbearing considering its 11% alcohol.

INTERLUDE

Clear light orange-gold with a very thin, very fine white head. Soft, pleasantly damp aroma with sour fruit characteristics—red apple, tart berry, and lemon pith. There are touches of malt, hops spice, and alcohol sweetness in the background as well. The flavor is quite sour with many of the aroma characteristics presented here too. The top layer is green berry tartness, followed by spicy hops and oak barrel-aged characteristics in the middle, with a baseline of sweet alcohol and nutty malt in the finish. Despite the relatively strong alcohol for a sour, the body retains the impression of lightness.

ALLAGASH

CURIEUX
ALE AGED IN OAK
BOURBON BARRELS

ALLAGASH

| interlude
ale aged in oak barrels

OPEN CAUTIOUSLY: CONTENTS UNDER PRESSURE
9.5% Alc. By Vol. ∾ 1 PINT 9.4 FL OZ (750 ML)

CAPTAIN LAWRENCE BREWING CO.—PLEASANTVILLE, NY

Scott Vaccaro, Brewmaster

The Captain Lawrence Brewing Company opened in January 2006 in suburban Pleasantville, New York. Its owner and brewmaster, Scott Vaccaro, at 33, represents a new generation of craft brewers who have established themselves in the flourishing craft beer scene. His story conveys a singular devotion to craft beer that might not have flourished in an environment less supportive of innovative brewing. Scott began homebrewing at age 17 under the guidance of a family friend and Charlie Papazian's classic tome, *The Complete Joy of Homebrewing.* He was enthralled by the work of beer scholar Michael Jackson whose books sought to broaden the awareness and appreciation of the great beers of the world. Scott went on to graduate from the well-known Fermentation Science program at the University of California, Davis, and one of his first brewing jobs was at the venerable Sierra Nevada Brewing Co. Scott's inspirational figures include craft beer giants Peter Bouckaert, formerly of Belgium's Rodenbach and currently of New Belgium Brewing Company, plus Vinnie Cilurzo of Russian River Brewing company, two of craft beer's contemporary godfathers. He also has great admiration for legendary Belgian brewers such as Cantillon and De Dolle, makers of historical Belgian beers. All of these influences attest to the fact that Scott and the Captain Lawrence Brewing Company are products of the creative exuberance found in the current craft beer renaissance. The development of Captain Lawrence Brewing Company describes a very deliberate path taken with passion fueled by the "greatest hits" of craft beer, and the knowledge that America's enthusiasm for craft beer would enable his success.

This climate of possibility is the greatest asset to craft breweries as they attempt to lure people over to their flavorful, artisanal products. Scott puts it simply: "I brew beer that I like to drink," and he describes these beers as "clean and decisive in character." Whether that beer's character is the crisp hoppiness of a pale ale, the lush fruity aromatics of a double IPA, the puckering tartness of a sour, or the funky aroma of a brettanomyces-fermented ale, it is that primary characteristic that should shine through and define the beer. Scott recalls poring over beer books, "reading about beers I never thought I would have a chance to drink," which clearly "imprinted the ideas of those flavors in my mind." He would never recover from it. During an early attempt at becoming an accountant, he found his days spent homebrewing to be the source of his greatest motivation. He left the accounting program, had a long talk with his parents, and headed west to brewing school. Scott explains it very simply, "My reason for brewing is it's all I've known. I've never thought about having another career."

In its first five years of operation Captain Lawrence has had great success. Scott is thrilled to have his beers served to the broad base of people in New York City. "It feels great to have our beers poured [there]," he says. "New York City is such a huge market . . . This is new to our generation—the embracing of craft beer by a larger group of people in general." Scott works hard to "react to the local palates and give them what they're looking for." "We sell the most pale ale," Scott says. "It's a classic, local, sessionable pale ale for the community." While such sturdy, workhorse beers like Pale Ale, and their popular Liquid Gold Belgian-style ale consistently please the masses and attract many new followers to the craft beer movement, Captain Lawrence has made its biggest mark with its series of barrel-aged special editions. One year after Captain Lawrence opened, in 2007, the "American-Style Sour Ale" category was added to the GABF competition. Scott entered the brewery's first sour beer, Cuvée de Castleton, which went on to win the gold medal. Two years later Rosso e Marrone won the brewery another gold medal in that category. This brought a lot of attention to Captain Lawrence. Scott credits these beers with "helping people online find out who we were," and their special edition bottle releases became major craft beer events. "All of a sudden we had a couple hundred people showing up for releases," he recalls. Cuvée de Castleton and Rosso e Marrone feature complex, tart fermentation profiles supplemented by the addition of fresh grapes to the oak barrels they are aged in—which were formerly used by a local winery.

Scott describes much of his brewing inspiration as a "reaction to what you're faced with every day." Passing by the small winery only blocks away from the brewery gave him the idea to age beers in some of their used barrels. While examining a bottle of Laird's Applejack liquor he noticed that it was produced nearby in New Jersey. He contacted the distillery to acquire some of their emptied apple brandy barrels. He now ages his Xtra Gold tripel-style ale, itself a GABF gold medal winner in 2008, in those barrels along with Amarillo hops for his special Golden Delicious ale, which also won a GABF bronze medal that year in the Wood and Barrel-Aged Strong Beer category.

The often unanticipated results of such experimental ales, along with the numerous accolades they have received, really scratch the creative itch for Captain Lawrence. But their quantity, and therefore their accessibility, is often quite limited. Scott also pursues new beers for which he has "a very specific notion of what [I] want to make. I knew I wanted to brew something crisp—something clean to toss back on a hot day," he says, so he brewed a kölsch. Different yeast strains were tried along with various American hops to develop a recipe for Captain's Kolsch that matched what Scott had envisioned.

These brewing endeavors—small experimental projects and large-scale, wide audience beers—balance each other out from a business perspective. The larger production beers penetrate the market more deeply and build a grassroots following for Captain Lawrence's skillfully produced, traditionally styled beers, while their side projects highlight the artistic, highly innovative side of craft brewing that garners prestige among aficionados. For the "small amounts of specialty beer [we produce] price isn't an issue," says Scott. He describes these "personal projects" as "an indulgence." "If it doesn't work, so be it. It's great to be small so we can keep experimenting." Scott notes that Captain Lawrence has "lots of different sour fruit beers in the works right now," saying "I love the depth [using fruits] adds to the sour flavors." A new IPA is in the works as well. This approach has been so successful that Captain Lawrence moved into a new 18,000 square foot facility in Elmsford, New York, a few miles up the road from the current brewery, at the end of 2011.

The list of Captain Lawrence's unique beers is extensive. "We're pushing the boundaries of barrel-aging by using many different types of casks," Scott says. One result is the "Smoke from the Oak" series of beers, which consists of various base beers aged in different types of oak barrels including bourbon, wine, rum, and port casks. Some of Scott's experiments do go on to reach wider audiences as seasonal production beers. Nor' Easter Winter Warmer was first homebrewed by Scott in 1998 while he was still working out West. He describes it as a "Belgian black ale dosed with elderberries." The current version now produced at the brewery each fall is aged in bourbon barrels. It is a special beer for Scott, who admires it for its "beautiful, winey berry-like notes that play off the dark roasted malt."

All of these efforts finally go toward creating what Scott considers to be his ideal brewery. "Overall, I want my brewery to be an inviting place for the public to come and feel at home and see what we're doing. My goal from the beginning is to create a brewery that is part of the community—something that people can call their own." It is this sort of dedicated and open-minded craft beer environment that Scott wants to maintain for people, so that they will be inspired to drink fine beer in much the same way that he has been inspired to brew it.

Captain Lawrence's lineup of year-round beers includes Pale Ale, Liquid Gold Strong Golden Ale, Smoked Porter, Captain's Reserve Imperial IPA, Kölsch, and Brown Bird Brown Ale.

Their seasonal and special release beers include Pumpkin Ale (fall); Rosso e Marrone (special release); Smoke from the Oak Bourbon, Rum, Wine, and Apple Brandy barrel-aged editions (special releases); Xtra Gold tripel-style ale (spring); St. Vincent's Dubbel (released on Fathers' Day); Nor' Easter Winter Warmer (winter); Cuvée de Castleton (special release), and Golden Delicious (special release).

Captain Lawrence's beers are distributed in Connecticut and New York.

Golden Delicious

Hazy yellow-gold with a medium-thick, loose white head. Lots of sweet fruity alcohol in the aroma that is a little boozy from the influence of the apple brandy barrels. This is pleasantly combined with softening oxidative characteristics and fresh orange hops notes. The clean, straightforward flavor profile comes across as dry but puts forth an emphasis on several forms of golden fruits—apple brandy notes, a fruity malt profile, and citrusy hop flavors—that, combined with the alcohol flavors, balances out to give an impression of moderate sweetness. The lightly structured body showcases a characteristic tripel-style alcohol profile with considerable warmth that conveys a richness in the mouth.

Nor' Easter

Dark brown-black mahogany with a thin, medium-fine light brown head. Aroma consists of caramel and vanilla bourbon barrel notes along with roasted malt and subtle dark fruit aspects with cocoa in the background. Dark flavor profile offers some roasted malt astringency with soft chocolate, caramel, and vanilla notes followed by subtle, tart blue fruit characteristics. Alcohol flavors are delicately assertive with some oak aspects rounding out the finish. The medium body conveys an excellent malt and alcohol balance which is supplemented by a final fruity lightness.

ROSSO E MARRONE

Beautiful hazy rosy coppery-gold with pale red highlights and a quickly dissipating, very fine off-white head. Fine strands of tiny bubbles gracefully stream up from the bottom of the glass. A deep, piercingly sour aroma tickles the nose at first and leads into a background of soft spice while expressing a hair-raising lactic sour verve. Vibrant vinous fruitiness is intermingled with soft oak and barrel oxidation, and a pleasant solvency only deepens the complexity. Taste bud-cramping sourness on the attack clears to reveal a multilayered dark grapy fruitiness and an uncanny wine-like complexity. Alcohol rises in the back end with deeply complex fermentation notes and a very slight spicy bitterness with a hint of light, nutty malt. The body is light but its nimble presence in the mouth conveys significant strength. The finish goes on and on as it slowly unfolds a profound complexity across the palate. This is truly a perfect hybrid drinking experience between beer and wine. Quite amazing.

VICTORY BREWING CO.—DOWNINGTOWN, PA

Bill Covaleski, Brewmaster & President

Speaking with Bill Covaleski, brewmaster and president of Victory Brewing, Co., one immediately senses his gratitude to the loyal fans of the craft beer community. As we discussed the evolution of the current craft beer-friendly climate in the United States, he takes obvious pride in the fact that the number of breweries in this country is back above pre-prohibition levels. "It takes guts to start," he acknowledges. "But the real heroes are the ones who buy the beer. Without an audience we'd be penniless homebrewers."

Building up the "guts" to start a new brewery began in 1990 as Bill worked with a German-trained Dutch brewmaster at an established Maryland brewery. In 1993 he traveled to Germany to take the International Course of Brewing Studies at the Doemens Institute in Munich. Bill's business partner and Victory co-founder, Ron Barchet, was trained in Germany as well at the Technical University of Munich at Weihenstephan. Together they built the original Victory brewhouse in 1996, just 14 miles from the headwaters of the East Bradywine Creek. It was a conscious decision to locate this close to a pristine water source. That first brewhouse was equipped with a 25 barrel system on which they were able to produce 1700 barrels in their first year. The original system was replaced in 2004 with one of double capacity, and by 2008 they were brewing over 42,000 barrels per year.

Bill credits the American craft beer resurgence in part to the growing sophistication of Americans' tastes. "The renaissance of American brewing has been exactly aligned with America's appreciation of flavor," he states. "The increase in coffee and cheese varieties available," for example, "is exactly analogous to the growth of craft beers. [Americans want] flavor in their foods." And, apparently, flavor in their beers as well, if Victory's continually increasing sales is any indication.

Victory's brewing philosophy appears to be working well. The classical German training undertaken in Europe and put to use in an American craft brewery has resulted in some unique Old-meets-New-World beers. While many new American brewers "rushed into IPAs," Bill and Ron created Prima Pils, a bold move considering that America has been drowning in near-flavorless pilsner lagers for decades. Although wary craft beer distributors initially balked at this "craft pilsner," it is now one of Victory's most lauded flagship beers, and the beer that Bill is still most proud of today.

Prima Pils is a uniquely American craft interpretation of a hallowed European beer style. To design this beer, Bill explained, "We used our European training and influence to reinvent a classic European style in the American vernacular." Indeed, one detects the classic European malt body, lager yeast notes, and the noble hop flavors, but these elements are presented in a distinctly American way. The recipe for Prima Pils is unusually liberal in its use of four noble hop varieties. The result is a beer that is both true to its classical roots and an original expression of American craft beer ingenuity.

The same principle of "concept vs. execution," as Bill describes it, is at work in Hop Devil, their biggest selling beer, which uses traditional German malts and whole-flower American hops. This beer's malt core is German-inspired and its hops are American, but applied in more of the English IPA fashion. The initial burst of citrusy American hop aroma fades into a toasted malt body that is supplemented by earthy and spicy hop bitterness.

Hops play an outsized role in the American craft beer scene. Shortages in recent years have caused hop prices to fluctuate dramatically. And while many breweries use high-quality pelletized hops, Victory has always remained committed to using, at considerable expense, whole-flower hops—a unique trait among breweries of its size. This commitment requires a significant investment not only in purchasing expense, but also in the form of cold storing an entire year's worth of hop inventory at any given time. But this dedication is reflective of Victory's uncompromising, product-driven business model.

Hops play the biggest role of all in Victory's Hop Wallop double India pale ale. This time a quintessentially American beer style was built around an Old World framework: a German lager-style grain profile. Bill describes the creative process behind Hop Wallop like this: "We're cognizant of what other brewers are doing, but improvement is a personal thing. We have to ask ourselves, 'What do we want *our* beers to taste like?'" The result is almost nothing like other double IPAs brewed on the East Coast. "We wanted to create a beer full of the juicy nuances of American hops, hung on a lean, pilsner-like body." It's a shockingly drinkable, hop-driven 8.5% ABV ale with notes of grass and fruit that is also unusually dry and crisp.

When asked what he was most excited about around the brewery these days, Bill mentioned Victory's newest brew, Headwaters Pale Ale. This hoppy American pale ale was created to commemorate the company's fifteenth anniversary and pay homage to the Brandywine River. "That fresh, clean water has undoubtedly contributed to the success we've enjoyed over the years," concedes Bill. In recognition of this debt to nature, proceeds from sales of Headwaters Pale Ale will be donated to watershed advocacy groups. In the first three months after the beer's release over $2,500 was raised from local sales alone. "It's a great educational platform for watershed stewardship," he remarked, then praised the outpouring of public support for the long-term project that resulted in the Headwaters Grant program.

The final recipe for Headwaters Pale Ale is the result of a two-year research project that consisted of a series of experimental beers called "Pursuit Pale Ales." Each version explored different combinations of American hop varieties in order to determine the perfect blend for this new type of pale ale. What *is* the perfect blend? It includes Simcoe and Cascade, Bill revealed, but the other two will have to be sussed out through diligent tasting.

One of the most vibrant places around the brewery is the 300-seat Victory Brewpub. Bill describes the atmosphere as an "unpretentious gastropub-type scene," and is proud of the "humble, working relationship" it plays in the "community-oriented culinary scene" of the Philadelphia area. Its menu contains all of the requisite pub classics, but also features a rotating selection of local Chester County, Pennsylvania cheeses as part of their "Victory for Local" initiative to support a sustainable community.

Bill's goal with the brewpub is to provide a center for "social discourse" where community members can meet and celebrate together. This atmosphere serves as "a platform for flavor discovery," and he relishes the fact that the "success of craft beer is supported by American consumers' palates, who are drinking these beers because of their flavor impact rather than their alcohol impact." He loves introducing people to new beer styles, in a "comfortable, family-oriented" setting whose ethos promotes respect for one another through the shared appreciation of their local craft beers. Yes, community building is another power possessed by great beer.

Bill also shares enthusiasm for food and beer pairing collaboration dinners with chefs. He feels that the one-on-one atmosphere that these events provide is ideal for educating people about craft beer. He also enjoys seeing the creative output of talented chefs inspired by his beers.

Victory now boasts a year-round lineup of 12 beers: HopDevil IPA, Prima Pils, Golden Monkey Belgian-style tripel, Storm King Stout Russian imperial stout, Hop Wallop Double IPA, Victory Lager German-style helles lager, Donnybrook Stout dry Irish stout, V-12 Belgian-style strong ale, Helios saison-style ale, Festbier Oktoberfest lager, WildDevil brettanomyces-fermented IPA, and Headwaters Pale Ale.

These are supplemented by another eight seasonal offerings which include: Moonglow Weizenbock (fall), Sunrise Weissbier Bavarian-style hefeweizen (summer), Whirlwind Witbier (spring-summer), Old Horizontal American barleywine (winter), St. Boisterous hellerbock (March), Summer Love Ale golden ale (summer), St. Victorious doppelbock (winter), Yakima Glory black IPA (fall-winter), and Baltic Thunder Baltic porter (special release).

Victory's beers are distributed in twenty-nine states including Alaska, California, Colorado, Connecticut, Delaware, Florida, Georgia, Illinois, Indiana, Maine, Maryland, Massachusetts, Michigan, Minnesota, New Hampshire, New Jersey, New York, North Carolina, Ohio, Oregon, Pennsylvania, Rhode Island, South Carolina, Tennessee, Texas, Vermont, Virginia, Washington, and Wisconsin.

Prima Pils

Clear, Bright, light yellow-gold with a thick medium-dense white head. Classic lager notes in the aroma with excellent spicy noble hops characteristics and a faint metallic edge in the background. The flavor is clean and bright with all of the aroma aspects carrying over along with a good level of crisp, spicy hop bitterness and very soft, dry toasted grain in the finish. The body is dry and light with very good structure making for an extremely refreshing drinking experience.

Headwaters Pale Ale

Clear bright orange-gold with a medium-dense white head. Light fresh citrus top notes in the aroma alongside soft pine and fresh grassy herbaceousness. This is followed by intriguing ripe apricot notes with faint spice and a hint of malt in the background. The flavor consists of a crisp malt core surrounded by mild earth and spice hops characteristics with inflections of orange peel and a mild, pleasant graininess. The dry body conveys a light but assertive malt presence that deftly balances the forward American hops profile.

Hop Wallop

Slightly hazy light gold with a fine, medium-thick head. Strong, vibrant, herbaceous, grassy hop aroma with notes of wildflowers and honeycomb. Bracing bitterness held up by some pleasantly understated malt notes with many of the aromatic elements showing up as specific flavors as well. This beer showcases a highly concentrated hops profile with a very crisp, light body and a well-integrated mild alcohol presence.

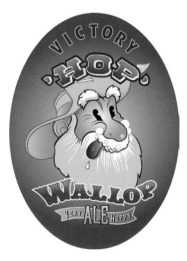

THE SOUTH

CIGAR CITY BREWING CO.—TAMPA, FL
Wayne Wambles, Brewmaster

Cigar City was the nickname given to Tampa, Florida, when it was the world's largest producer of hand-rolled cigars. In 1885 the neighborhood of Ybor City was established by cigar manufacturers who needed to house the thousands of immigrants they employed in their factories. Though no longer the "Cigar Capital of the World," the old neighborhood is now a National Historic Landmark District that draws many tourists. Tampa's Cigar City Brewing Company is reviving a sense of that golden age as it draws on the city's diverse cultural traditions to promote its innovative beers.

Joey Redner, a Tampa native, homebrewer, beer writer, and local history buff fell in love with the diversity of craft beer he found when traveling to Portland, Oregon. Historically, Tampa's brewing tradition consisted of breweries that focused on light beers for tourists to drink out in the sunshine. He returned home inspired to bring flavorful craft beers to Florida and slowly began preparations to start his own brewery. After many years of planning and raising capital he realized that his improvisational approach to homebrewing might not translate well into a viable commercial operation, and that he enjoyed the development side of the business more than the brewing itself. He had the concept firmly in place—knew he wanted the brewery to serve as a cultural ambassador for Tampa by celebrating its rich cultural history while supplying the community with flavorful beers—and he knew he wanted to call it Cigar City.

Enter Wayne Wambles, whom Joey hired as his brewmaster in 2008 before any decisions about the types of beers they would brew had been made. Together they developed what the signature flavors of Cigar City would be. Even though Wayne liked hop-driven beers and Joey preferred malty ones, the two wholeheartedly agreed that Cigar City's beers would represent the town's distinctive history. "Our beers are definitely influenced by the local culture," says Wayne. "Joey and I talked about the concept and I learned more and more about how vibrant the local culture here is. As long as we stay true to our concept we'll be able to export Tampa's culture along with our beers."

Cigar City brews two flagship beers. The hoppy Jai Alai IPA and the malty Maduro Brown Ale were created as its standard bearers. *Jai Alai*, the highly athletic Basque game played in a court at terrifyingly high speeds, has maintained popularity in pockets of Florida, especially within its Hispanic communities. Jai Alai the beer is a densely constructed, powerful American IPA with caramel malt underpinnings. Wayne explains: "We use six different hop varietals to give the beer a layered complexity."

Maduro, when referring to a cigar, signifies that it has been rolled in a dark brown wrapper and offers a robust smoking experience. Maduro Brown Ale has robust chocolate malt notes and is brewed with flaked oats for a silky-textured body.

Beyond these solid core offerings the beers of Cigar City tend to turn to the unconventional. "We do it all," says Wayne, "but some of our beers express different values. The way that I approach the recipes and the formulations is strategically structured to make the beers more complex. Some represent compromise and balance. Others are very culinary-influenced beers." The latter approach expresses the confluence of Wayne's two passions in life: cooking and brewing. He feels no reason to keep these two areas separate. "We practice culinary zymurgy," says Wayne, referring to the branch of chemistry dealing with brewing. "I always have food ideas in mind while formulating recipes." In his earliest brewing days "my first homebrewing experiments weren't very well received," he says. While the rest of his brewing circle was churning out classic standards, Wayne was pushing the limits with hybrid styles. Those who tasted them weren't sure how to react to beers like ginseng hefeweizen, India brown lager, and a Mounds Bar Christmas beer brewed with coconut, cinnamon, and Ghirardelli cocoa. Though these beers certainly showcased his creativity, Wayne admits that they were "a bit outlandish for their circumstances." But even as he shifted his focus to the fundamentals of producing classic beer styles, he still maintained his desire to brew food-related beers. Working at Cigar City with Joey proved to be the perfect balance for him to brew traditional styles with modern twists. "We try to make beers that don't directly compete with other brands. They're not straight styles; they have a Cigar City twist on them. We just want to make beers that are fun to drink and not necessarily true to a style."

Cigar culture has influenced a number of Cigar City's beers. At one point Joey encountered another homebrewer who had used cedar cigar sleeves in a batch of beer. He liked the results so much he asked if he could implement the idea in his brewery. In order for Wayne to turn this idea into a production beer, "I had to understand what [the cedar] would do to the beer and decide what would be the best base beer to use," he says. He brewed a few test batches and it seemed clear that a hop-driven IPA would best combine with the unique characteristics of Spanish cedar. Wayne explains that "the wood adds this big white grapefruit expression that goes great with American hops varietals. It adds elements that you just can't get from hops alone—sandalwood, white pepper, clove . . . " The result of this process is Cigar City's Humidor Series IPA. "We've had an incredible response to that beer," says Wayne, referring to the gold medal it won at the 2009 GABF and the many other local awards it has received.

Aging beer with Spanish cedar is a decidedly non-traditional brewing method. But Wayne finds this fact very exciting: "I'm in favor of using many different types of woods [in brewing]." He recently conducted a seminar on the use of exotic woods to get brewers to "think outside the oak barrel," as he puts it. Wayne is currently at work on a series of special edition beers in which a Belgian-style strong golden ale is aged with other non-traditional woods including lemon and grapefruit. With such distinctive characteristics coming from the wood the base beer needs a similarly high level of complexity to be able to handle them. "The yeast byproducts [from the Belgian strain] are going to add a lot of layers to the beer," says Wayne, who constantly asks himself while brewing, "How many layers can I put into this and still make an eloquent product?"

A solid answer to this question can be found in a glass of his Hunahpu's Imperial Stout. This is the beer that has captivated beer geeks around the country and has brought wider fame to Cigar City. Named for the Mayan deity whom, legend tells, gave cocoa beans to humankind, Hunahpu's presents a complex, multilayered flavor profile that is shockingly well-balanced. Each element can be tasted both individually and together as a whole within its dense onslaught of flavors. The ingredient list—which includes Peruvian cocoa nibs; pasilla and ancho chilies; Ceylon cinnamon; and Madagascar vanilla beans—reads like a recipe for an haute cuisine fusion dessert. "It was a long-held idea that I never had a chance to make," says Wayne. "I was researching what the Mayans were using in chocolate production and was digging for what would be necessary to make a Mayan chocolate imperial stout." After formulating a beer recipe based on this research Wayne brewed an initial batch on his pilot system. "It fell together almost the first time we brewed it," he says. "With the chilies, I wanted just a little bit of heat on the back end. They also lent some tobacco and deeper fruit notes. Threshold levels of cinnamon would complement the chocolate and the chilies, and the Madagascar vanilla gives it another level of depth. It drinks like a dessert mole sauce." When he brought a cask of Hunahpu's to the Atlanta Cask Festival it won first place and he knew he had come up with something special. "That sealed the deal for me."

Another beer that incorporates some improbable ingredients is Guava Grove, a saison brewed with guava puree. Before cigars became synonymous with Tampa, New Yorker Gavino Gutierrez, who worked in the fruit packing business, traveled to the region following rumors of wild guava trees. While the trees he found there were not feasible for commercial use, the trip did bear fruit in the form of a recommendation to his friend, Vicente Martinez Ybor, to consider Tampa as a potential sight for a new cigar factory.

Guavas are widely enjoyed in Tampa today and play a significant role in the local Cuban cuisine, but using guavas in a beer posed some unique brewing challenges. "Guavas are interesting," says Wayne. "We expected them to lend more sweetness to the beer, but they actually lent a tart character. It was a good revelation." Wayne concluded: "We needed a yeast that kicks off some esters and phenols to contribute to the fruitiness. Some classic saisons have a slight tartness to them. The guavas' tart funkiness resembles this, so we decided to use a saison yeast [for this beer]."

These innovative beers are proving very successful for business, and the brewery is planning to expand production. "My inspiration comes from many sources," says Wayne. "Whether I'm brewing a straight style with a strict formulation or a beer that tastes like an idea I had with no plan—I know what my ingredients do."

Cigar City brews Jai Alai IPA and Maduro Brown ale year-round.

Seasonal offerings include Warmer Winter Winter Warmer old ale (Jan.-Feb.), Big Sound Scotch Ale (Mar.), Guava Grove Belgian-style saison brewed with guavas (June-July), Marshal Zhukov's Imperial Stout (Aug.), Puppy's Breath Porter (Sep.), Humidor Series cedar-aged ales in varying styles (varying release), Bolita Brown Double Nut Brown Ale (varying release), 110K+OT over-the-top experimental ales (varying release), and Improvisación Oatmeal Rye India Brown Ale (varying release).

Hunahpu's Imperial Stout brewed with cocoa nibs, chilies, cinnamon and vanilla is released each year in March at the brewery.

Cigar City's beers are distributed in Alabama, Florida, Georgia, New York, and Pennsylvania.

HUMIDOR SERIES IPA

Hazy orange-gold with a thick, fine light tan head. Cedar wood is clearly evident in the aroma. Digging deeper reveals white pepper and spicy, earthy nuances. Some citrus hops eek out from underneath the wood profile along with a touch of alcohol sweetness. Lots more cedar notes in the flavor with intriguing bitter white grapefruit and more white pepper and dark spices. Hops spice and caramel malt play supporting roles to the complex, up-front wood notes. The medium body conveys the deeply packed flavor profile with good structure and leaves a long finish with spicy hop bitterness. This is a completely unique take on an IPA. Very interesting.

Guava Grove

Hazy bright orange with a very thick, loose white head. Lots of carbonation. The aroma consists of faintly spicy fermentation notes alongside sweet-tart guava fruit notes which, rather than being overpowering, offer a muted, ripe unctuousness with a very faint whisper of vegetal wintergreen. Subtle hints of dry grassiness and toasted grain are present in the tail end. Very soft funky fruitiness in the flavor overlaying a delicate malt structure with some bitter and spicy hops notes and a bit of sour fruit in the background. The very light body comes across quite delicately with a touch of spice and soft alcohol in the finish.

HUNAHPU'S IMPERIAL STOUT

Thick, pure black with a thin, medium-fine dark brown head with intense deep golden highlights around the rim and a viscosity that coats the glass with glycerin. Huge aroma of smoky chili barbeque and a whiff of cinnamon. Bitter dark chocolate, sweet caramel, and toffee are also present amidst the huge roasted malt profile with a bit of soft alcohol in the background. The flavor is full of bitter

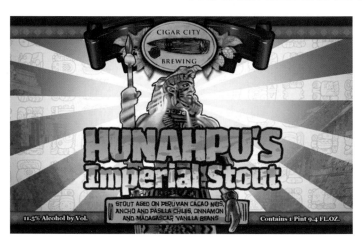

cocoa with accents of cinnamon and smoky chili. Dark fruit notes reside underneath along with an earthy hops edge. All of these flavors are balanced quite harmoniously—the unique ingredients do not take over, but meld very well with the sweet and bitter dark roasted malt framework. This beer has a huge presence in the mouth with a lot of dimension. It is multifaceted with dark roast and sweet flavors playing off of one another.

TERRAPIN BREWING CO.—ATHENS, GA
Brian "Spike" Buckowski, Brewmaster & Co-Founder

Surveying a selection of beers from the Terrapin Brewing Company, one is met with the image of a bright green turtle on each label, its hooked bill grinning while engaging in a variety of activities. A bespectacled turtle wears a red bandana and tattered straw hat while plucking a banjo and chewing a stalk of barley on the label of Rye Pale Ale. A turtle's beady eye gleams from behind an executioner's mask while preparing to drop the blade of a hops-stuffed guillotine for Hopsecutioner India Pale Ale. And my personal favorite: a toque-wearing turtle wields a frothy pint and a spatula before a steaming tray of cookies fresh from the oven for Wake-n-Bake Coffee Oatmeal Imperial Stout.

Terrapin brewmaster and co-founder Brian "Spike" Buckowski is quite fond of the whimsical turtle-themed artwork used by his brewery, whose name was inspired by a Grateful Dead album. "We have a great local artist that does all of our artwork for us," he remarks, after acknowledging the importance of high quality beer inside the bottle. "The liquid has to be solid," he says—a fitting incongruity akin to turtles producing baked goods—"and the packaging dynamite as well." But whimsy aside, Spike cautions that a brewer has to "know [his] home market" while being "aware of the transient nature of craft beer drinkers. Craft beer drinkers want to try new craft brews." Grabbing their attention in the beer cooler is the first step to gaining new customers. "Catch their eye and keep them coming back," he says, summarizing the one-two punch of label and beer. He stresses the importance of fostering loyalty in his customers while encouraging exploration. To do this, Terrapin maintains a diverse selection of year-round offerings that is supplemented by numerous seasonal and specialty releases. These specialty releases range from his own explorations into hybrid beer styles to fund-raising editions for the historic Georgia Theater in downtown Athens, which was destroyed by fire in 2009.

When designing a new beer—perhaps one of his single-batch "Side Project" editions, which now number at 15— he tells me the ultimate goal is to "make well-balanced beers that tell a story." The first part of that goal, the concept of balance, plays a huge role in Terrapin's philosophy of brewing. Spike likes to talk about "brewing in 3D," meaning that all aspects of the tasting experience need to be considered together and balance one another out. "Balance the 'fun' beers by making them solid beers as well," he warns. He takes into consideration how the "old guys" brewed traditional beers to style, "but then I add my own twist," he says. He sites Terrapin's Pumpkinfest as an example of this. It's a traditional Oktoberfest lager brewed with pumpkin and pumpkin pie spices, and a very clear mash-up of old and new brewing traditions.

The second part of his goal, presenting the back-story as a part of the experience of enjoying the beer, is another way of keeping people's attention focused on a beer's unique individuality. We discussed several engaging beer back-stories, but perhaps the most significant one is that of Terrapin's flagship beer, Rye Pale Ale. Its original recipe, developed during his homebrewing days, "came out of the bathtub" and became the "first one out of the gate" for Terrapin, Spike recalls. It was the brewery's first and only production beer, and just six months after its introduction, beer judges awarded it a gold medal at 2002 GABF. Spike is still very proud of that first beer, which remains "cemented in my heart as my favorite," he says. Additionally, he feels that this beer embodies the culture and sentiment of the brewery, right down to its label—"The farmer, the banjo, the straw hat . . . That label best describes Terrapin as a southern brewery."

Rye Pale Ale "put rye on the map" as a hot ingredient in American craft beer, adds Spike. The rye adds a unique twist to an otherwise classic, hoppy American pale ale. Rye's subtle toasted flavors round out the specialty malt bill and balance out the prominent citrus hops profile. But rye isn't the only ingredient used in Terrapin's lineup of beers with roots in the culinary arts. Another interesting story can be found behind the suggestively named Wake-n-Bake Coffee Oatmeal Imperial Stout—breakfast in a bottle. Spike wasn't a huge fan of coffee as he began working with Jittery Joe's Coffee, an Athens staple, on a custom blend of roasts for a new beer he wanted to make. He undertook a deliberate tasting process, comparing different roasts and blends, both hot and cold brewed, and tested their flavors in combination with a base control beer. By the end of it Spike was buying quality coffee and drinking it black. The process had taught him to appreciate the nuances expressed by the right beans and the right roast.

The same thing happened again, but this time with chocolate, when he teamed up with Olive and Sinclair, an upstart artisanal chocolate company in Nashville, Tennessee, to produce Terrapin's new seasonal offering, Moo Hoo Chocolate Milk Stout. In addition to the customary dark roasted malts, cocoa bean shells are steeped in the beer, and raw cocoa nibs are added, along with lactose to make it a milk stout, giving the beer a deep chocolate flavor with a rich mouthfeel. "Experimenting with food to put in beer has turned me onto some great stuff," recalls Spike as he thinks about how his bachelor diet has changed over the years—"I'm a foodie."

Several other Georgia-grown products play a role in Terrapin beers. Both Sunray German-style wheat and Gamma Ray imperial wheat use locally produced tupelo and sourwood honeys from the Savannah Bee Company. These traditional single-source honeys are quintessentially Georgian products, and are highly regarded all over the South for their unique flavors.

The memorable back stories possessed by these beers, in addition to the innovative brewing processes used to produce them, give these beers enhanced appeal and a special resonance with Terrapin's local consumers. The fact that they involve regional artisans adds additional cachet. Spike is very conscious of the importance of involving the community in the big picture of running a brewery. His favorite events are the brewery's weekly tour days that "bring everyone in town over to Terrapin." Families will come and picnic on the brewery's massive lawns, bands play live music, and people can cycle through the brewery on detailed tours of the facility. Two to three hundred people would not be unusual on a given tour day, "with maybe up to 600 on a home-game night" for the Bulldogs,

Spike adds. It's this sort of community involvement that really solidifies the bonds between a brewery and its local patrons.

Spike also views these occasions as a prime opportunity to educate and relate to people. "Education is huge," he says. "The more they learn about beer the more apt they are to try different styles." One thing he'd like to change is the "fear of color" in beer he encounters in some people. It seems that people often shy away from stouts just because of their dark color, thinking that they'll be "too heavy." He's also surprised to find that many women have a "higher bitterness tolerance than men . . . Women really seem to like IPAs." In fact, Hopsecutioner IPA is quickly becoming Terrapin's best selling brand. He likens this expansion of peoples' palates to graduating up through different levels of hot sauce: "You start with ketchup, then move on to pepper, then maybe to Texas Pete, to Tabasco, to some 'insanity' sauce—your palate gets used to it." Spike's voice rises with enthusiasm when he declares, "Beer is not just fizzy yellow water anymore. There is a beer out there for everyone," and he really enjoys helping people find their beer. "Once you move into craft beer, you never go back."

Terrapin brews a year-round selection of four beers: Rye Pale Ale, Golden Ale session beer, Hop Karma Brown IPA, and Hopsecutioner IPA. Three widely released seasonal beers include Sunray German-style wheat (spring-summer), Pumpkinfest (fall), and Moo Hoo Chocolate Milk Stout (winter). Five additional limited-release seasonals are produced as part of the "Monster Beer Tour" series which include Rye Squared double IPA (Feb.), Monk's Revenge double IPA-meets-Belgian-style tripel (Mar.), Gamma Ray imperial wheat beer brewed with local tupelo and sourwood honey (June), Big Hoppy Monster imperial red ale (Aug.), and Wake-n-Bake Coffee Oatmeal Imperial Stout (Nov.). Other special releases include the Side Project series and So Fresh & So Green, Green wet-hop ale.

Terrapin's beers are distributed in Alabama, Florida, Georgia, New Jersey, North Carolina, Pennsylvania, South Carolina, Tennessee, and Virginia.

RYE PALE ALE

Slightly hazy orange-gold with a loose off-white head. Candied orange peel hop aroma is followed by softly sweet malt and alcohol notes with some lightly toasted nutty grain on the back end. Toasted malt flavors combined with a slight sweetness present themselves up front and then give way to a dry, nutty graininess. A mild, well-integrated light citrus and spice hops profile maintains throughout. The light body offers nice malt through the mid-palate with a dry, softly spicy finish.

HOPSECUTIONER

Hazy medium orange-amber with a fine, buff-colored head. Sweet malt and alcohol aromas dominate followed by caramelized citrus hops, a bit of earthiness, and faint spice in the very end. The flavor offers a medium malt character surrounded by pleasant alcohol notes with a vein of resinous bitterness running through the center of it. The medium-full body has a slight sweetness and prominent alcohol that balances out the malt to create one big mouthful of an IPA.

WAKE-N-BAKE COFFEE OATMEAL IMPERIAL STOUT

Opaque brown-black with a thin, fine mocha-colored head. Strong coffee aroma with dark roasted malts, sweet caramel, and creamy dark chocolate in the end. Some soft dark fruit alcohol notes are also present. Lots of dark roasted grain bitterness in the flavor with a bit of delightful astringency. Dark coffee and bittersweet chocolate flavors are quite strong with a distinct creaminess that remains on the tongue. The big body conveys a full mouthfeel that is not overwhelming. The oatmeal contributes a lovely plushness that gives way to dark malt and coffee bitterness in the finish.

6 The Greater Craft Beer Community

The rise of craft beer is just one part of the growing interest people are taking in their food and drink. The culture of craft beer in many ways embodies the ideals of the local, sustainable, and artisanal food movement, making it an inviting and easily accessible entry point into this broad community. Whether you feel like drinking something local or want to cook with unique seasonal ingredients, there are many resources available to assist you in making the most informed and satisfying decisions. What these sources all share is the belief that honest, fresh, community-oriented products are the ideal, and that to support their production is to participate in the most rewarding way of eating and drinking. Adding more flavor to life's experiences enhances our enjoyment of daily pleasures and provides us with a deeper connection to the sources of our food and drink. What follows are the most useful resources I have found to help explore the burgeoning new food and beverage communities.

ONLINE CRAFT BEER COMMUNITIES

RATEBEER.COM
BEERADVOCATE.COM

Given the rate at which new craft breweries and brewpubs are opening and the ever-growing list of beers produced by them, the quick-to-respond nature of the Internet has proved to be the ideal medium for keeping up on the diversity of the craft beer movement. Two sites have emerged as the primary go-to databases for craft beer: RateBeer, based in Santa Rosa, CA, and BeerAdvocate, based in Boston, MA. Each features comprehensive, user-generated, administrator-reviewed databases of craft breweries and beers, extensive discussion forums, and educational materials on beer-related topics. Both sites provide a detailed beer evaluation template for users to document their tastings, including separate rating categories for a beer's appearance, aroma, flavor, and mouthfeel. The individual scores are processed into an overall score for the beer—RateBeer uses a 100-point scale while BeerAdvocate applies a letter grade— and the beers are then ranked against all others on the site. Lists of the world's best beers, both overall and for individual styles, are closely watched within the online beer community, are the subject of countless heated discussions, and fuel a hype-machine that can elevate a new beer to cult status or relegate it to insignificance.

The influence of these sites on the craft beer community has been immense. Obscure one-off brewery-only releases have developed nationwide followings. Rare limited edition bottles are collected and traded throughout the country. And a traditional Trappist ale, brewed in tiny quantities and available (on certain days) only from the Belgian monastery where it is brewed, became the top-ranked beer in the world on both sites for many years.

Founded in 2000, RateBeer's mission is "to provide independent, unbiased, consumer-driven information about beer and breweries and to enhance the image and worldwide appreciation of beer." Joseph Tucker, RateBeer's owner and operator and self-described "tech geek," told me "I'm often surprised when people tell me their new craft beer business would not have been possible without RateBeer, that RateBeer shelf tags have increased sales in their bottle shop, or that it has helped their little brewery enter new markets." He's pleased with the international following Rate-Beer has developed. "I never thought craft beer would grow to the point that we would see RateBeer shelf tags in El Salvador." The site currently has 70 volunteer administrators around the world who verify beers, attend events, and meet with brewers. An events calendar lists happenings across the country and guides followers to local pubs, breweries, and bottle shops, and can assist in planning craft beer tourism trips.

BeerAdvocate was founded in 1996 by brothers Jason and Todd Alström. As listed on the site, BeerAdvocate's goals are to: "Wake the masses to better beer options. Give beer consumers a voice. Empower them to learn, share, and advocate. Rally to support the beer industry. [And] put the Respect back into Beer."

Their motto, "Respect Beer," is a call-to-arms for beer fans throughout the world to discover the joys of craft beer and the community that surrounds it. In a 2007 New York Times article by Eric Asimov featuring the brothers, Todd stated that, "One of our main goals is trying to raise the image of beer as a whole and bring back the beer culture . . . We find a lot of people who [are learning that] this culture has nothing to do with the beer culture they're used to." The site pursues its mission by providing an outlet for fans to discuss, rant, and praise all aspects of craft beer; discover new beers and breweries as soon as they appear; and share information with one another about craft beer festivals and special events.

BEER JUDGE CERTIFICATION PROGRAM
BJCP.ORG

Even if you never intend to judge a homebrew beer competition, the official style guidelines put forth by this organization are an invaluable resource for learning about the intricacies of the most common beer styles brewed around the world. The website states: "The purpose of the Beer Judge Certification Program is to promote beer literacy, the appreciation of real beer, and to recognize beer tasting and evaluation skills." Meticulously researched and authoritatively written, the BJCP Style Guidelines are regarded by many as the gold standard for detailed beer style information. Though the carefully worded entries are quite technical, they are easily understood and provide clear explanations of, for instance, the differences between porters and stouts or English and American IPAs. Detailed descriptions of a beer's color, aroma, flavor, and history are provided along with commercial examples considered to be the most representative of each style. Mead, cider, and similar fermented beverages are also covered, including obscurities such as braggot (mead made with malt) and cyser (cider made with honey). The entire style guidelines are available free online in a document that can be printed and placed directly into a binder for easy reading and referencing, something that should be a part of every craft beer enthusiast's library. The BJCP style guidelines are the basis for developing a strong understanding of the differences among beer styles and a command of the vocabulary used to describe them.

For those who do wish to pursue becoming a certified beer judge with this organization, the website serves as home base for information on exam prep classes, exam dates, and testing locations. Whether or not you plan to judge competitions, the tasting skills covered in the training classes are extremely valuable for developing a discerning palate, including the ability to recognize common beer flaws.

THE BREWERS ASSOCIATION
THE GREAT AMERICAN BEER FESTIVAL, WORLD BEER CUP, AND SAVOR: AN AMERICAN CRAFT BEER & FOOD EXPERIENCE

The Brewers Association is an advocacy group that works to promote craft beer across the United States on behalf of its membership of brewers, distributors, and many other individuals associated with the craft beer industry. Their stated purpose is: "To promote and protect small and independent American brewers, their craft beers, and the community of brewing enthusiasts." Raising awareness of the vibrancy of this growing industry through political advocacy and education is central to that goal. Julia Herz, the Brewers Association Craft Beer Program Director, spends most of her days working directly with consumers, distributors, and the brewers themselves conducting educational seminars, speaking at conferences, and organizing tastings. "I certainly do have the best job in the world, in my opinion," she says. "We are all leading the change in our own way. Together we're the conduit to help nurture and energize the beer community, but it's the consumer who is the true motivator of this movement."

One of the biggest ways that the Brewers Association celebrates the culture of craft beer is through the several highly popular events it organizes for beer fans. The Great American Beer Festival, held annually in Denver, Colorado, is the preeminent event for American beer. The World Beer Cup, held in even-numbered years, is the most prestigious international beer competition and the largest commercial beer competition in the world. In competition years the winners are announced at the Craft Brewers Conference, a trade conference for industry professionals that is also organized by the Brewers Association. Medals earned at these competitions are among the most highly regarded awards in the craft beer industry.

Beginning in 2009, the Brewers Association also organizes a major festival centered on craft beer and food. Savor: An American Craft Beer & Food Experience is held each year in Washington, D.C. and features hundreds of craft beers paired with specially created food samples. It also provides opportunities to speak directly with brewers and chefs, and additional educational salons for even more detailed trips into the world of beer and food. Its comfortable, classy atmosphere combined with the quality of the breweries in attendance has made it the benchmark for food-and-beer events in America.

Another significant role the Brewers Association plays is to compile craft beer industry statistics to help with marketing and publicity. "We are a nation of beer drinkers," says Julia proudly. In 2010, "with $101 billion in overall beer sales, craft beer accounted for $7.6 billion [or 7.5 percent]. This represents an 11 percent volume increase and a 12 percent sales increase over the previous year." These numbers are not atypical; the market for craft beer has experienced robust growth year after year. "Since 1970 the segment has continued to blossom with positive growth numbers," says Julia, and many of the gains in recent years have been in the double digits. This information, as well as much more, including a library of articles and resources on enjoying craft beer, is available on their website: craftbeer.com.

CICERONE CERTIFICATION PROGRAM

CICERONE.ORG

Ray Daniels had the unique experience of being inspired by bad beer. As an author, beer judge, and former director of the Brewers Association Craft Beer Marketing Program, he has dedicated his career to beer education and promotion. Despite the growing awareness of and appreciation for craft beer, Ray was tired of "going into bars serving 30 craft beers on tap with no idea about what they had or how to handle them." How could this situation be improved? One half of the battle is to get craft beer served in more establishments. The other half is to ensure that the beer is served correctly to the guests in those establishments. The first part of this scenario is covered by craft brewers and its promoters, including the many sales representatives striking out each day to sell great beer. But part two is much less well represented. Much is left to the individual establishment owners to know and execute proper beer service and train their employees to do the same. As craft beer expands, so does the need for a more detailed understanding of its unique and diverse characteristics. Ray asked himself "What should people who serve beer know?"

In 2007 Ray answered that question when he established the Cicerone Certification Program with the goal of training people who sell and serve beer professionally to manage and present beer in a simple, straightforward way. "While beer should be and can be very simple for the consumer, the people serving it need to know a lot to do it right and really serve them," Ray explains. In addition to making sure the perfect pint is served to each customer, "they also need to be able to accommodate people who are more knowledgeable about beer," says Ray. "The more sophisticated the consumer gets the more you can explore the less commonly trod areas of the beer world and really open up new things for them."

Though the term "beer sommelier," and others similar to it, has been applied to knowledgeable individuals in the beer service industry, it is self-applied and has no formal standards of knowledge or experience. A Certified or Master Cicerone, named after the term used to describe a person who guides guests through museums and explains the significance of the exhibits, are protected trademark titles that can only be applied to those who have completed the official training and testing process. Though a Cicerone may be similar to a sommelier in terms of responsibilities, Ray wants to be clear that "we're not modeling ourselves after the sommelier system. We don't want to ride on their coat tails in any way. We should be our own unique thing. We're a different beverage; we need a different program."

The entire "Master Syllabus" can be found online at cicerone.org. It contains all of the topics covered in the Certified and Master Cicerone examinations, including information on draught systems, service techniques, beer production, style information, beer tasting, and pairing beer with food. The Cicerone Program also awards the title of "Certified Beer Server" to individuals who pay for and complete an online test that covers the fundamentals of beer and beer service. Over 10,000 people have passed the test, and some larger companies with an emphasis on serving beer have even gone so far as to require their employees to become certified.

BOOKS YOU SHOULD READ

BOOKS ABOUT BEER

Here are a few books that should be a part of every enthusiast's beer library. While the ranks of books on craft beer are not nearly as deep as those on wine, there are nonetheless some important titles available to assist you in rounding out your craft beer education, with more being published each year.

Garrett Oliver, the brewmaster of Brooklyn Brewery and craft beer champion, produced *The Brewmaster's Table: Discovering the Pleasures of Real Beer with Real Food* (New York: HarperCollins, 2003), the original tome surveying beer and food. It is primarily centered on the classic European brewing traditions and provides detailed information on classic beer styles as well as the production of beer itself. This is combined with some solid recommendations for traditional beer and food pairings.

Oliver has also completed the monumental task of editing the first edition of the stalwart *Oxford Companion to Beer* (New York: Oxford University Press, 2011). This authoritative reference contains over 1,100 alphabetical entries on every aspect of the brewing industry throughout the world solicited from experts on each topic. It is an indispensible resource for researching the intricacies of beer.

For a good overview of the breadth of craft beers produced in America, Andy Crouch's *Great American Craft Beer: A Guide to the Nation's Finest Beers and Breweries* (New York: Running Press, 2010), provides one-paragraph descriptions of hundreds of examples arranged by style along with informational sidebars. One can't help but work up a thirst while taking a "couch tour" of many of America's most famous and creative craft beers and breweries. This book serves as an excellent starting point for planning tasting forays into new flavor territory.

Randy Mosher has given us an excellent all-purpose guide to beer enjoyment with *Tasting Beer: An Insider's Guide to the World's Greatest Drink* (North Adams, Massachusetts: Storey Publishing, 2009). It covers the brewing process, a history of beer styles from around the world, beer tasting strategies, beer with food, and information about everything in between. The presentation ranges from trivia to technical terminology, with the bulk of the book devoted to general beer information along with beer judging and style tasting methods. This is a highly useful, entertaining, and enlightening craft beer offering.

BOOKS ABOUT FOOD

There are legions of excellent cookbooks available on every topic in the culinary world. The work of farm-to-table restaurant pioneer Alice Waters is closely aligned with many of the goals of the craft beer movement and presents the type of food and cooking ideals expressed throughout this book. Her Chez Panisse series of books are seminal works on seasonal, ingredient-driven cooking, but her recent volume, *The Art of Simple Food* (New York: Clarkson Potter, 2007), offers both guidance on how to shop for and prepare the finest seasonal ingredients in flavorful, straightforward ways and an overview of the philosophy behind this type of cooking and eating. This book is much more than a collection of recipes; it is a manual on obtaining the most pleasure and satisfaction from each meal opportunity.

Though not a cookbook at all, Michael Pollan's *The Omnivore's Dilemma: A Natural History of Four Meals* (New York: Penguin, 2007), is perhaps the most important book written about food in the last decade. In it we are presented with both a celebration of the many wonderful aspects of the food culture in America today and a frank look into the brokenness of our industrial food complex. This is a must-read for everyone wishing to fully understand the true implications of the way America eats, for better and for worse. Well-researched and articulate, Pollan's book lays out a compelling case for considering deeply how we participate in the larger food community. With an issue this important, which affects so many aspects of our daily lives, it is critical that each of us gains an awareness of how our choices make a difference in the future of our food. This is the best source that I have found for doing so.

For a detailed, comprehensive reference on cheese, Max McCalman is your go-to guy. His experience as both restaurateur and educator gives him a broad perspective on the many facets of artisanal cheese. His most recent book, the authoritative *Mastering Cheese: Lessons in Connoisseurship from a Maître Fromager* (New York: Clarkson Potter, 2009), is extremely useful and informative in its coverage of all aspects of cheese, from terroir to production to selecting and serving. His two previous books, *The Cheese Plate* (2002), and *Cheese: A Connoisseur's Guide to the World's Best* (2005), are works of a different sort, focusing primarily on wine pairings and cheese "reviews" respectively, but also serve as valuable references.

BOOKS ABOUT BREWING

Interested in brewing your own? Homebrewing is how many of today's most successful craft brewers first found their inspiration and developed the creative skills necessary to start their own breweries. Even if you never brew yourself, having a working knowledge of the brewing process and how different recipes and techniques affect the final product is very useful for learning to taste craft beer. One seems to be able to taste kettle caramelization, for instance, more clearly while picturing boiling wort in one's mind—either from an actual brewing experience or a detailed description of the process. And you haven't experienced the true glory of hops until you've actually handled them in the raw, smelled the resin left on your fingers, and let the warm vapors of steeping hops permeate your senses.

Charlie Papazian is the father of homebrewing in the United States. In 1978 he, along with Charlie Matzen, founded the American Homebrewers Association with the publication of the first issue of Zymurgy magazine. It announced the new organization, publicized the recent legalization of homebrewing, and called for entries into the organization's first national homebrew competition. Papazian's reassuring call to "Relax. Don't worry. Have a homebrew!" echoes throughout *The Complete Joy of Homebrewing: Third Edition* (New York: HarperCollins, 2003), a somewhat-dated looking but still very relevant manual on the basics of making your own beer (the book is now in its third edition). Charlie's infectious enthusiasm is also spread throughout a companion volume, *The Homebrewer's Companion* (1994), which provides additional advanced information on recipes, techniques, and equipment.

The aforementioned Ray Daniels, founder of the Cicerone Certification Program, has also written many excellent books on craft brewing. For the advanced brewer, or the extremely dedicated drinker, his *Designing Great Beers: The Ultimate Guide to Brewing Classic Beer Styles* (Boulder, CO: Brewers Publications, 2000), presents detailed technical information on creating recipes for any classic beer style, along with historical and ingredient information. Detailed charts and graphs serve as valuable references for serious brewers, including professionals like Peter Zien, who recommends this book.

There's nothing like the aroma of freshly steeped whole-flower hops—pictured here in AleSmith's hop back after a batch of wort for X Pale Ale has been run through it.

CLOSING THOUGHTS

Craft beer is but one of the options available to diners today wishing to experience a high quality, flavorful beverage with their meal—boutique wines and specialty cocktails have become increasingly popular and available as well. The point is that we can now expect many pairing options to choose from when sitting down to enjoy a fine meal. Wine, of course, has had well-established academies devoted to training experts, and many chefs and mixologists have achieved celebrity status through dedicated cable channels and publishing houses. Although humankind has produced beer since the development of agriculture many thousands of years ago, beer culture in America has not consistently been focused on providing flavor and quality. This is changing.

Recent years have marked dramatic growth for beer in this country—not in the roughly 95 percent market share held by just a few large corporations, but by the record number of small, independent breweries now in operation which make up the dynamic craft segment. Now is the time for advocates of high quality beer to step forward and lead a grassroots effort to spread awareness of and appreciation for the bounty of flavorful options becoming available in more and more local communities. Drinking craft beer is not only in good taste—it's a statement in support of local artisans and craftsmen. This choice satisfies on multiple levels. It is a choice for full-flavored beers, but also one that inspires us to consider what can yet be achieved in the way we come together to share meals with one another. Celebrate quality. Build community. Enjoy craft beer.

ACKNOWLEDGMENTS

Special thanks to my agent, Angela Rinaldi of The Angela Rinaldi Literary Agency, whose belief in this project from its earliest days has resulted in the book you now hold. Thank you also to my editor, Joseph Sverchek, at Skyhorse Publishing for his valuable assistance and his commitment to increasing awareness of the joys of craft beer.

Thank you so much to my photographers, Bryan N. Miller and Casey Barbula, whose generosity with their talents, time, and hard work has been a major contribution to this book. Thank you also to John Schulz of StudioSchulz photography for access to his catalog of craft beer images.

Thank you to Bob Howald and Kristen Sande of Valley Cheese and Wine in Henderson, Nevada, for their assistance in acquiring all of the necessary cheeses, for sharing their professional expertise, and for the use of their "studio."

Thank you to all of the brewers, owners, and staff who took time out of their busy schedules to share their stories and their beers with me. You are the engine of the craft beer movement.

Thank you to Peter Zien and the AleSmith team for the support and friendship they provided during this project. Your shared dedication to quality and craftsmanship has been a foundational inspiration for me.

And thanks to my Las Vegas chefs, Patrick Higgins and Joseph Burns, whose belief in me as a chef, and in the success of fine dining craft beer dinners, helped me gain the experiences necessary to conceive this project.

PETER ZIEN'S RUSSIAN IMPERIAL STOUT HOMEBREW RECIPE

The Russian imperial stout has become a cult favorite among beer geeks. Its high octane flavor profile and alcohol content make it a serious beer not only to consume, but also to brew. The following eight pages feature the original recipe from Peter Zien's handwritten homebrew journal and offer a glimpse into the inspiration which would later be poured into classic AleSmith brews.

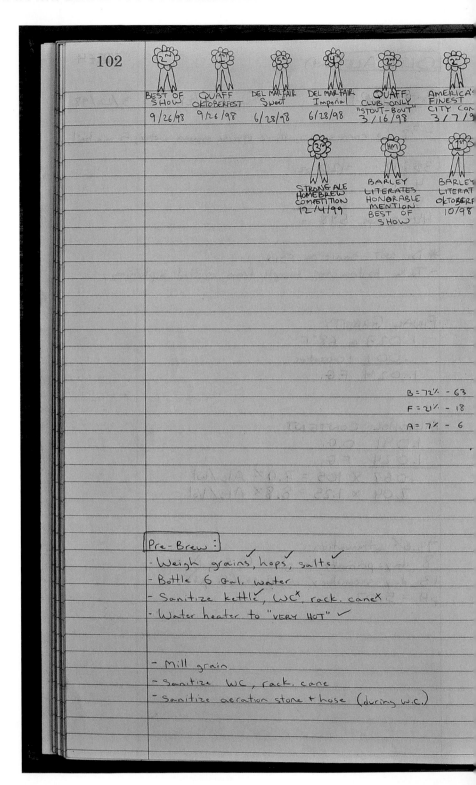

102

BEST OF SHOW
9/26/98

QUAFF OKTOBERFEST
9/26/98

DEL MAR FAIR Sweet
6/28/98

DEL MAR FAIR Imperial
6/28/98

QUAFF CLUB-ONLY "STOUT-BOUT"
3/16/98

AMERICA'S FINEST CITY Com
3/7/9

STRONG ALE HOMEBREW COMPETITION
12/4/99

BARLEY LITERATES HONORABLE MENTION BEST OF SHOW

BARLEY LITERAT OKTOBERF
10/98

B = 72% - 63
F = 21% - 18
A = 7% - 6

Pre-Brew:
- Weigh grains, hops, salts
- Bottle 6 Gal. water
- Sanitize kettle, WC×, rack, cane×
- Water heater to "VERY HOT"

- Mill grain
- Sanitize WC, rack, cane
- Sanitize aeration stone + hose (during W.C.)

BREW DATE: 1/25/98
103-1

IMPERIAL STOUT 1.085 O.G. 87 IBU 231 SRM 1.02 BU:GU

	MILL DIAM.	LB's	MALTED BARLEY	SRM	VALUE	GRAVITY POINTS
*	1.9	3 1/2	Great Western 2-row Klages	1.8	30	105
*	1.9	2 1/2	U.S. Pale 2-row Harrington	3.4	30	75
*	1.9	3 3/4	Weissheimer Acid malt	1.8	30	113
*	1.9	1/2	Bamberg Dark Crystal	150	22	11
	3.5	1/2	DeWolf-Cosyns Chocolate	400	22	11
	3.5	1/2	Bamberg Karaffe	595	22	11
	3.5	1/2	Franco-Belges Roasted Wheat	370	22	11
	3.5	1/4	Franco-Belges Kiln-Coffee	160	22	11
	—	1/4	Lyle's Black Treacle syrup	350°	36	9
	3.5	1/2	Briess Roasted Barley	450	22	11
	—	3 1/3	Northwestern Gold extract	6	36	119

12 1/2 LBS GRAIN BILL / 16 1/10 TOTAL

$$IBU = \frac{(.7489)(aa\%)(oz)(U\%)}{5} \qquad \underset{SRM}{231} = \frac{1153}{5} \qquad \underset{O.G}{1.097} = \frac{487}{5}$$

[illegible] %	oz:IBU	HOPS / ADJUNCTS / BOIL MINS:	W/P	P/W BkU: AA%	32/25 90	32/25 75	26/21 60	23/18 45	20/15 30	14/10 15	0/0 2ND-ARY
53	1:46	Magnum	W	14		1/2:26	1/4:11	1/4:9			
24	1:21	Northern Brewer	W	7.8			1/2:12		1/2:9		
3	2:20	Mt. Hood	W	3.7	*FWH 1:14					1:6	
	4:87	Licorice (Italian)					1"/3 gr.				
		Irish Moss							1/2 Tsp.		
		Isinglass (lq.)									1 oz.
					①	②	③	④	⑤	⑥	

WATER TREATMENT

	Ca	SO_4	Mg	Na	CO_3	Cl
STYLE: Dublin ⟹	115	55	4	12	200	19
5 gr. Chalk	106				159	
1 gr. Epsom Salt		21	5			
1/2 gr. Kosher salt				11		16
5 GAL./PPM TOTALS:	106	21	5	11	159	16

* = Add Salts to boil

YEAST

- White Labs WLP004 Irish Stout Yeast

(38°F) REFRIGERATED: 1/23/98

(65°-68°F; 69%-74% atten.) 12:50p (72°F) PITCHED: 1/25/98

104

IMPERIAL STOUT (cont.)

MASH/SPARGE

	Lb's	Qt:s/Strike Temp.	Heating Schedule	Stabilize Temp.	Time
(8:00a)	10¼	10¼/106°F	DOUGH-IN	104°F	25
TEMP. RAISE #1		2½/104°F	Add Boiling Water + Heat	140°F	25
TEMP. RAISE #2		1¼/140°F	Add Boiling Water + Heat, 2¼ lb. grain	158°F	25
(9:45a)	SPARGE	18/185°F	RACK SPARGE WATER DURING 10 MIN. LAUTER-TUN REST	170°F	—

BOIL SCHEDULE

		TIME
(10:30a)	① Add bag #1, salts, bring to boil	15
(10:45a)	② Add bag #2,	15
	③ Add bag #3, licorice, extract, + treacle	15
(11:22a)	④ Add bag #4,	15
	⑤ Add bag #5, ½ Tsp. Irish moss	15
(11:52a)	⑥ Add bag #6, copper racking cane	15
(12:07p)	⑦ END BOIL	CHILL WORT

(12:10p) WORT CHILL (72°F)
- Sanitize w/ 15 min. hot water run

HYDROMETER
1.084 @ 71°F
.001 + correction
1.085 Original Gravity

AERATION (72°F)
- Sanitize stone + hose in 15 min. boil
- Submerge stone; turn knob 2⅛ turns for 3 min's.

(12:50p) YEAST PITCH (72°F)
- Warm yeast to room temp., shake well,

106

PRIMARY FERMENTATION)

(<9 hr, start-up)

DATE	TIME/COMMENTS	BEER TEMP.	
1/25/98	12:50p, YP, foamy, infrequent B	72°F	
	4:45p, reduced foam, occasional B	72°F	
	9:50p, 1 B/55 sec's, light foaming, some clearings	71°F	
1/26/98	6:50a, 4 B/10 secs, 2" krausen	70°F	
	12:50p, 9 B/10 sec's, 4"+ krausen (nearing top*)	71°F	
	9:30p, 7 B/10 sec's *BLOW-OFF TUBE, 9"+ krausen	71°F	6
1/27/98	6:50a, 15 B/10 sec (removed↑) 2" krausen (affixed airlock)	71°F	6
	1:50p, 18 B/10 sec's, 2" krausen	71°F	6
1/28/98	6:50a, 5½ B/10 sec's, ½" krausen	69°F	6
1/29/98	6:50a, 1 B/7 sec's, thin cover	68°F	6
	7:50p, 1 B/12 sec's, clearing, (DAY #4)	68°F	6
1/30/98	6:45a, 1 B/15 sec's, clearing	69°F	6
1/31/98	7:50a, 1 B/19 sec's, clearing	69°F	6
2/1/98	7:15a, 1 B/25 sec's, clearing, thin cover	68°F	6
2/2/98	7:50a, 1 B/55 sec's, clearing,	69°F	6
2/3/98	7:10a, 1 B/35 sec's, areas cleared	69°F	6
2/4/98	6:50a, 1 B/105 sec's, areas cleared (DAY #10)	69°F	6

SECONDARY FERMENTATION

DATE	TIME/COMMENTS	BEER TEMP.	R TE
2/4/98	7:15p, occ. B, slight foaming	68°F	6
2/5/98	6:15a, infrequent B, slight foaming	68°F	6
2/6/98	3:00p, infrequent B, reduced foaming	68°F	6
2/7/98	7:00a, infrequent B, still	68°F	6
2/8/98	7:00a, " " " " "	68°F	6
2/9/98	6:50a, still DAY # 5/15	68°F	6
2/11/98	6:50a, still	68°F	68
2/12/98	6-8:00p, BOTTLED DAY #8/18	68°F	68
	— carbonating	—	66
2/24/98	2:00p, REFRIGERATED	—	36

IMPERIAL STOUT (cont.)

NOTES:

- Heated Dough-in strike temp. of 106°F on inside stove, burner set @ 150°F, during grain milling...;
- During WC: tilted kettle + shook racking cane to increase flow, also pinched hose @ neck of racking cane; Increased flow dramatically!*
- Efficiency factor missed by 13% (.13 gravity points), acid malt < 30? 2¼ specialty malts insufficiently mashed?, mash times too short? pH too low?
- Mashed base malts, acid malt, + dark crystal separately, added specialty dark malts @ 140°-158° heat rise, lost conversion?...
- 1st temp. raise boiling water raised to 116°F;
- 2nd temp. raise hardly raised at all w/input of specialty grains, used external heat;
- Took kettle off burner when added extract + treacle; warmed extract to help run from bag;
- * = affixed blow-off tube to fermenter 1/26, 2:30p, foam moving through tube into water...; wrapped fermenter neck w/saran wrap around tube;
  - Removed tube, re-attached airlock 1/27, 6:30a;
- Somewhat dificult sparge; needed to stop, stir, + re-open valves to get run-off...; (2¼ lb finegrind)
- Recirculated 6 Qt.'s thru lauter-tun before sparging;
- Possible under-sparge resulting in lost O.G. pt's? Consider taking hydrom. readings during sparge...;

SECONDARY FERMENTATION | Day #10   2/4/98

- No hop additions
- Siphon, then add approx. 1 oz. liquid Isinglass, stir, affix airlock;

108

IMPERIAL STOUT (cont.)

BOTTLING: Day #8/18   2/12/98

- $\frac{3}{4}$ cup corn sugar primer, 5 min boil, 16 oz;

40 : 12 oz = 480
 5 : 22 oz   110
 6 : 7 oz   42 $\Rightarrow$ 632 oz <8 oz>
51 : 632 oz

- Soak OA caps in Iodophor solution.

FINAL GRAVITY
 1.028 @ 68°F
  .000 + correction
 1.028 Final Gravity

ALCOHOL CONTENT
 1.085 O.G.
 1.028 F.G.
  .057 x 105 = 6.0% Alc/wt.
  6.0 x 1.25 = 7.5% Alc/Vol.

67% attenuation
10 days primary in glass
 8 days secondary in glass

GLOSSARY

- A -

abbey ale—A beer which emulates the styles originally brewed by Belgian Trappist monks but not brewed within a monastery. They are characterized by their fruity fermentation flavors, robust malt profiles, and high alcohol content.

ABV—Abbreviation for "alcohol by volume." This is typically expressed as a percentage measuring the strength of a beer.

acetic—A fermentation aroma and flavor descriptor used to express the presence of a vinegary quality. Acetic aromas and flavors are sometimes found in wood-aged sour beers or those with an unwanted bacterial infection.

acidity—The acidic character of a beer's flavor. A certain amount of acidity can add dimension to a beer.

adjunct—Additional grains other than malt which are used to brew beer. Adjuncts are generally used in conjunction with malted grains in order to decrease the cost of a beer and/or to lighten a beer's flavor and body.

alcohol—A class of compounds composed of carbon, oxygen, and hydrogen, which has an intoxicating effect on humans. Ethanol (C_2H_5OH) is the primary alcohol produced by saccharomyces yeasts during fermentation.

alcohol content—The amount of alcohol in a beverage. It is most often measured by volume and expressed as a percentage ABV.

ale—A category of beer brewed with top-fermenting yeast, as opposed to lagers brewed with bottom-fermenting yeast.

alpha acid—Bitter compounds found in lupulin, the resin produced by the flower cones of the hop vine. Hops with high levels of alpha acids can contribute greater levels of bitterness than those with low levels and are prized by brewers.

appearance—A description of how a beer looks, and one of the key categories in which a beer should be evaluated. Characteristics such as color, clarity, size, color, and shape of the head should be considered when assessing a beer's appearance

aroma—How the beer smells and one of the key categories in which a beer should be evaluated. Aroma is very closely linked to a beer's flavor.

aroma hops—Types of hops which are valued for their specific aromatic properties rather than their alpha acid content. They are typically added later in the brewing process and during dry hopping.

astringency—A physical sensation in the mouth often described as a flavor that is caused by the presence of polyphenols similar to that found in strong black tea and red wines. Pleasant in certain beer styles in small amounts, an overabundance is considered a flaw.

attack—The very first sensations experienced when the beer enters one's mouth.

attenuation—The degree to which fermentable sugars in wort have been consumed by yeast. Low attenuation results in beers with high levels of residual sugars.

- B -

balance—A characteristic of high quality beers which display an even and complimentary distribution of aromas, flavors, and body characteristics. The hop, malt, and fermentation characteristics, along with the presence of alcohol and the way the beer feels one's mouth, all contribute to a beer's balance or lack thereof.

barley—A cereal grain that serves as a key ingredient in the brewing of beer that, after the malting process, provides the fermentable material for yeasts.

barrel—1. A wooden vessel traditionally made from oak which is used to age wine, spirits, or beer. Barrels which formerly held spirits or wine are often then used to age beer, which imparts the beer with its particular flavor. Barrels also allow oxygen to come in contact with the beer and produce oxidative flavors. 2. A standard measurement for volumes of beer, known as "beer barrels," or bbl. A U.S. beer barrel is equivalent to 31 gallons and is the main unit for measuring commercial beer production in America. A standard size "keg" is one half barrel.

beer—A fermented beverage whose source of fermentable material is grain, as opposed to fruits or honey.

bittering hops—Types of hops, usually chosen for their high alpha acid content, which are boiled for lengthy periods during the brewing process to add bitterness to a beer rather than a particular flavor or aroma.

body—How a beer presents itself in one's mouth and one of the key categories in which a beer should be evaluated. A beer's body may be negatively described as "flat," "dead," or "thin"; positively as "balanced," "dynamic," or "lively"; and objectively as "full," "light," or "structured"; to name only few of the many applicable descriptors. A beer's viscosity, alcohol content, bitterness, and carbonation are all considered when assessing its body.

bottle conditioning—A process by which a beer is carbonated via a secondary fermentation which takes place after it has been bottled.

brettanomyces—A naturally-occurring wild yeast used to make lambic-style beers and other "wild" and/or sour ales. Unwanted brett infections can be ruinous to brewers and winemakers alike due to its uncanny resilience, however, under the right circumstances it can add incredible complexities to a beer. It is a vigorous fermenter responsible for the "horse blanket" and "barnyard" aromas found in beers.

brew kettle—A container in which wort and hops are boiled together to combine their flavors.

brewpub—A restaurant where casual food is served and fresh beer is brewed onsite in small batches.

buttery—A flavor descriptor use to describe the presence of diacetyl in beers. It is most often, but not always, an undesirable characteristic.

- C -

carbonation—1. The process of dissolving CO_2 gas into a beer usually achieved through bottle conditioning or force carbonation. 2. The amount of CO_2 dissolved in a beer.

cask—A traditional vessel from which beer is served using either the force of gravity or a hand pump, or "beer engine," without the use of any pressurized CO_2.

cask conditioning—The process of carbonating a beer through a secondary fermentation within the keg or cask itself, often with the inclusion of additional hops.

cheesy—A flavor and aroma descriptor used to describe the presence of isovaleric acid that is often found in aged hops.

chocolate malt—A dark brown roasted malt that can often impart a chocolaty flavor to a beer.

complimentary pairings—Pairings which feature food and beverages that share flavor similarities that taste good together.

contract brewing—A business arrangement in which a brewer produces beer for another individual to market and sell rather than doing so him- or herself.

contrasting pairings—Pairings that feature food and beverages that do not share flavor similarities but whose differing flavors taste well together.

crystal malt—Varieties of specialty roasted malts used to add body and flavor to beers by contributing certain unfermentable sugars. Crystal malts undergo a specific malting process to crystallize these sugars and come in a variety of shades which add color to beers.

- D -

diacetyl—A strong flavor component produced during fermentation which is mostly reabsorbed by the yeast cells. When present in detectable quantities it gives a beer undesirable buttery and/or butterscotch flavors.

dimension—An often elusive characteristic found in beers that possess a set of complex, well-balanced aromas, flavors, and body characteristics. A one-dimensional beer may only display a single primary aroma, flavor, and body characteristic, while a multidimensional beer will exhibit a complex array of primary, secondary, and possibly, tertiary sensory characteristics. Such characteristics can bring about varied experiences throughout the enjoyment of a beer. Multidimensional beers are ideal for use in food pairings.

double—A prefix added to a beer style to denote that it has been brewed to stronger specifications than the style traditionally calls for. Synonymous with the prefix "imperial."

draught beer—Beer served from a keg or a cask through a draught system rather than from a bottle.

dry hopping—A technique used to impart additional hop flavors and aromas to a beer without adding bitterness. This is achieved by adding whole flower hops directly to the tank or cask.

- E -

esters—A large group of flavor and aroma compounds which are formed during fermentation. Ester flavor and aroma descriptors are often described as "fruity"—resembling apples, bananas, and pears—and "spicy"—resembling aniseed and clove. Various yeasts produce different ester profiles that are affected by many factors, but perhaps most of all by the temperature they are fermented at.

extreme beer—A beer that possesses an intense flavor profile, substantial body, high alcohol content, and/or some other unconventional, nontraditional characteristic. Certain examples of double IPAs, Russian imperial stouts, and barleywines are often considered to be "extreme beers."

- F -

fermentation—The process by which yeast or bacteria converts one substance to another including sugar into alcohol, CO_2, and other important byproducts.

final gravity—A measure of the specific gravity of a beer after the fermentation is completed. This reading, combined with a reading of a beer's original gravity, can be used to estimate a beer's ABV.

finish—The flavors, aromas, and sensations that remain in the mouth, throat, and soft palate after a beer has been swallowed. It should not be—though it often is—used interchangeably with the term "aftertaste" which, strictly speaking, only refers to taste remaining on the tongue and can carry negative connotations.

flavor—In simplest terms, how a beer tastes. It is one of, if not the key, categories by which a beer should be judged. The overall perception of flavor, however, is a complex interplay of tastes and aromas.

food-friendly—A beer that can be easily paired with a wide variety of foods. These beers are often complex and multidimensional with diverse flavor profiles.

force carbonation—A process for carbonating beer by which CO_2 is dissolved into beer held under pressure

fresh hop ale—A seasonal beer made with freshly-harvested and dried hops.

- G -

grain bill—The grains used in a given beer recipe.

- H -

head—The layer of foam that forms on the top of a beer as the beer is being poured. A proper head is essential to the enjoyment of most beer styles as it contributes to a thicker, smoother mouthfeel.

head retention—The length of time a significant amount of head remains on a glass of beer. This is an important indicator of a beer's quality and for anticipating its mouthfeel.

hop back—A vessel used to infuse hot wort with additional hop aromas and flavors after the boil by running it through a bed of whole-flower hops while under pressure. The hops also naturally filter the beer.

hops—One of the four essential ingredients for brewing beer. Hops are the cones (strobiles) of a hop vine which contain a bitter resin known as lupulin, which, when boiled, imparts bitterness to the beer and also contributes distinctive flavors and aromas. Certain hop varieties are prized for their particular flavor and aroma qualities. They also serve as a natural preservative for beer.

- I -

IBU (International Bittering Unit)—An IBU is a unit used to measure the level of bitterness in a given beer. It is especially useful for comparing the relative bitterness of different beers and setting the bitterness guidelines for various beer styles.

imperial—A term originally applied to specially brewed strong stouts meant for export from England to the Russian imperial court of Catherine the Great, it is now often used as a prefix for many examples of beers which have been brewed to stronger specifications than their styles traditionally call for—synonymous with the prefix "double" in this case.

infection—An unwanted bacterial or wild yeast fermentation in a beer which is often caused by poor sanitation procedures.

isomerization—In brewing, the process during which alpha acids in hop oils are made soluble in the wort during the boil.

- L -

lactobacillus—A group of common lactic acid bacteria, along with *pediococcus*, whose fermentation imparts a sharp sourness to beers. Revered in styles where this is called for, it can otherwise spoil beer as an un-wanted infection.

lactose—An unfermentable sugar derived from milk that is used in brew-ing to add body and a slight sweetness to beers including milk, sweet, and lactose stouts.

lager—A type of beer produced using bottom-fermenting yeast, as op-posed to ales made with top-fermenting yeasts.

lauter tun—A vessel in which sparging takes place. The mash is pumped over a perforated bottom so that the wort can drain out while the mash serves as a filter.

lightstruck—The presence of "skunky" flavors in a beer caused by hop-derieved compounds being exposed to light. This is often a problem for beers that are packaged in clear or green bottles or ones which have not been stored properly.

Lovibond, degrees—A measure of the color of beer and grain. SRM is now a more common measurement system though the lovibond scale is still often applied to malts.

- M -

malt—Barley or wheat grains that have been germinated in order to re-lease the enzymes necessary to convert their starches to sugars, which are then dried at the precise moment to halt this process and then roasted to varying degrees.

mash—The porridge-like combination of ground malt and water pro-duced during mashing.

mashing—A precise, temperature-controlled cooking process during which malt is combine with hot water to convert the starches and pro-teins in the malt to sugars and enzymes that can be fermented by yeasts.

mash tun—A brewing vessel in which the mashing process takes place.

mouthfeel—How a beer feels in a one's mouth. This aspect may generally be described as light, heavy, flat, lively, dead, weighty, thick, thin, or watery.

- N -

nitrogen, or "on nitrogen," "nitro," or "nitrogenated"—Refers to a beer infused with and dispensed using a blend of N_2 and CO_2 gasses. Beers served this way have very fine, creamy heads with good reten-tion. They are less carbonated than other beers resulting in a creamier mouthfeel. This method is often associated with Irish-style stouts and certain English-style pub ales.

- O -

original gravity (OG)—The concentration of sugars in the wort before fermentation begins.

oxidation—The process by which oxygen affects a beer's aroma, flavor, and body by breaking down certain aromatic compounds. Flavors and aromas produced by oxidation are often described as musty, damp, or resembling cardboard, and are considered a serious flaw. Under very specific, controlled circumstances, such as barrel or extended bottle aging, oxidative flavors can be desirable in certain beer styles which can lend a particular mellowness to strong beers.

- P -

palate—1. The parts of the mouth where flavor is experienced including the "soft palate" at the back of the roof of the mouth, which separates the cavities of the nose and the mouth, and the tongue. The term can also refer to where a flavor is experienced in the mouth. The "front" of a person's palate is usually associated with the attack of the beer, while the "back" is associated with the beer's finish, and the "mid" is what's referred to between the attack and the finish. 2. A person's experience with and ability to discern and describe flavors and aromas.

pediococcus—A group of common lactic acid bacteria, along with *lactobacillus*, whose fermentation imparts a sharp sourness to beers. Revered in styles where this is called for, it can otherwise spoil beer as an unwanted infection.

phenols—Flavors and aromas in beer, generally derived from fermentation, that are often described as fruity, spicy, or medicinal. Considered undesirable in many beer styles known for their "clean" flavor profiles, phenols are encouraged in certain, highly complex beers.

pitch—Adding yeast to cooled, aerated wort during the brewing process.

polyphenols—A group of aromatic molecular compounds in beer derived from malt and hops that can contribute astringent qualities. Different from the balancing astringency of tannins, low levels of polyphenols can contribute to a beer's body but are usually considered undesirable in larger amounts.

primary fermentation—The first, vigorous fermentation that takes place when brewing beer, during which most of a beer's alcohol is produced.

primary flavors—Those flavors experienced first and most prominently in a beer.

- R -

real ale—Generally speaking, high quality craft beer that has been cask conditioned and served without the use of pressurized draught systems. It is also a term adopted by CAMRA (Campaign for Real Ale) to refer to beers served in this way that adhere to their strict guidelines for production and service.

Reinheitsgebot—The name used to describe the German purity law which states that beer can only be made using water, malt, hops, and yeast, which was first enacted in 1516.

- S -

saccharomyces—Scientific name for top- and bottom-fermenting yeasts used for brewing beer.

seasonal beers—Certain beers produced and sold over a limited period of time during the year. These beers are typically made to celebrate holidays, anniversaries, and other events—or simply beers which are best enjoyed during a particular time of year. They may also be produced to highlight certain ingredients, which are freshest during certain seasons.

secondary fermentation—A fermentation that takes place after the primary fermentation, for which the beer may or may not be transferred to a secondary fermentation vessel, such as a barrel. Secondary fermentations are typically longer and slower and may involve fermentation agents other than *saccharomyces* yeasts, such as bacteria or brettanomyces and may include other types of non-alcoholic fermentations. Secondary fermentation can also refer to a fermentation which takes place inside a bottle, keg, or cask, in order to carbonate the beer inside.

secondary flavors—Flavors that are experienced more subtly following a beer's primary flavors.

session beers—This term refers to various styles of beers that generally contain less than 4.5% ABV and do not have strong or intense flavors, thus facilitating the consumption of multiple servings throughout a "session."

solventy—A flavor and aroma descriptor used to describe unpleasant harsh, acrid, and/or chemical elements in a beer resembling acetone, rubbing alcohol, or other solvents that may leave a strong warming sensation in the mouth. This is usually the result of a contaminated equipment or improper fermentation.

sparge—The process of washing the mash with additional water to extract any remaining sugars. This process most often takes place in the lauter tun.

specific gravity (SG)—A measure of a beer's density as compared to the density of water using a hydrometer.

SRM (Standard Reference Method)—A measurement of a beer's color.

starch—Produced by plants as an energy store, starches are broken down during malting and mashing to produce sugars that can then be fermented.

starter—Propagating a large batch of yeast in a separate vessel so that a greater amount can be pitched into the wort and fermentation can begin more rapidly.

- T -

tannins—A polyphenol with a characteristic astringency derived from hops and barley husks. Is desirable in certain beer styles when present in small amounts.

tertiary flavors—Extremely faint or delicate flavors which are experienced after primary and secondary flavors. Experiencing tertiary flavors in a beer is rare and noteworthy and marks a highly complex and sophisticated beer.

Trappist breweries—Breweries within Trappist monasteries that are tended to by, or under the direct supervision of, monks. Beers marked with the hexagonal "Authentic Trappist Product" logo must abide by the following rules:

1. They are produced within the walls of the monastery or in the vicinity of the monastery.
2. The monastic community determines the policies and provides the means of production. The whole process of production must clearly evidence the indisputable bond of subsidiarity, with the monastery benefiting from the production, and must be in accordance with the business practices proper to a monastic way of life.
3. The profits are primarily intended to provide for the needs of the community or for social services.

There are currently seven Trappist breweries—six in Belgium and one in the Netherlands.

- V -

viscosity—The thickness of a beer. Viscosity is an extremely important aspect of a beer's mouthfeel.

- W -

weiss—German term meaning "white" used for beers made with wheat—*weissbier* or *weizenbier*. It refers to the pale, cloudy color these beers possess. Similar to the Belgian term *wit*, which also refers to a different style of beer made with wheat.

wet hop ales—Seasonal beers made with hops that are freshly-picked and used immediately after harvest before they begin to degrade.

wheat—A cereal grain that serves as a key ingredient in brewing certain styles of beer that, after the malting process, provides the fermentable material for yeasts and is often used in combination with barley.

wort—Prior to the addition of yeast and commencement of fermentation, wort is the liquid that has been extracted from the mashing process.

- Y -

yeast—A type of microscopic fungi used to convert carbohydrates and sugars into alcohol. Special strains are propagated for use in brewing with each one contributing unique attributes to a batch of beer.

- Z -

zymurgy—The branch of chemistry that studies the science of alcoholic beverage fermentation.

PHOTO CREDITS

Front cover photo by Bryan N. Miller

Pages 2–3: photo by Bryan N. Miller

Pgs. 10–11: photo by Bryan N. Miller

Pgs. 16–17: photos courtesy of StudioSchulz

Pg. 19: photo by Bryan N. Miller

Pg. 22: photo by Bryan N. Miller

Pg. 25: photo courtesy of StudioSchulz

Pg. 26: photo by Wikipedia user Phyrexian

Pg. 28: photo courtesy of Dogfish Head Craft Brewery

Pg. 29: photo courtesy of StudioSchulz

Pgs. 31–33: photos by Bryan N. Miller

Pg. 34: photo by Amy K. Mein

Pgs. 35–36: photos by Bryan N. Miller

Pg. 37: photo by Schuyler Schultz

Pg. 84: photo by Schuyler Schultz

Pg. 85: photo by Bryan N. Miller

Pg. 96: photo by Casey Barbula

Pg. 100: photo by Schuyler Schultz

Pgs. 104–114: photos by Casey Barbula

Pg. 117: photo by Bryan N. Miller

Pg. 123: photo by Bryan N. Miller

Pg. 125: photo by Bryan N. Miller

Pg. 126: photo courtesy of StudioSchulz

Pg. 127 (top): photo courtesy of StudioSchulz

Pg. 127 (bottom): photo by Bryan N. Miller

Pgs. 128–130: photos by Bryan N. Miller

Pgs. 132–133: photos by Bryan N. Miller

Pg. 134: photo courtesy of StudioSchulz

Pgs. 135–136: photos by Bryan N. Miller

Pg. 137: photo courtesy of StudioSchulz

Pgs. 140–141: photos courtesy of StudioSchulz

Pg. 143: photo by Daniel Norwood

Pgs. 145–151: photos by Bryan N. Miller

Pg. 158: photo by Tim Stahl

Pgs. 164–165: photos courtesy of StudioSchulz

Pg. 166: photo courtesy of The Brooklyn Brewery

Pgs. 227–228: Photos courtesy of Captain Lawrence Brewing Company

Pgs. 246–247: photos courtesy of StudioSchulz

Pg. 259: photo by Bryan N. Miller

Pgs. 262–269: photo by Casey Barbula

Back cover photos by Bryan N. Miller

Unless otherwise noted, brewery logos and beer label images courtesy of their respective breweries.

COOKING UNIT CONVERSIONS
(units rounded for convenience)

Ingredient	U.S. Measure	Metric
almonds	8 ounces	230 grams
baking powder	1 teaspoon	3.5 grams
baking soda	½ teaspoon	2.5 grams
	1 teaspoon	5 grams
bread, torn into chunks	1 ounce	30 grams
butter	1 cup=16 tablespoons=2 sticks	230 grams
	1 tablespoon	14 grams
capers	2 ounces	60 grams
cashews	2 cups	225 grams/475 milliliters
chopped dates or raisins	¾ cup	115 grams
pitted prunes or dried apricots	8 ounces	215 grams
corn syrup	½ cup	120 milliliters
flour	1 cup	125 grams
	1 tablespoon	8 grams
ginger (fresh), peeled, minced	1 ounce	30 grams
liquids: almond milk, beer, cream, lemon juice, chicken/pork stock, water, etc.	¼ cup/2 fluid ounces	60 milliliters
	1 cup/8 fluid ounces	240 milliliters
olive oil	¼ cup/2 fluid ounces	60 milliliters
popcorn (unpopped)	1 cup	200 grams/24 milliliters
pork	2–2.25 pounds	1 kilogram
salt	1 teaspoon	6 grams
	1 tablespoon	18 grams
spices: allspice, cinnamon, coriander, cumin, paprika, Piment d'Espelette, red pepper flakes, saffron, smoked paprika, white pepper, etc.	¼ teaspoon	1.25 milliliters
	½ teaspoon	2.5 milliliters
	1 teaspoon	5 milliliters
sugar, brown, firmly packed	1 tablespoon	12 grams
	¾ cup	150 grams
	1 cup	200 grams
sugar, white	1 tablespoon	12.5 grams
	1 cup	200 grams
vanilla extract	1 teaspoon	4 grams/5 milliliters

OVEN TEMPERATURE CONVERSIONS

Fahrenheit	Celcius	Gas Mark
225°	110°	1/4
250°	120°	1/2
275°	140°	1
300°	150°	2
325°	160°	3
350°	180°	4
375°	190°	5
400°	200°	6
425°	220°	7
450°	230°	8

INDEX